Samuel G.W Benjamin

The Story of Persia

Samuel G.W Benjamin

The Story of Persia

ISBN/EAN: 9783743316546

Manufactured in Europe, USA, Canada, Australia, Japa

Cover: Foto ©ninafisch / pixelio.de

Manufactured and distributed by brebook publishing software (www.brebook.com)

Samuel G.W Benjamin

The Story of Persia

The Story of the Nations

THE

STORY OF PERSIA

BY

S. G. W. BENJAMIN

LATELY UNITED STATES MINISTER TO PERSIA

NEW YORK
G. P. PUTNAM'S SONS
LONDON: T. FISHER UNWIN
MDCCCLXXXVIII

COPYRIGHT BY
G. P. PUTNAM'S SONS
1887

Press of
G. P. Putnam's Sons
New York

PREFACE.

The author wishes to call attention to the fact that the scope of this work is entirely different from that of the volume recently published by him, entitled "Persia and the Persians." The latter work is intended to give a description of Persia as it is; while the present volume is a history of Persia, as it has been, offering a narrative of the most noteworthy characters and events of that ancient empire from its foundation in prehistoric times.

This work differs from other histories of Persia in giving more proportionate attention to the legendary period of her history than is usual with those who have dealt with this subject, as well as to the great career of the House of Sassân, which, in the opinion of the author, has never received full justice from those Christian historians who have undertaken a connected history of Persia. On the other hand, the long period between the Saracen invasion and the rise of the Sefaveans has been presented so fully elsewhere, and offers so few really salient points that are distinctly connected with the development of Persia as an independent monarchy, that it hardly seemed best to give more than a mere outline of that period in a volume whose limits are circumscribed.

It seems to be the established rule for historians to refer to the authorities they have consulted. The author may therefore state that he has, in the preparation of this volume, made use of the various well-known authorities on the subject; but it is scarcely worth while to present a list of them here. Those writers who are dead will not be disturbed by any departure from their opinions or any new presentation of the facts they recorded; while living authorities can see for themselves whether the author has agreed or disagreed with their conclusions.

In several instances, as in regard to the character and career of Chosroës Parveez, or the quality of Persian military talents and courage, the author has found it impossible to arrive at exactly the same conclusions as many writers on Persia. A long residence in various parts of the East, including several years in Persia, has led the author to form a higher and, he thinks, a more just estimate of the character of Orientals than many European writers are willing to concede to them. For the rest, the author commits this little work to the reader with the hope that he may find "The Story of Persia" not unworthy a place by the side of the histories of Greece and of Rome.

S. G. W. BENJAMIN.

CONTENTS.

I.

FERIDOON 1–23

Founders of Persia, 1—Shah Djemsheed, 2–5—Royal standard of Persia, 8—Imprisonment of Zohâk, 10—Daughters of Yemen, 12—Treachery of Serv, 15—Feridoon's test, 17—Murder of Iredj, 21—Feridoon's vengeance, 23.

II.

ZAL 24–33

Minoutchehr ascends the throne, 24—Sahm's white-haired son, 25—Zal, governor of Seistân, 26—Roodabêh's love, 27—Wedding festivities, 33.

III.

RUSTEM 34–42

Capture of Sipend, 35—Death of Minoutchehr, 36—Turkish invasion, 37—Keï Kaoos, 38—Soudabêh's adventures, 39—Afrasiab defeats the Syrians, 40—Embarkation of Rustem, 41—Rustem's victory, 42.

IV.

SOHRAB 43–50

Loss of Kaksch, 43—Marriage of Rustem and Tehmimêh, 44—Birth of Sohrab, 44—Sohrab seeks his father, 45—Siege of White Castle, 46—Gurdaferid, 47—Treachery, 48—Royal missive, 49—Reconciliation of Rustem and Keï Kaoos, 50.

V.

SOHRAB AND RUSTEM 51–65

Death of Zendeh Rezm, 52—Conflict between the Persians and Touranians, 56—Meeting of Rustem and Sohrab, 57—Death of Sohrab, 64—Tehmimêh dies of grief, 65.

VI.

SIAWUSCH 66–81

Finding of a queen, 66—Birth of Siawusch, 67—Trial by fire, 69—Siege of Balkh, 70—Hospitality of Afrasiab, 71—Marriage of Siawusch, 73—Accusations, 74—Death, 75—Keï Khosroo, 76—Piran-Wisa's deceit, 77—Rustem kills Soudabêh, 78—Victory of Keï Khosroo, 81.

VII.

KEÏ KHOSROO, OR CYRUS 82–97

Territory of Persia, 83—Touranians, 84—Cyaxares and the Medes, 86—Sect of fire-worshippers, 87—Zoroaster, 88—Subduction of Media, 89—Crœsus, 90—Capture of Babylon, 91—Warning of Belshazzar, 94—Death of Belshazzar, 95—Death of Cyrus, 96—Cyrus' tomb at Passargadæ, 96.

VIII.

FROM CYRUS TO DARIUS I. 98–111

Succession of Cambyses, 98—Subjugation of Egypt, 99—Smerdis beheaded, 100—Death of Cambyses, 101—Election of Darius, 102—Inscription at Behistoon, 103—Extension of Persian empire, 105—Expedition against Greece, 107—Battle of Marathon, 109.

IX.

XERXES 112–125

Personal appearance and temperament, 113—Army, 114—Canal through Mt. Athos, 115—Thermopylæ, 116—Battles at Artemisium, 117; at Salamis, 118—Retreat of Xerxes, 121—Battle of Platæa, 122—Defeat of Persians at Mycalé, 124—Xerxes assassinated, 125.

X.

PERSIA UNTIL THE INVASION OF ALEXANDER . 126-140

Artaxerxes Longimanus, 126—Rebellion of Megabyzus, 127—Xerxes II., 128—Degeneracy of Persian monarchy under Darius Nothus, 129—Treachery of Tissaphernes, 130—Cyrus the Younger purchases services of Greek mercenaries, 132—Battle of Cunaxa, 133—Retreat of the Ten Thousand, 135—Ochus, 136—Siege of Sidon, 138—Murder of Artaxerxes III., 139—Darius Codomanus, 140.

XI.

DARIUS CODOMANUS AND ALEXANDER . 141-157

Rout at the river Granicus, 141—Reduction of Phœnicia, 142—Defeat of Persians on the plains of Arbela, 143—Alexander enters Persepolis, 144—Alexander's feast, 145—Assassination of Darius, 146—Intermarriage between Macedonians and natives, 147—The mystic plane-trees, 148—Death of Alexander at Babylon, 149—Pitho, satrap of Media, 150—Seleucia, capital of the Greco-Persian empire, 151—Elements of discord, 151—Revolt of Diodatus, 154—Shepherds of Parthia, 156—Rhages or Rheï, 157.

XII.

THE PARTHIANS 158-170

Arsaces I., 158—Mithridates the Great, 161—Murder of Phraortes, 162—Defeat of the Romans, 163—Ctesiphon, 164—Campaign of Marc Antony, 166—Final check to the Romans, 167—Vologeses I., 168—Destruction of Seleucia, 169.

XIII.

THE HOUSE OF SASSÂN . . . 171-178

Rise of the Neo-Persian power, 172—Artaxerxes or Ardeshir declares Persia independent, 173—War with Rome, 174—Faith of Ormuzd, 175—The Zendavesta, 176—Religious character of the Persian revolution, 177.

XIV.

PAGE

SAPOR I. 180–189

Daughter of Manizen, 180—Recovery of Nisibis, 181—Imprisonment and death of Valerian, 182—Cultivation of the arts, 183—Dyke of Shuster, 184—Manichæism, 185—Death of Sapor, 186.

XV.

PERSIA UNTIL THE REIGN OF SAPOR II. . 190–206

Death of Manee, 190—War of Sapor II. with Rome, 192—Julian the Apostate masses his forces at Antioch, 194—Rejects peaceable propositions of Sapor, 195—Massacre of population at Hit, 197—Race for Ctesiphon, 199—Julian burns his fleet, 200—Death of Julian at Samarah, 202—Retreat of the Romans, 203.

XVI.

FROM SAPOR II. TO CHOSROËS I. . . 207–225

Death of Sapor I., 207—Isdigerd I., 208—Boyhood of Varahran, 209—Peace with the Romans, 210—Ephthalites or White Huns, 211—Victory of Varahran, 213—Refinding of an old love, 216—Perozes, 217—Restoration of Zoroastrianism in Armenia, 218—Mazdâk the reformer, 219—Deposition of Kobâd, 220—Restoration to the throne, 221—Destruction of the Mazdâkites, 223—Renewed hostilities with Rome, 224—Death of Kobâd, 225.

XVII.

CHOSROËS I., SURNAMED ANURSHIRWAN . 226–236

Conspiracy against Chosroës crushed, 226—Execution of Mazdâk, 227—Justice of Chosroës, 228—Establishment of fixed taxes, 230—Chosroës founds university of Shapoor, 231—The Augustan period of Persian history, 232—Expulsion of Abyssinians from Arabia, 233—Lazic war, 234—Siege of Petra, 235—Death of Chosroës, 236.

XVIII.

CHOSROËS PARVEEZ 237–266

Insult to General Bahram Shobeen, 237—Death of Hormazd, 238 — Coronation of Chosroës II., 240 — Flight from Ctesiphon, 242—Seeks aid from the emperor at Constantinople, 243—Defeat of Bahram, 244—Revolt of Vastam, 245—Shireen, 246—Friendly relations with Maurice, 247—War in Syria, 248—Siege of Jerusalem, 249—A proud hour for Persia, 250—Dastagerd, 252—Oath of Heraclius, 254—The star of Persia wanes, 255—Retreat of Chosroës, 256—Campaigns in Asia Minor, 259—Siege of Tiflis, 260—Battle near Nineveh, 261—Heraclius sacks Dastagerd, 262—Conspiracy of nobles, 265—End of the "Great King," 266.

XIX.

THE MOHAMMEDAN CONQUEST OF PERSIA . 267–282

Coronation of Siroes, or Kobâd II., 267—Murder of all the brothers of Kobâd, 268—Pestilence, 270—Insurrection and death of Shahr Barz, 271—Coronation of Isdigerd III., 272—Campaign against the Saracens, 273—Repulse of the Persians, 274—"Day of Concussion," 275—Rustem slain, 276—Fate of the leathern standard of Kaweh, 278—Fall of Rheï, 279—Defeat of the Persians near Nehavend, 281.

XX.

PERSIA UNDER THE MOHAMMEDANS . . 283–294

Crushing of Zoroastrianism, 283—Firdoüsee, 284—Ismail, Shah of Persia, 288—Shah Abbass the Great, 290—Rule of the Afghans, 291—Aga Mohammed Khan, 292—Feth Alee Shah, 294.

LIST OF ILLUSTRATIONS.

	PAGE
RUINS OF PERSEPOLIS	*Frontispiece.*
PALACE GUARD .	7
CONE OF MT. DEMAVEND	11
KING SLAYS EVIL GENIUS	19
REPRESENTATIONS OF PERSIAN MYTHOLOGY .	29
ANAHITA, OR PERSIAN VENUS .	38
AHRIMAZDAO	41
CYRUS—ANCIENT SCULPTURE . . .	47
GATEWAYS, PALACE OF DARIUS, PERSEPOLIS	53
ANCIENT PERSIAN ARCHITECTURE .	63
FIRE-ALTAR	69
PILLAR, BASE AND CAPITAL, PERSEPOLIS	73
RELIEF AT BEHISTOON .	79
TOMB OF CYRUS .	85
DARIUS HUNTS	93
MAP—PERSIAN EMPIRE UNDER DARIUS . *face*	98
GATEWAY OF XERXES (PERSEPOLIS)	100
HEAD OF DARIUS . .	106
PERSIAN ARCHITECTURE . .	109
XERXES' SEAT AT SALAMIS	119
RELIEF—PLATFORM OF XERXES AT PERSEPOLIS	123
TOMB OF ESTHER AND MORDECAI	131
RELIEF ON THE STEPS OF XERXES .	137
DARIUS AT ISSUS	143
ALEXANDER AND FAMILY OF DARIUS	153
COIN OF MITHRIDATES I. .	161
RUINS OF PALACE AT HATRA . . .	165

COIN OF ORODES	167
COIN OF ARDESHIR I.	173
ORMUZD	175
RUINS OF CASTLE OF THE FIRE-WORSHIPPERS	179
HEAD OF SAPOR I.	183
ROCK SCULPTURE NEAR SHAPOOR	187
SAPOR I.—PERSIAN SCULPTURE	189
PERSIAN CAVALRYMAN	195
SCULPTURE AT TACHT-I-BOSTÂN	205
COIN OF SAPOR II.	209
HOUSEHOLD FIRE-ALTAR	211
VARAHRAN V. IN BATTLE	215
COIN OF VARAHRAN V.	223
COIN OF CHOSROËS I.	225
PALACE OF CHOSROËS I., CTESIPHON	229
CEMETERY OF THE ZOROASTRIANS	235
RATSCH-RUSTEM	241
COIN OF PEROZES	243
COIN OF CHOSROËS II.	247
DOMESTIC FIRE-ALTAR	249
COIN OF ISDIGERD III.	255
TOMB OF AVICENNA	257
SHAH ABBASS THE GREAT	263
MOSQUE AT KOOM	269
NADIR SHAH	277
MAP—MODERN PERSIA	face 283
AGA MOHAMMED KHAN	285
FETH ALEE SHAH	289
YOUNG PERSIAN GOVERNOR (MODERN)	293

In the preparation of the illustrations for this volume, use has been made of the plates in "History of Persia from the Most Early Period to the Present Time," by Col. Sir John Malcolm, K.C.B., K.L S., London, 1815, and "Geschichte des Alten Persiens," von Dr. Ferdinand Justi, Leipzig, 1879, to the publishers of which works we desire to express our acknowledgments.

G. P. PUTNAM'S SONS.

THE STORY OF PERSIA.

I.

FERIDOON.

The legendary period of Persian history begins far back in the mists of time. It is the custom to assume that legend means fiction; but historians are now beginning to perceive that the legends of a nation are often not only more interesting and poetic than what is called its authentic history, but that they really suggest actual facts, while nothing can be more fascinating than the study of such legends. No country has more attractive legends than Persia; and to judge from them we cannot avoid the conclusion that no nation now existing has such a continuous vitality as the old land of Cyrus and Xerxes.

The founder of the Persian nation was Kaiomurs. He also had the title of Gilshah, or king of the world. He established his capital at Balkh. The wild beasts of the forests acknowledged his sway. They paid obeisance at his throne. Kaiomurs made it his ambition to civilize the savage tribes of Asia. In these noble efforts he encountered violent opposition from the barbarians called Deeves; and he sent against them his handsome son Siamek, with a powerful army; among his auxiliaries were lions and tigers eager for the fray. But Siamek was slain in the battle which followed among the mountains, and great was the lamentation of all.

Siamek had a son named Houscheng. He was placed at the head of a host that went forth to avenge the death of his father; and the Deeves were at last subdued. Kaiomurs died soon after this event, and Houscheng, wise, prudent, and just, succeeded to the throne. It was in his reign that the Persians became fire-worshippers, adoring flame as the symbol of God. Thamauras succeeded Houscheng, and he in turn was followed by Shah Djemsheed, who is one of the most celebrated monarchs of Persia. Djemsheed, during a reign of many years, accomplished much for the advancement of his people. He introduced the use of iron, and the weaving and embroidering of woollen, silk, and cotton stuffs; and divided his subjects into four castes or classes: priests, warriors, and traders; the fourth caste was composed of husbandmen, who bore the name of Nesoudi. Of this class the Persian poet, Firdoüsee, wrote: "They render homage to no one; they labor, they sow, they harvest, and are nourished in the fields of the earth without injury to any one. They are subject to the orders of none, although their clothes are humble, and their ear is never struck by the clamor of slander. They are free; and the tillage of the earth is their right; they have no enemies; they have no quarrels." It must be admitted that this is a somewhat poetic and rose-hued description of a farmer's condition.

Shah Djemsheed also enlisted the subject Deeves into the service of making bricks, of which the invention is attributed to him. He is likewise credited with the employment of hewn marble in the construction of buildings, with the discovery of perfumes, the arts of healing, the invention of ships, and many other useful means for benefiting the race. It was Djemsheed also who instituted the No Rooz, or New Year, at the time of the spring solstice, a festival still celebrated in Persia with many ceremonies during ten days. He seems indeed to have been a most puissant, beneficent, and glorious king for many peaceful years, until, as the legend records, his head was affected by the height of power which he had reached; then he became arrogant and recognized no other greater than himself, and forgetting his Creator, assumed himself to be the sole architect of his greatness. The priests and people trembled when they heard his high utterances, for they foresaw that it meant his downfall. They realized what a later king wisely said: "Pride goeth before destruction."

The favor of God was withdrawn and Persia became torn with discord. It was in vain that the haughty monarch besought the divine pardon when it was too late. On the western boundaries of Persia was a nation whose armies flew to battle on swift horses and bearing long spears. They had for king, Mardas, widely known for his valor and virtues.

To him was born a son who was named Zohâk, who at first seemed destined to rival the noble qualities of his father. But ambition proved the ruin of his character—ambition of which a great poet had said, "by that sin the angels fell." The Evil One in human form came to Zohâk and tempted him to slay his father and seize the throne. Zohâk first hesitated, but ended by carrying out this fell design. Having led him thus far in inquity, the dark spirit continued his influence over Zohâk, who was now in his power, having sold himself to evil.

Having reached this point, the Devil, in the guise of a favorite servant, said to Zohâk: "O king, live forever, full of content and power! my heart is full of love for thee, and to behold thee is all that I desire. I have but one desire to ask of the king, even if this honor be above my deserts; it is that he permit me to kiss his shoulders, and that I touch them with mine eyes." Zohâk perceived not the design of the Evil One in making this seemingly simple request, and therefore granted it. An extraordinary result followed, for from each of the shoulders of the king sprouted a black serpent. Struck with horror, Zohâk searched everywhere for a remedy, and finally caused the reptiles to be cut off at the shoulders. But behold they grew forth again like branches of a tree. At last the Evil One, in the guise of a skilled physician, presented himself before Zohâk, and advised him to do no injury to the serpents, but to feed them with the brains of men, in the hope that they must thus ultimately perish. Was this a subtle design to cause the destruction of mankind? Thus early do we see the superstition of man selling himself to the Devil illustrated in Persia as in Europe. All are familiar with similar tales in European legends of the dark ages.

It was after these remarkable events that great disturbances broke out in Persia; on all hands was discord and strife. Djemsheed, belying his former character, became an odious tyrant; pretenders to his throne raised insurrections. Finally, a faction, in despair, turned to the west and implored the aid of Zohâk against the sovereign who had now become the greatest enemy of his people. Zohâk invaded Persia, and Djemsheed, defeated in battle, took flight, abandoning his throne to Zohâk. For many years he abode in exile concealed. When all supposed him dead and had quite forgotten him, the exile returned, hoping to create a rising in his favor. But Zohâk caused him to be seized unawares and sawn asunder.

Thus was the fall of the great Djemsheed. But the good deeds he accomplished in the first half of his reign have caused his memory to live, and to the present time the Persians look back with pride to the splendor of their country in the days of Shah Djemsheed. But Persia groaned under the tyranny of Zohâk. She had simply exchanged one tyrant for another, and that one worse than his predecessor. Each day two young men of the flower of Persia's youth were slain to gratify the furious hunger of the serpents of Zohâk. But in time the servitors, who acted as executioners and cooks, devised a scheme of slaying a sheep in the stead of one of the human victims, and permitting him to escape, on condition that he fled the country in order that their stratagem might not be discovered.

Finally Zohâk dreamed a dream which caused him to summon all the mobeds, or wise men, into his presence to interpret his vision. Long they hesitated, until one of their number, Zirêk, stood forth and dared to tell the king that the dream foretold the coming of a great and good prince, who should hurl him from the throne and bind him in chains on the mountains. On coming to his senses after falling into a swoon from fear, Zohâk sent messengers into every quarter of his empire to search out and bring to him the fateful prince. They sought in vain. But Feridoon, for such was his name, was daily growing in strength and preparing for the noble task assigned to him by Providence. He was the son of Abtin, grandson of Shah Djemsheed, and Firanêk, daughter of Thehour, king of the isles of Madjin.

Learning that a glorious son had been born to Abtin, Zohâk caused Abtin to be seized and executed. But Firanêk escaped with Feridoon, and placed him in charge of a gardener, who had a cow of extraordinary beauty and lineage, named Purmajeh, which secretly nourished the infant for three months. But the secret became divulged, and when the mother heard that the servants of Zohâk were coming to snatch her child from the garden, she flew hither, and was able to carry Feridoon to the mountains of Elborz before the coming of the king's executioners.

Years went by and Feridoon reached manhood, and descended to the plains to try his fortune. About that time Zohâk, oppressed by the terrors of conscience, called an assembly of his nobles, and required them to sign a document asserting that his reign had been beneficial to Persia. While this transaction was in progress a cry of justice was heard at the palace gate, and a man named Kaweh, a blacksmith, was brought into the presence of the king. "Who hath wronged thee?" demanded Zohâk. Kaweh replied, that he asked justice and redress for the sixteen sons who had been slain one by one to appease the serpents of Zohâk. But one remained, and he in turn was doomed to the same fate. With frantic and terrible words the blacksmith made the proud and cruel monarch tremble.

PALACE GUARD.

Appalled by the rage and sorrow of a father, whose language seemed like the cry of doom, Zohâk ordered the only remaining son of Kaweh to be restored to him. And then he bade him sign the document which the noblemen had already signed. On learning its purport, Kaweh burst into fierce invectives against the craven nobles who had yielded to the wishes of Zohâk, and tearing the document in twain, rushed forth from the palace with shouts of vengeance.

In the market-place a throng gathered around the blacksmith, who summoned the world to rise and restore justice to her throne. Placing his leathern apron on a spear he proceeded through the city, calling on all to follow this standard and summon Feridoon to deliver them from the chains of Zohâk. Feridoon accepted the invitation of the insurgents, and proclaimed the leathern apron as the royal standard, causing it to be adorned with gold and precious stones and fringed with gayly colored embroideries. From that day, until the Mohammedan conquest many centuries later, the rude leathern apron of Kaweh the blacksmith, under the name of Kaweianee, was the standard borne at the head of the armies of Persia.

Feridoon having carefully laid his plans, collected an army, and accompanied by his two brothers, set out against Zohâk, fired with a lofty zeal to free his country and avenge his father's death. His warriors were mounted on swift steeds. On the way he was visited by an angel from paradise, who came to him in his tent at night to foretell the varied fortunes that he was to encounter and bestow on him a magic power to overcome the wiles of his foes. But the brothers of Feridoon, aware of the visit of the celestial messenger, were smitten with envy, and conspired to slay their more fortunate brother. While he was still sleeping calmly in his tent they hurled an enormous rock from the brow of a precipice, intending it to fall on the tent. But Feridoon was awakened by the sound of the rolling rock, and by instantly using the magic power given him by the angel, arrested the stone in its course.

The army of the insurgents arrived at last on the shores of the Tigris, and Feridoon with his mounted host swam across the turbid flood of that famous river and arrived at the gates of the proud capital of Zohâk, whose palace raised its towers to heaven. Feridoon bore an iron mace with a head shaped like a cow's head, in remembrance of the cow Purmajeh which had nourished him. Since that time the form of a cow has been a talismanic sign, an omen of good fortune, in Persia, engraved on seals or appearing on maces and shields. The prince smote the great gate with his mace, and at the signal his army stormed the walls, burst in the gates, and put the garrison to flight. Feridoon entered the palace of Zohâk, but that proud monarch was gone. In the apartments of the women the victor found two daughters of Shah Djemsheed, whom he at once liberated. From them he learned the hiding-place of Zohâk, who it seems was seeking to retrieve his tottering fortunes by secret conference with magicians.

A swift messenger bore to Zohâk the strange tidings of the fall of his capital. Quickly raising an army, the usurper rushed home to expel Feridoon from his palaces. A terrible battle ensued in the streets; the populace themselves fought against Zohâk, so weary were they of his tyranny. But he succeeded in penetrating to the palace, and, furious with jealousy, was about to slay the captive daughters of Djemsheed whom Feridoon had rescued and married, but he was met by the young hero, who, instead of killing Zohâk, made him his captive and reserved him for a more dreadful doom.

When the battle was over and the victory of Feridoon was complete, he marched toward the great mountain Demavend in the north of Persia, bearing with him the deposed tyrant in chains. On arriving at the mountain, Feridoon caused search to be made for a deep, narrow, sunless defile in the heart of the Demavend, where was a bottomless cavern. Iron clamps were made; Zohâk was stretched on the edge of the precipice over the abyss, and bound alive to the rock by the clamps, and there they left him to fill the air with his shrieks and groans during the coming ages.*

The first act of the good Feridoon, after mounting the throne of his ancestors was to send a herald to his mother Firanêk, who was dwelling in a secret hiding-place, to ask her blessing, and announce to her the good fortune which Heaven had vouchsafed to him and to Persia. Good fortune favored Feridoon for many years; his reign was prosperous, and his people happy after their release from the tyranny of Zohâk. Three sons were born to Feridoon, and when they reached the age of manhood he caused search to be made for three princesses worthy of alliance with the line of Djemsheed. The nobleman who was deputed to this task was Djendil,

* The study of comparative history makes it clear that the story of Zohâk is a record in poetic form of an invasion of Persia by the Assyrians at a time when the reigning dynasty of Djemsheed had fallen into degeneracy

CONE OF MOUNT DEMAVEND, TAKEN FROM AN ALTITUDE OF 10,000 FEET.

noted for his intelligence and discretion and famed for his travels. Far and wide over many lands Djendil made inquiry for three maidens suited by birth and character to become the daughters-in-law of Feridoon. But nowhere did he find what he sought until he arrived at the court of Serv, the king of Yemen. Seeing that in the three fair princesses of Yemen he had at last found the objects of his quest, Djendil in many lofty and learned phrases, conveyed to the king of Yemen the purpose of his coming, and in the name of Feridoon proposed their alliance with the three princes of the royal house of Persia.

The king of Yemen turned pale when he heard this message, but replied, good father as he was: "I will consult with my daughters and learn what is their will in this matter." He was filled with anguish when he thought of having his daughters go away from him to a far-off land, whence they might never return, although he well knew that a marriage alliance with the king of Persia was a glory to be sought after, and also that it is the lot of parents to see their daughters leave them for other homes when they reach years of maturity. On the other hand the king of Yemen hesitated to affront so great a monarch as Feridoon by refusing the honor. He therefore summoned his nobles in council and asked their advice.

The nobles advised a course rather more haughty than he felt justified in pursuing, and he therefore followed his own judgment. He took a middle course. Instead of definitely accepting or rejecting the offer, he stated that he must first see the three brothers; if they would come to his court, and he found them suited to marry his daughters, he would not withhold his consent. This was an unusual proceeding in an Oriental country, for Persia was more powerful than Yemen, and it is customary there for the bride of a prince to go to the home of her husband without a previous interview with the father-in-law.

Djendil having received the response of the king of Yemen, kissed the throne, and returned to his royal master, who summoned his three sons when he heard the reply, and advised them as follows: " The king of Yemen is head of a numerous people; he is a cypress that casts a shadow afar. He has three daughters like pearls; he has no sons, and these maidens are his diadem. I have asked them for you. But it is now necessary that you repair to Yemen, and that you conduct yourselves with prudence and circumspection; pay careful attention to all that he shall say to you; remembering that you are the sons of a king. Listen, therefore, to my counsel, and if you act accordingly you shall reap happiness.

" The king of Yemen is a man of great shrewdness. He is wise, upright, and powerful. He must on no account discover you to be lacking in intelligence, for he will undoubtedly employ devices to test your character and ability. He will decree a banquet on the first day in your honor. His three fair daughters, lovely as gardens in spring-time, will be present. He will seat them on the throne-royal, and in height and appearance they will strongly resemble each other.

The youngest of the three will enter first, the oldest will come last, and the second will come between them. He will place the youngest next to the oldest of you; the eldest next to the youngest prince, and the second in age will be seated next to the one of you whose age is between his brothers. Note this point well; for thus you will avoid a disastrous result. He will ask you, then, to designate the princesses according to their age. If you reply correctly he will decide in your favor."

Carefully pondering the words of Feridoon, the three princes set out on the long journey to Yemen, escorted by numerous warriors clad in glittering mail. When Serv, king of Yemen, learned that they had entered the borders of his dominion, he sent forward a troop of his bravest chieftains to accompany them to his capital; and when the princely brothers entered the gates of the city, all the people came forth sprinkling them with amber and saffron, and pouring out wine scented with musk. The manes of the steeds were fragrant with sweet odors, and they trod upon coins of gold scattered broadcast over the pavement. The palace was decorated like paradise; the bricks of its walls were covered with silver and gold and hung with embroideries of price.

Here the king of Yemen received the princes and as Feridoon had predicted, he now brought his three daughters hither, glowing in their beauty. They were seated exactly in the order the king of Persia had foretold, and the king of Yemen then asked: "Which of these stars is the youngest, which is the second, and which the eldest?" The princes replied as they had been advised by their father, and thus at one stroke warded off the wiles of enchantment. Serv, the king of Yemen, and his nobles were astounded. He perceived that artifice was of no avail to keep his daughters at home, and he awarded them, according to their ages, to the three princes. After conversing a while as to the future and the plans of their lives, the three sisters arose and retired to their apartments, blushing with mortification at the discomfiture of their father.

After this event, being still unresigned to giving up his lovely daughters, Serv ordered wine to be brought and singers to enliven the watches of the night, and when the three brothers yielded to the wine and fell asleep, he caused them to be laid on couches by the side of a fountain of rose-water, under the stars, where the roses diffused balm over their slumber. And then the king retired and, master-magician as he was, devised enchantments that would relieve him of the sad necessity of losing his daughters. He caused a great cold and a piercing wind to arise, and a frost able to kill the flowers of the gardens, hoping that in their sleep the princes might be frozen to death. But instead of this they were awaked by the terrible cold, and by their superior intelligence at once divined the cause of this change in the weather, and thus they took means to resist and overcome the treachery to which they had been exposed.

When the sun burst above the mountain tops, the royal magician flew to the garden expecting to find the three princes stiff and stark and dead, and thus his daughters would be left to comfort him in his old age. But he found the brothers seated on their couches blooming and alive, and perceived at last that against them no arts of his magic could avail.

Then the king of Yemen ordered his halls of audience to be prepared and the nobles of his realm to assemble. And there, too, came the three maidens, who had hitherto dwelt in seclusion; they were adorned with crowns and jewels, and until now had never known sorrow. Never yet had trouble touched their fair, dark tresses. And there he bestowed the three treasures of his heart on the three princes. But in the bitterness of his soul he said: "It is not Feridoon who is the cause of my grief, but I myself. Know that he who hath no daughters shall be spared the pain of parting with them." Then he said to the wise men of the kingdom: "Kings are worthy to be husbands of stars like these. Know that I have given my beloved daughters to these princes, according to our rites and customs, to cherish and love them like their own souls."

Then the order went forth to prepare all things agreeably for the journey of the sisters to their new home. The king spared no trouble nor expense nor gifts that would add to the comfort of the journey of his daughters. Litters carefully arranged for them were placed on the backs of strong camels, and when all was in readiness the king of Yemen bade farewell to his children and returned alone to his palace, while they started forth with the three princes on the long journey to Persia.

When Feridoon learned that his sons were returning successful, he went forth to meet them. Anxious to put their courage to the test, he took the shape of a terrible dragon, roaring and vomiting flames, and attacked the eldest of the brothers. But the prince said to himself: "A prudent man fighteth not with dragons," and turned and fled. Then the dragon flew at the other brothers; and the second brother said: "What matters it whether it be a dragon or a warrior?" and he drew his bow; but the youngest son tarried not afar, but full of fire and fury rushed at the dragon, crying: "Flee from our presence, for we are the sons of Feridoon, lions that it is fatal for thee to resist!"

Feridoon having thus divined the characters of the three princes, vanished. But having resumed his former shape, he advanced to meet them with great pomp, and returned thanks to the All-giver for their safe and happy return. On arriving at the palace he summoned the brothers into his presence and informed them of the ruse he had practised. He rejoiced at the opportunity he had seized of testing their characters, and now for the first time did Feridoon give names to his sons suited to the opinion he had formed of them. The eldest he called Selm, the next he called Tour, and the youngest Iredj. As he named them in turn he invoked for each the blessing of God.

After this ceremony Feridoon consulted the horoscope to divine the destiny of his sons. He learned that the two eldest were destined to success and renown, but Iredj, the youngest and best beloved, although possessed of such brilliant qualities, was doomed to misfortune and a tragical end. Feridoon, deeply pained by this declaration, now proceeded to divide the government of his vast empire among the three brothers. To Selm was awarded the dominion of the western portion, and to Tour the eastern provinces reaching even to China; this division of Asia has, since this event, been called after him Tourân. But notwithstanding that the stars were adverse to the destiny of Iredj, Feridoon selected him as the ablest to preside over the heart of the empire, or Persia itself.

The brothers took charge of the reins of government, and years passed on during which the empire was at peace. But Feridoon was growing old and full of years, and in proportion as their father became feeble the two eldest brothers became jealous of their brother Iredj, who was destined to take precedence of them on the death of Feridoon. Consulting together they wickedly conspired and sent an insulting message to Feridoon, demanding that Iredj be deprived of the throne of Irân, and declaring that if this were not done, they would together lead an invasion into Persia for the purpose of destroying Iredj and razing the capital to the ground. This haughty message was borne to Feridoon by a herald mounted on a swift dromedary.

Entering a palace whose towers arose toward heaven, and awed by the pomp and magnificence of the royal abode, the herald was admitted to the presence of Feridoon, who was seated on his lofty throne, proud and venerable, with a snow-white beard

KING SLAYS EVIL GENIUS.
SCULPTURE AT PERSEPOLIS.

reaching to his waist. The monarch graciously inquired after the health of his royal sons, and whether they continued true to the faith of their fathers and enjoyed prosperity and peace in their borders. The envoy replied: "O glorious king, live forever on thy throne of splendor! I, the unworthy slave of a king, bring unwillingly to the emperor a hard message; he who sends it is responsible, but I am innocent. I will repeat, with the king's permission, these inconsiderate words." Feridoon replied: "Speak on." He listened attentively, and his soul kindled with fury. He sent a message in reply to his sons, advising them to repent without delay from the rebellious course they had chosen.

After this, Feridoon communicated the matter to his beloved son Iredj; he informed him that in this world we can look for no defenders unless we are prepared to defend ourselves, and that his innocence and rights were a strong armor to him. Homer uttered the same sentiment in the Iliad when he said: "Thrice armed is he whose cause is just." Feridoon advised Iredj to collect an army and prepare to resist the attack of his brothers, and promised him all the resources of the empire in the conflict.

But Iredj replied that it was the desire of his life to imitate the noble example of his royal father; to do good and not evil was his aim; he did not care for glory and power at the expense of bloodshed, nor did he seek fratricidal strife. Instead of resorting to arms, therefore, he asked the permission of Feridoon to go to meet his brothers Tour and Selm, attended only by a few retainers, hoping by words of friendship and peace to abate their jealousy and hate. Finding Iredj firm in his purpose, Feridoon granted the request, but with gloomy forebodings. He gave him a letter-royal for Tour and Selm, and then Iredj set forth on his journey, strong in the justice of his cause and the purity of his motives. The two brothers were in council surrounded by a great army, when Iredj approached without suspicion of impending danger. He met them with a countenance showing brotherly affection and kindness; but they received him with lowering looks. The hate of the two brothers was deepened when they saw their troops gazing with admiration on the noble bearing of their younger brother. They upbraided him with usurping, as they said, the throne of Persia. He replied that the right had been conferred on him unsolicited by their royal sire Feridoon. But rather than be the cause of war and blood he would willingly resign his rights to them. This generous reply, instead of allaying only increased the wicked fury of the two brothers. Tour drew a dagger and smote Iredj to the heart. The brothers then embalmed the head of their poor victim, and sent it with an insulting message to their aged father Feridoon.

Anxiously looking for the return of Iredj, the old monarch had the walls of his palace re-adorned to give him a joyous welcome home. Musicians and dancing-women and banquets were in readiness for the happy occasion. But Feridoon, watching from the saddle at the head of his expectant army, only discovered a solitary dromedary coming from the dusty horizon, and a rider with sorrowful eyes. The rider bore a case of gold which he presented to the king. With a grim presentiment he caused the case of gold to be opened. They took thence a cloth of silk, and when the silk was unrolled the aged monarch looked on the head of his beloved son. Feridoon fell from his horse in a swoon. When he came to his senses again he returned to the city on foot, followed by his army lamenting, and with banners rent in twain.

Pressing the head of Iredj to his bosom, the old man bent his steps to the now forsaken palace of Iredj. After invoking the curse of the All-just upon the slayers of his son, Feridoon threw himself on the grass, and with locks wet with dew lay night after night under the stars, and all the land wept and bemoaned the sorrow which had come on the great king.

Although their father was old, yet Tour and Selm dared not lead an open revolt against him, for he was still a hero, and in his despair was a dangerous foe. And soon a son was born to Iredj by his favorite wife, Mahaferid. He was named Minoutchehr. But when Tour and Selm heard that the son of Iredj was a manly youth, who would in time seek to avenge the murder of his father, they devised a scheme to get him into their power. A messenger was sent by them to Feridoon, bearing rich gifts and words of deep remorse for the cruel assassination of Iredj. In token of their repentance they now begged Feridoon to send to them Minoutchehr, the son of

Iredj, who should receive from them ample amends for the wrong done to his father. But the aged king discerned the craft and wickedness of the brothers. He bade the messenger return and say to them that they should not again have it in their power to deceive him, but to prepare for the sure retribution that awaited them. Conscience-stricken, and well knowing the power of Persia, the brothers made ready their forces to repel the vast host which Minoutchehr was leading against them. The young hero had inherited the wisdom of Feridoon and the virtues of Iredj, and the leathern standard of Kaweh, resplendent with jewels, which never yet had recoiled before the foe, was carried before them. His heart was nerved, too, with a stern resolve to destroy the murderers of his father. Victory attended the arms of Minoutchehr. Tour was first defeated and slain, and after him Selm was completely overthrown, and his head was cut off by the redoubtable sword of Minoutchehr.

Having seen his son avenged, Feridoon, the great and good king, descended in turn to the tomb, old and full of years, and Minoutchehr succeeded him on the throne.

The greatest poet of Persia has beautifully said: "Feridoon the glorious was not an angel; he was not made of musk and amber; it was by his justice and his generosity that he won his great renown. Be just and generous, and thou shalt be like Feridoon."

II.

ZAL.

WHEN Minoutchehr assumed the crown of the dynasty of the Keïanides, he announced his intention to reign over his vast dominions with humanity and justice, and as a servant of God, the ruler of the universe. In the name of all the nobles assembled on this august occasion, the great Pehlevân or warrior Sahm, the son of Neriman, arose and promised their allegiance and aid in all the plans and enterprises which the young monarch should undertake for the good of his subjects.

The nobles then dispersed, and Sahm returned to Seistân, the hereditary province which was under his control. The house of Sahm is perhaps the most celebrated in the legends of Persia, and had vast influence in shaping her destinies. It is therefore a pleasure to give here a narrative of the many romantic events and heroic characters which marked the career of the great family of Sahm, the son of Neriman. It came to pass, after the return of Sahm to Seistân, that a son was born to him of extraordinary beauty. But although Sahm had longed for a son to perpetuate the line, yet for seven days no one dared announce to the father that a son was born to

him, for the hair of the infant was white. All the
women of the household were in tears, for they
dreaded the result when Sahm should learn of the
white hair of his child,—such an unfortunate omen is
it considered in Persia to have light hair and blue
eyes.

At last a nurse was found of courage sufficient to
enter the father's presence, who, after saying,
"May the years of Sahm the hero be happy, and
may the heart of his enemies be rent asunder!" proceeded to tell him of the little son that was in the
apartments of the women. Sahm followed her hither
but when the curtain was raised and he saw that the
fair infant was white-haired, his senses seemed to
depart from him with horror at what he deemed
an ill-portent to his fortunes, he dreaded also the
mockery of men when they should hear of it.
Nothing could appease his rage. He doomed the
poor infant to be exposed on the summit of the
Elborz mountains. But a great bird, called the
Simurgh, had its nest there, and when it heard the
wailings of the child, the bird tenderly lifted him
from the rocks, and carried him to its nest, and fed
him on tender venison until he grew to manhood,
hardy and well-formed. But Sahm had a dream,
which the mobeds, or wise men, interpreted to mean
that his son was still alive on the Elborz, and that,
after asking the forgiveness of Heaven for his cruelty
to his son, it was his duty to reclaim and bring him
home from the wild eyrie of the Simurgh.

Sahm listened to the words of the mobeds. He
hastened to the Elborz and found his son dwelling

on the pinnacles of the mountain. From the foot of the inaccessible rock Sahm beheld his son, a youth of heroic mould, standing on the nest of the Simurgh and gazing like a king over the world. But there was no way to reach him, and while Sahm was impatiently searching for a means to communicate with his son, the Simurgh beheld the father and divined for what purpose he had come. He told the youth, who yet knew nothing of men, that the hour had come for him to return to his native land; the faithful bird plucked a feather from its plumage and bade the youth carry it with him; in after life, if sore beset by trouble, he was to throw the feather into the fire, and immediately the Simurgh would come to his aid and show him a way out of the difficulty. Then it took him on its wings and bore him to his father. Sahm received his son with joy; he begged him to forgive his early sin in exposing him, and bestowed on him the name Zal-Zer. The cymbals and the kettle-drums of the army pealed a welcome, and, clad in purple and mounted upon a noble steed, the youth returned, crowned with honors, to the palace from which he had been driven a naked and wailing infant.

After these events King Minoutchehr ordered Sahm to march with an army against the rebels who had arisen in the north of Persia. Sahm constituted Zal the governor of Seistân during his absence. Zal found this a fit opportunity to make the acquaintance of some of his neighbors, and, among others, visited Mihrab, the king of Kabool. He was tributary to Minoutchehr, but owing to his being connected with the line of Zohâk, the deposed tyrant and usurper, there seems to have been little cordiality between the king of Persia and his feudatory viceroy, Mihrab. While at Kabool, Zal learned of the extraordinary beauty and accomplishments of Roodabeh, the daughter of Mihrab and Sindocht. Roodabeh likewise heard her maidens sing of the manly virtues of Zal, the son of Sahm, the son of Neriman. The result can easily be foreseen; they were a pair worthy of each other; and without having yet met, were already madly in love. The maidens of Roodabeh contrived to inform the young hero of the state of the feelings of their mistress towards him, and a secret interview was planned. It may be asked why such secrecy between a prince and princess of equal rank? but her descent from the house of Zohâk made it highly improbable that either the king of Persia or Mihrab would consent to their union.

When Zal arrived at the foot of the tower where Roodabeh was awaiting him, his difficulties only began. The gates were closed, and he had no ladder. The maiden loosened the long tresses, of which she had such store, and, leaning out of the window, bade him raise himself by her hair. But he unloosed the lasso, which the warriors of Persia used so skilfully in those times and flung it over one of the battlements instead, and thus he was able to pull himself up to the top of the wall. But Mihrab and Sindocht were filled with wrath when they learned of the secret interviews of the lovers, and utterly forbade all hope of their marriage. Fortunately it occurred to Zal in this predicament to lay the whole matter before

Sahm, his father, in a letter sent by a swift messenger. The matter appeared of such importance to Sahm that he called his wise men before him to give him their advice, for such was his love for his son that he did not wish hastily to decide against the ardent hopes of the young viceroy. The wise men consulted the stars long and carefully; they returned to Sahm with smiling countenances and announced that a happy issue was destined for the marriage of Zal and Roodabeh; and Sahm caused gold and silver to be bounteously distributed to the wise men, for their decision had given his troubled heart repose.

When the good tidings that Sahm had given his consent was received, Roodabeh caused the woman who brought the news to her to be showered with coins of gold, and ordered her to be clothed in new vestments. But Mihrab was furious on learning this decision, desiring no alliance between the line of Zohâk and the race of Persia.

Word of these transactions also came to the ear of King Minoutchehr; although greatly disturbed at the possibility of any of the race of Zohâk regaining influence in Irân, yet he decided to act with moderation and wisdom. But reflection only increased his wrath against Mihrab, who seemed to him to be subtly acting in such a way as once more to bring Persia under the hated influence of the house of Zohâk. Forthwith he ordered Sahm to return with his victorious troops from the north, and march against and overthrow and destroy Mihrab and all his family. It was as Mihrab had foreseen. The love of Zal and Roodabeh seemed about to prove his

REPRESENTATIONS OF PERSIAN MYTHOLOGY, FROM AN ANCIENT RECORD.

destruction. When Zal heard of the approach of Sahm, he swore a loud oath that even if a dragon breathing fire were to come against Kabool, they must first cleave off his own head before he could capture the place. And then he went forth to meet his father, confident in the promise that Sahm had given, to permit the marriage of Zal and Roodabeh.

When Zal entered the presence of Sahm, he saluted him with all honor, and in passionate but respectful terms upbraided him for the course he was taking. He reminded his father that, when he was an infant, he had exposed him on the top of a mountain, regardless that it is God who giveth black hairs and white, and had left him to be sustained by the mercies of a wild bird of the peaks, to whom indeed he was more indebted for life than to him. And, now that his son had reached years of manhood and lived a true life, again it was the father who, in spite of his promise, was thwarting him and bringing sorrow to his heart by seeking to destroy Kabool, where Zal sojourned and was happy.

Sahm listened attentively, and acknowledging the justice of what Zal had said, replied that a remedy must be found to settle the difficult question with which he had to deal. He decided to send Zal himself to King Minoutchehr, with a letter, there to plead his own cause with the stern but not unreasoning monarch. While Zal was gone on his hazardous errand, Sahm and his army reposed amid the vineyards and rose-gardens of the well-watered land where they were encamped. Swift as arrows from the bow the impatient young lover and his attendant warriors flew over mountain and plain, until their panting steeds brought them to the lordly gates of Persia's capital.

While these events were occurring, Mihrab was filled with rage and anxiety, for the large army of Persia, under the redoubtable chieftain Sahm, was on his borders, and he expected daily to be attacked and destroyed by an overwhelming host. Thus brooding, Mihrab vented his fury on his wife Sindocht, and their lovely daughter Roodabeh. To appease her husband, and perhaps save her life and her daughter's, Sindocht offered herself to carry a present, composed of the most valued treasures of Kabool, to Sahm, and urge him to treat them kindly. It was no small thing for a princess to go thus to the camp of an enemy. But the result proved favorable, for Sahm not only received her graciously, but also, in the name of Zal, accepted the magnificent presents she brought. He bade her return reassured to Kabool, saying: " Let not your heart be troubled, for all will end according to your desires."

Immediately on arriving at the court, Zal was summoned to an audience of King Minoutchehr, who received him graciously. After reading the letter of Sahm, the king smiled, and said: " Although this is a question which arouses my fears of future difficulties, yet all that you desire shall be granted."

After this a royal banquet was served, with dishes of silver and gold, on a table covered with beaten gold. Minoutchehr invited Zal and the great nobles of the court to sit with him; after the banquet, wine was brought in another hall, and the feasting continued until late. Then Zal mounted his steed and returned to his quarters, leaving the king well pleased with the bearing of his young and noble subject. At early morning, according to the custom of a warm country like Persia, King Minoutchehr seated himself again on his throne, and the nobles and warriors gathered before him to consult of the affairs of the empire. On this occasion the king commanded the mobeds, or wise men of Persia, to put Zal to a supreme ordeal. The ordeal consisted of five riddles, proposed in poetic language and requiring a high degree of intelligence for their solution. Zal acquitted himself with such success that the king of kings himself condescended to express his gratification, and ordered another banquet to be served.

At the audience of the following morning Zal respectfully requested the king's permission to depart. But Minoutchehr replied that a final test of the merits of Zal must yet occur. He must have an exhibition of the athletic skill and heroism of the young warrior before he could grant a free permission to his request. The champions of the empire were summoned to meet on the grand square before the palace, to compete with Zal. It was a severe test, and many a time, doubtless, the heart of the hero trembled with dread lest he should fall short of the approval of the monarch, and thus fail of winning his bride. But in the exercises with the bow, the javelin, and the mace, and in exhibitions of horsemanship, Zal outstripped every competitor, and by the remarkable feats of his skill and strength and courage, aroused the amazement of the king and the entire court.

Minoutchehr blessed Zal, and ordered his servants to spread before him a truly noble present of ornaments of gold and gems, of slaves and horses, and all manner of precious things; and Zal bowed to the earth before the king, and kissed his feet. And Minoutchehr condescended to write a letter to Sahm full of graciousness, and informing him that he had granted all the wishes of his great son Zal.

Swift messengers were sent in advance to announce the return of Zal to Kabool, and Mihrab and Sindocht caused their palace to be gloriously adorned and prepared for the marriage of Zal and Roodabeh. For seven days the wedding festivities continued. At the end the horses and the camels were made ready, and Roodabeh, blooming and happy, accompanied her bridegroom to the bowers of Seistân. In due season a son was born to Zal and Roodabeh. At his birth Zal threw the feather given him by the Simurgh into the fire, and the Simurgh appeared; by her aid the infant had a happy entrance into life. He proved to be a child of wonderful size and beauty, and they called him Rustem. Before returning to the mountain eyrie, the Simurgh blessed the infant, predicting for him a long and glorious career, and again left one of her feathers for use in case another time of need should come to the house of Sahm.

III.

RUSTEM.

WE head this chapter with the name of the great hero of Persia, because during four reigns he was engaged in all the leading events which occurred in that country. By his powerful arm her monarchs were strengthened on the throne, or rescued from the difficulties in which their own follies had thrown them; by his prowess the enemies of Irân were over and over again repelled from her borders. The mighty deeds of Rustem and his noble charger Raksch have made an indelible impression on the legends of Persia, and his name has rung over many a battle-field since then as a watchword of triumph.

Although it does not appear from the legends that there was a formal division of the Persian empire after Minoutchehr succeeded to the throne of his grandfather Feridoon, yet we are left to infer that the somewhat loose bonds that united the provinces to the parent country gradually became without force, notwithstanding the victories of Minoutchehr over Selm and Tour. The regions under the sceptre of Tour, which are now called by the general name of Tartary, began to be called Tourân, and came under the rule of Afrasiab, who, during a long reign, waged terrible wars with Persia, in which the victory was sometimes on one side and sometimes on the other. In these wars it was that Rustem was chiefly engaged.

The first exploit of Rustem was the capture of Sipend. This was a place situated on a steep eminence, and impregnable; it was guarded by a strong garrison. The young warrior hid a number of his braves in cases, such as were used for carrying salt, and loaded them on camels. In the guise of a camel-driver, Rustem led the caravan to the gates. To the demand as to what was on the camels, the reply was, salt. As the people of the beleaguered town were in need of this article, the governor gladly admitted the caravan. From the fact that more care was not taken to ascertain the character of the loads, it is evident that stratagem was not often resorted to in the wars of that period. The people gladly welcomed the supply of salt, but as it was now toward night the opening of the cases was deferred until the following days, and the people gave themselves up to feasting. But when the town was asleep, Rustem arose at dead of night and released his companions, and a furious attack on the garrison at once began. A furious fight in the streets resulted in the slaughter of the governor and the greater part of the people in Sipend. On the return of Rustem to Seistân, his mother, Roodabeh, clasped him to her arms, and with motherly pride gave him her blessing; but when Sahm heard the tidings he bestowed a robe of honor and a steed of price on the herald who brought the good news.

About this time King Minoutchehr died and was succeeded by his son Newder, who began his reign by such injustice and tyranny that the nobles revolted. In this crisis of affairs Newder called upon Sahm to render assistance in restoring order to the kingdom. Sahm obeyed the summons of a sovereign whom in his heart he could only regard with contempt, and returned home from the wars in which he was engaged. On the way he was met by the nobles of Persia, who, loudly complaining of the tyranny of Newder, offered the crown to Sahm, who was now old and venerated by all. But the hero who for so long a period had faithfully served his country, was not at the last to prove unfaithful to his duty. Sahm sternly declined the proffered honor; instead of this, he proceeded to advise the nobles to return to their allegiance, and gave King Newder some wise counsel, which for a time had some effect. But after this the kingdom of Persia was invaded by Afrasiab, who defeated Newder and captured him in a severe battle. Afrasiab put his royal prisoner to death, which was doubtless an advantage to Persia in one respect, for it freed her from the authority of a sovereign ill-fitted to command her destinies.

Zal now came to the rescue of the throne, and instead of retaining it for himself, as it appears he might have done, placed on it, instead, a collateral descendant of Feridoon, named Zeff, who for five years ruled wisely, and somewhat restored Persia after her misfortunes. He was succeeded by Guerschap, who had immediately to repel an invasion of the Turks of

Tourân, under the redoubtable monarch Afrasiab. It was in this campaign that Rustem, who now first entered into a great war, rode his famous roan charger Raksch. From a large troop of horses he selected this noble colt, threw a lasso over his head, and mounted him in spite of the fierce struggles of the dam, who proudly sought to protect her offspring from the saddle.

Guerschap died childless during this campaign, and Persia was again without a king. Rustem was immediately despatched to summon a chieftain of the house of Feridoon who dwelt in concealment near the Elborz mountains, to ascend the throne. His name was Keikobad. The young king immediately took the head of his army and led his host against the invaders. Rustem performed prodigies of valor, and Afrasiab was forced to sue for peace. But the glorious reign of Keikobad was of short duration. He died at his capital, Istakhar, better known in other lands by the name of Persepolis, and was succeeded by Keï Kaoos, who reigned for many years, but proved himself a weak and capricious monarch, who might have ruined the empire he had inherited but for the powerful support of Rustem and other chieftains of renown.

Keï Kaoos began his reign by undertaking an ill-advised war with the hardy mountaineers of Mazanderan, as it is called in Persia, but known in our histories as Hyrcania. From the time of Shah Djemsheed, the kings of Persia had been engaged in indecisive conflicts with the people of that region, who, in their mountain fastnesses, could resist the strongest armies. Keï Kaoos thought that his own inexperienced arm could wage war against Mazanderan unaided by the great leaders of his armies. But he found his mistake to his cost, for he was surrounded by the mountaineers and was forced to send swift messengers to Zal and Rustem to hasten to his rescue. Rapidly collecting an army, father and son urged their forces northward, and after much severe fighting succeeded in extracting Keï Kaoos out of the predicament in which his folly had brought him. In this war Rustem distinguished himself especially by several great exploits which in the legends of Persia are called the seven adventures of Rustem. The chief of these adventures seems to have been the overthrow of the Deeve Sefeed, or White Demon, a name the Persians applied to a tribe of unusual ferocity, who, from their light complexions and hair, received the title of white.

ANAHITA, OR PERSIAN VENUS.

Having been delivered from this great peril, Keï Kaoos decided to set out on a journey through his dominions with great pomp, attended by an immense train of warriors, nobles, wives, and slaves, and with the music of trumpets and cymbals and drums, exactly as the monarchs of Persia have been accustomed to take their journeys from that time to this day. But while the king of Persia was engaged in these pageants, word came to him, like a flash of lightning out of a clear sky, that the people of Syria, on the borders of the Mediterranean, one of the provinces of Kaoos, had revolted under the leadership of a powerful chieftain, who had declared his independence of Persia. With an immense army, Keï Kaoos marched against the rebels, and graciously granted pardon to the satrap who had rebelled. But he demanded, as a condition of peace, the daughter of the king of Syria, whose name was Soudabêh. Her father was reluctant to part with his only daughter, but Soudabêh was of an ambitious nature, and gladly availed herself of the opportunity to become queen of a monarch who at that time was the most powerful sovereign in the world. After seven days' feasting, Soudabêh was sent to King Keï Kaoos, attended by six hundred slaves, and of camels, mules, and horses one thousand each, laden with treasures beyond computation; the princess herself was mounted on a glittering litter, and all manner of perfumes loaded the air about the royal train. Thus a bloody war was followed by the triumphs of love.

But the king of Hamaverâm, or Syria, had yielded his daughter to Kaoos with great sadness and reluctance. And after she had gone to the camp of Kaoos, he devised a stratagem for regaining possession of his child. In pursuance of this design, the king of Syria sent an invitation to Kaoos, his son-in-law, to accept of a banquet in the halls of Syria's king. But when Soudabêh heard of this, she urged her royal bridegroom to decline the invitation, as she divined that her father meant no good by the proposal. But Kaoos would not be convinced, having, after his easy victory over the Syrians, formed a mean opinion of their courage to dare any further attacks against him. The result was as Soudabêh had predicted. After several days of feasting in the capital of Syria, seeing the suspicions of his guest lulled by the bounteousness of his hospitality, the king of Syria commanded Keï Kaoos and his chief warriors to be seized and thrown bound into the dark dungeons of a fortress which stood on the pinnacles of an impregnable height. Happily, Zal and Rustem were not present at the time. A band of veiled women was then ordered by the king of Syria to bring his daughter from the camp to his palace. But Soudabêh, with wild reproaches for the treachery her father had shown, demanded to be led to her husband. Furious that she now preferred her husband to a father who doted on her, the king of Syria permitted her to share the captivity of Kaoos.

Great was the confusion that everywhere broke forth in Persia when the tidings spread that her king was enchained in a dungeon. On all sides was heard the clangor of arms. The king of Syria, on the one hand, led an army into that unhappy country to subjugate it, while from the opposite direction, like an inundation, the hordes of Tourân, led by the implacable enemy of Persia, Afrasiab, burst over the borders, defeated the Syrians, and made a conquest of Persia.

Once more did the Persians have recourse to the great house of Scistân, and Zal and Rustem were summoned by the popular voice to redeem their land from its chains. Rustem sent a secret messenger, who in disguise found his way to the dungeon of Keï Kaoos, and bade him keep up good courage, for a great army was coming to his rescue. Another messenger was sent to the king of Hamaverâm, summoning him to yield up the royal prisoner he had won by treachery, or prepare for the destruction that awaited him when Rustem should appear at the head of an invincible host.

The king of Hamaverâm sent back reply that never again should Keï Kaoos step forth from his dungeon, and that he was ready to hurl back Rustem and his army. As the frontiers of the king of Hamaverâm extended as far as the blue sea we call the Indian Ocean, and the way was long by land, Rustem embarked his forces on a fleet of galleys and succeeded thus in reaching the country of the enemy safely. The sequel may be foreseen, for Rustem was there; and hardly had the combat

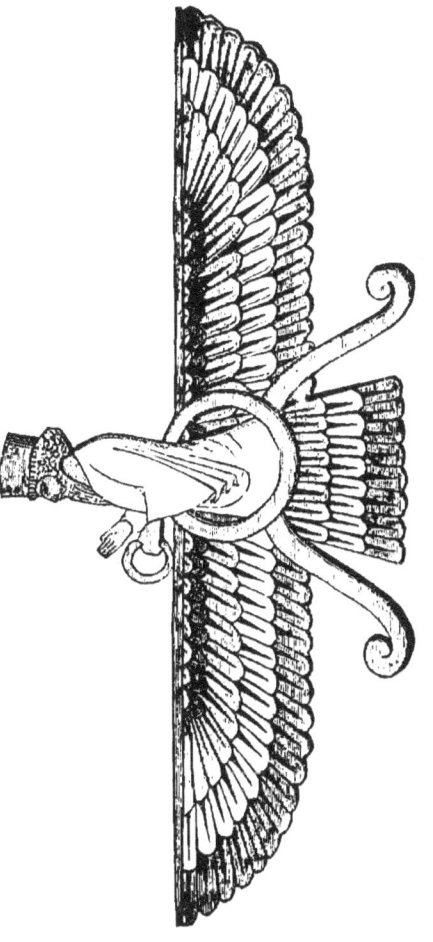

AHRIMAZDAO.

begun when the enemy fled in dismay before Rustem and his redoubtable charger. But the king of Hamaverâm sent swift runners to his neighbors the kings of Egypt and Barbary, beseeching their aid. They answered his appeal, but the same result followed in the great battle they fought with Rustem. The king of Hamaverâm was forced to sue for peace, and restored Keï Kaoos and his warriors to liberty, together with Soudabêh. Thus once more had Rustem proved the savior of his country and king. In addition to this success, Rustem compelled the king of Hamaverâm and his allies to furnish two hundred thousand men to aid Keï Kaoos to expel Afrasiab from Persia. Heralds were also sent to demand the assistance of Greek auxiliaries in the great contest that was now close at hand.

Having completed the arrangements for recovering his throne, Keï Kaoos sent a royal letter to Afrasiab ordering him to abandon Persia without delay. Afrasiab turned pale with rage and sent a haughty and insulting reply. In the campaign which followed, the great Rustem once more led his troops to victory, and Afrasiab and his armies were expelled from Persia with great slaughter. For some years after these events Keï Kaoos devoted himself to restoring his dominions to their former prosperity, having apparently profited by the hard lessons of misfortune. Among other works, he caused several magnificent palaces to be built, and this seems to have been an important era in the progress of architecture in Persia. Keï Kaoos had once more reached a lofty pinnacle of power and splendor, but the hero of his reign who had reaped the glory of the wars was Rustem.

IV.

SOHRAB.

IN his early adventures in the north, Rustem once on a time came to the capital of the feudatory king of Semenjân. While he was asleep in the meadows his horse Raksch strayed away and Rustem proceeded to Semenjân in hope of finding him there. There he learned that Raksch had been found by some of the servants of the king and was stabled at Semenjân as he had surmised. But when about to depart, Rustem yielded to the urgent invitation of the king to tarry awhile and rest himself in feasting and repose. He little thought of the results that would follow his visit to Semenjân. But his experience was that of many. The most trifling incidents often give occasion to events of far reaching importance.

The king of Semenjân had a fair daughter named Tehmimêh. She had heard of the great Rustem — and who had not, for the fame of his exploits and his virtue and grandeur of soul had already spread far and wide, although he was yet in early manhood. Susceptible as she was beautiful, the noble maiden of Semenjân made her preference so evident that the young hero, who was ardent as he was brave, readily yielded to the power of her fascinations. The consent of the king of Semenjân having been obtained, Rustem and Tehmimêh were married with all the rights prescribed by law. A peculiar feature of this alliance, of which the results will appear further on, lay in the fact that the king of Semenjân was feudatory to Afrasiab the deadly enemy of Persia, while Rustem was her greatest champion. At the period of this event the two countries were at peace.

But the hour came when Rustem must leave his blooming bride for awhile at least. Before he bade her farewell, to return to his home far in the south, he gave her an onyx which he wore on his arm, bidding her, if she should have a daughter from their union, to twine the gem among the tresses of the child under a fortunate star. But if the child should prove to be a boy, he bade her bind the onyx to his arm as his father had worn it, predicting for him a glorious career. With many sighs and tears Tehmimêh parted from Rustem, and then he mounted Raksch and returned to Seistân.

The months went by, and then to the lonely bride of Rustem was born a son, large and handsome; his eyes and his mouth were lit with a smile when he was born, and so his mother called him Sohrab. She sent word to Rustem that a child was born from their love, but she told him it was a girl, lest when the boy grew older his father should send for him, and thus rob her of her treasure. In the East, strange as it may seem, boys are more prized than girls.

All these incidents indicate an age when Persia and

the neighboring lands were thinly peopled, and communications between different districts were rare and tardy.

While still of tender years, Sohrab showed signs of his noble lineage. He quickly displayed a love for horses and feats of arms; he was of a proud and haughty spirit, and conscious of his lofty descent, insisted that his mother, who had concealed the fact, should inform him of the name of his father. She had kept the affair a secret, lest Sohrab should wish to go forth and seek his father, Rustem. Then Tehmimêh revealed to Sohrab the secret of his birth, and showed him a bracelet, composed of three superb rubies and three emeralds, which Rustem had sent when he learned that Tehmimêh had a daughter. "It is thy father who has sent this to you, my noble son; thy father Rustem, the greatest warrior on the earth, and he the scion of a great race." And then she enjoined Sohrab to keep these things secret, lest Afrasiab, the enemy of Rustem, should slay Sohrab, or lest Rustem should send for his son, and thus break the heart of his mother with grief.

Sohrab grandly replied: "This is not a secret that can be kept; for the whole world resounds with the mighty deeds of Rustem. Since he is my father, I shall go to his aid; he shall become king of Persia, and together we shall rule the world." After this, he caused a steed worthy of him to be found, and with the aid of his grandfather, the king of Semenjân, made preparations to go in quest of Rustem, his father, attended by a mighty host. But when Afrasiab heard of these events, he held counsel with his wise men, and decided openly to assist Sohrab in his enterprise, in the expectation that in the war which ensued both Rustem and Sohrab would fall, and Persia be then at his mercy. He sent an army of auxiliaries to Sohrab, and also two astute courtiers, named Houman and Barman. They were, under the guise of friendship, to assume the position of counsellors to Sohrab, who was still a mere youth, although full grown, tall, and of great ability and courage. They were to conceal from Sohrab the identity of his father, if they should meet on the field of battle, in the hope that Sohrab, as the younger, would be able to slay Rustem, and after that it would be, as Afrasiab reasoned, comparatively easy to destroy Sohrab by treachery that his young mind would not suspect.

Sohrab, with his army and that of Afrasiab, set out for the south, intending to fight his way until Rustem should be sent against him; then he would make himself known to the great chieftain, and form an alliance with him that would place the line of Seistân on the throne. Here again we gain a clear idea of the peculiar system of society in those remote times. In order to find his father, a son, whose mother belonged to another nation, was obliged to lead a host against his father's country.

The first operations of the army of Sohrab were directed against a fortress called the White Castle. It was the key to the heart of Persia. Guzdehem, an old and famous warrior, was lord of the place, but he had a younger captain, named Hedjir, to lead his forces. Little suspecting what a champion was at the head of the invading army, Hedjir sallied boldly forth, and was at once discomfited by Sohrab, who made him prisoner. Guzdehem had a lovely daughter, who was skilled in athletic sports, an amazon famed for her exploits in war. Her name was Gurdaferid. Filled with fury by the defeat of Hedjir, she delayed not to put on a complete suit of mail, gathering up her heavy tresses under an iron helmet. Mounted on a fiery steed, Gurdaferid rode forth from the gates of the White Castle, and fiercely challenged the host of the enemy to send a champion to meet her, and decide the fate of the fortress by single combat. But no one of the enemy dared to encounter this redoubtable heroine, until Sohrab, who was reposing in his tent, chanced to behold her defying the army of Tourân.

With a smile of exultation Sohrab rode forth to a fresh encounter. As he approached, Gurdaferid shot arrow after arrow against his ringing mail. Rapidly wheeling her horse from side to side, now retiring, and now advancing, and smiting her shield with her spear to frighten his horse, it seemed at first that Gurdaferid, by her dexterity, was about to gain the advantage. Mortified and enraged, Sohrab made a supreme effort, and succeeded in driving his spear-head under her coat of mail, and lifting her in the saddle. Drawing her

CYRUS,
ANCIENT SCULPTURE.

scimitar, Gurdaferid clove the spear in two, but then panic-stricken by the extraordinary power he had displayed, she turned her steed and fled. Sohrab pursued, and seizing her helmet, wrenched it off her head. To his amazement, he discovered, as her wealth of hair fell over her shoulders, that he had been engaged in combat with a maiden. Putting up his sword, Sohrab threw his noose around her waist, and made her his captive.

Gurdaferid secured her liberty by a truly feminine stratagem. Showing her face to Sohrab, she reminded him that both armies would make sport of him if they learned that his courage had been displayed in overcoming a woman; and, rather than lay himself open to such mockery, it were far better to release her. Thus he would guard his reputation and she solemnly promised in return that the White Castle, with its garrison and treasures, should be promptly surrendered.

Perhaps these suggestions had some weight with Sohrab, but it is more likely that he was unable to resist the soft pleading of her lips, and the expressive glances of her gazelle-like eyes. At any rate, he allowed her to re-enter the gates of the White Castle, firmly convinced that he would soon be master, not only of the fortress, but of the fair heroine whom, as the legend records, he had already begun to love. But when Gurdaferid was once more safely within the gates, she mounted the battlements, and mocked Sohrab, who now saw that he had been trifled with, like many a man since then. He vowed vengeance on the morrow; when the sun should arise again, he promised to burst in the gates, to raze the walls, and slay young and old without mercy. But she laughed, and bade him beware of Rustem, who, when he arose in his might, would sweep Sohrab and the hosts of Tourân from the face of the earth.

Sohrab having returned to his camp, Guzdehem immediately wrote a despatch to Keï Kaoos, which was sent by a swift messenger before dawn, informing him that the armies of Touran had once more invaded Persia, led by a hero of vast stature and irresistible power. He warned Keï Kaoos to make instant preparations to meet the foe, or Sohrab would devour the kingdom. The messenger having departed, Guzdehem escaped from the White Castle with all his people, by a secret passage, being well aware what fate awaited them if they tarried until Sohrab should storm its walls. Great was the mortification of Sohrab to find the fortress abandoned; greater still was his regret at the escape of the fair Gurdaferid, who was indeed a fit mate for the young eaglet, who had flown hither from the heights of Semenjân.

When Keï Kaoos received the despatch of Guzdehem he was greatly troubled, and by the advice of his chieftains and counsellors decided to summon Rustem once more from his retirement to come to the rescue of Persia.

The great Guiv was deputed to bear the royal missive to Rustem, with orders to delay not an hour either in going or returning, for the occasion was critical. Guiv was received with great honor, and Rustem agreed to the mandate of Keï Kaoos. But when Guiv urged their immediate departure, Rustem, with entire confidence in his own power to overcome all who attacked Persia, bade him tarry several days in feasting. Greatly disquieted by the delay, Guiv finally persuaded Rustem to depart with him for the court.

But when Rustem presented himself to Keï Kaoos, the monarch, in a great rage, ordered Thous to lead Rustem and Guiv at once to the gallows. Thous laid his hand on the shoulder of Rustem, but the chief of Seistân smote him dead with one blow of his fist. He then reminded Keï Kaoos of all that he owed to him, his life and his throne, and with loud defiance strode out of the presence of the monarch, and hastened back to Seistân, scorning Kaoos, and caring not for the fate of Persia. The enemy meantime were approaching, and the king, trembling for his security and repenting his injudicious wrath, permitted Gouderz, who was great and wise, to go to Seistân and apologize to Rustem for the error of Keï Kaoos, and plead with him to lend his powerful aid before the redoubtable Sohrab should lay Persia at the feet of Tourân. After much expostulation Rustem finally yielded, and the hosts of Persia, led by Keï Kaoos and Rustem, set forth to encounter Sohrab. The return of Rustem to the court was hailed with great feasting and rejoicing. The king, by his conduct, did every thing to efface from the heart of the hero the impression of his base ingratitude.

V.

SOHRAB AND RUSTEM.

KEÏ KAOOS put an immense host into the field. One hundred thousand horsemen in glittering mail, and a troop of mighty elephants accompanied the army. When the tents were pitched at evening, and the torches gleamed in the canvas streets, the camp seemed like a great city. Day by day the army drew nearer to the White Castle, where Sohrab still remained, preparing his forces for an advance to the capital of Iran. The watchmen on the high towers announced the appearance of the serried spears of a great host, and Sohrab, with Houman, climbed to the battlements to reconnoitre the platoons of the enemy. At the sight, Houman showed some apprehension, but Sohrab bade him take courage, for he felt assured of victory.

When night came on Rustem repaired to the pavilion of the king and begged permission to go forth unarmed to spy out the force of the enemy, and learn the character of the chieftains opposed to them, especially Sohrab, whose renown aroused a certain dread in the Persian host. Permission being readily granted, the dauntless Rustem clad himself in the disguise of a Turk, and succeeded, in the dark, in entering the gate of the fortress, where he soon penetrated into the very presence of the great Sohrab, who was seated at a banquet with his chieftains feasting the night before the battle. At his side was his uncle Zendeh Rezm, who was acquainted with Rustem, and to whose care the mother of Sohrab had confided him, with the request that when they should discover Rustem in the hostile army, he should point him out to Sohrab, who had planned this campaign expressly with the purpose of meeting the father of whom he was so justly proud.

One hundred brave warriors were seated around the brave scion of Semenjàn, and musicians sang his glory while the red wine went round, and the torches in the high halls of the castle gave back the flash of arms and the gleam of eyes eager for the combat of the morrow. Rustem watched the scene, standing in the shadow of the door. Zendeh Rezm, having occasion to go forth, discovered the Persian hidden there, and well aware that in the army of Tourân there was no man of such stature and build as he, demanded sternly who he might be. Rustem gave him one blow on the back of the neck and he fell where he stood, dead.

Sohrab waited long for the return of his uncle, seeing his place empty. But when search was made they found the warrior cold on the pavement. Sohrab, followed by all the guests and slaves, rushed with a bound to behold this terrible scene, and all were struck dumb with amazement and dread, until Sohrab cried out, "There is no repose for us this

GATEWAYS.—PALACE OF DARIUS, PERSEPOLIS.

night, my brave warriors, for a wolf has entered the fold, and defied the shepherd and the dogs. Sharpen your blades, for I swear before God, to avenge Zendeh Rezm when the sun rises!"

But Rustem returned to the camp and reported to Keï Kaoos all that had occurred, adding that rumor had not exaggerated the qualities of Sohrab, who in person and soul was undoubtedly the most dangerous champion who had yet led an army against Persia. Then the king ordered musicians and wine, and they drank to success when the clash of arms should ring over the plains at return of day.

When the sun arose Sohrab put on his coat of mail and his helmet of steel decorated with gold. A scimitar was suspended at his side from a band that passed over the shoulder. From the pommel of his saddle was hung a lasso, such as the warriors of those days used with so much effect. It was so long that it was coiled sixty times around the pommel. Accompanied by Hedjir, one of the captains of Afrasiab, he rode forth to a rocky eminence from whence he could well observe the hostile army. Sohrab enjoined his companion to point out to him the chief warriors of the Persian host, and especially Rustem, adding with great sternness that if Hedjir should deceive him he should throw him in chains for the remainder of his life. One after another, Hedjir indicated to Sohrab various chieftains of renown, their tents and banners. But when Sohrab called the attention of Hedjir to a great tent before which was planted the standard of Persia, the leathern apron of Kaweh, and a warrior of vast stature and commanding presence who was there, and a great steed neighing by the tent door, and eagerly demanded to be informed who it could be, Hedjir, remembering the purpose for which he had been sent by Afrasiab, refrained from telling Sohrab that this was none other than his famous father, Rustem; but in an indifferent tone replied that it must be some foreign ally who had joined the army of Keï Kaoos. Sohrab showed much disappointment when he failed to discover Rustem in the army of Persia, but as the legend says, "It was destined otherwise by the decree of Him who changeth not."

Dissatisfied with the reply of Hedjir, Sohrab continued to ply him with questions and surmises, saying that it must be impossible for Rustem to be absent from the seat of war on the eve of so important a conflict, for he was ever at the front of battle, eager for the din of arms and for glory. Hedjir replied again that it was now the feast of roses in Seistân, and Rustem had probably tarried to enjoy its festivities. But Sohrab stoutly maintained that Rustem was of no such stuff as to prefer feasting to war; and reminded Hedjir of the threat made to him in case he told not the truth; Sohrab then added that if he failed to be rightly informed about Rustem, he would surely hew Hedjir into fragments. Hedjir, close-pressed by the questions and threats of the young warrior, evaded a direct reply by saying that it was folly for Sohrab to seek to meet Rustem in battle, for there could only be one issue to such an unequal combat, even though the Persian were now advanced in years. "Better," said

Hedjir, "that thou encounter him not, for he would utterly destroy thee on the battle-field."

When Sohrab heard these words, he turned away hesitating and perplexed; then from the saddle he felled Hedjir to the earth, and returned to the White Castle. He was greatly disheartened, for he had opened this campaign with the earnest longing that it might make him acquainted with his father; and he found himself baffled and disappointed. The mysterious words of Hedjir made it evident that it was impossible to learn through him the exact truth regarding Rustem. But, as Sohrab was the leader of the Touranian army, he could not remain idle; and, therefore, like a careful general, made all the preparations necessary to win success.

Taking off his coronet of gold, Sohrab replaced it with a massive helmet; his mighty arms and chest he encased in a coat of chain mail; his thighs and arms were protected with greaves and armlets of steel; he took his lasso, his bow, his scimitar, and his tremendous mace, and defiled his sturdy warriors, many and brave, forth from the castle to the plains. Taking the Persians unawares by the swiftness of his onset, Sohrab hurled the army of Tourân against the entrenched camp of Keï Kaoos, and penetrated to the very pavilion of the king. It was magnificent to behold the irresistible charge of this stripling, who, yet a mere youth, seemed like a god of war.

In this dire extremity, when all seemed lost, Keï Kaoos sent for Rustem. Impatiently exclaiming that Kaoos never sent for him except when he had got himself into trouble, the hero of Seistân put on his armor, mounted Raksch eagerly, and rushed to the combat. But when Rustem reached the spot where Sohrab, with his mighty mace, was dealing death on all sides, he said to him: "Let us leave this place and go beyond the lines of the two hosts." "Yes," replied Sohrab, "we'll go together alone to a retired spot; we are both heroes, and you and I will decide this war between ourselves; but know that in the shock of arms you will not be able to withstand me, although you are large of stature and of great strength."

Rustem looked at this young man so tall, so broad in the shoulders, so firmly knit, and sitting his steed with such ease and skill, and he replied in a pleasant voice: "O young man, still of tender years! the earth is dry and cold; the air of heaven is soft and balmy. I am old, and have seen many a battle-field; I have destroyed many an army; never have I been overthrown. Assuredly, if you survive me, you will be able to encounter dragons. The stars have witnessed my prowess, the world has been at my mercy. But I have a tenderness for you, and I seek not to rob you of life. Leave the people of Touran, for there is none like you in Persia."

While Rustem was thus speaking, the heart of Sohrab beat fast, and yearned towards Rustem; for a vague instinct made him think that the father whom he was seeking was before him. He said: "I will ask you a question, and must have the truth. Tell me frankly your birth, and rejoice my heart with glad tidings; I think that you are Rustem, of the great race of Neriman." But Rustem replied: "I am not Rustem, nor of the race of Neriman; for he is a chieftain, and I am only an ordinary man, having neither palace nor princely diadem." The heart of Sohrab sank within him as he heard these fatal words, and the light of day became dark before his eyes in his despair, for he remembered the words of his mother, and his soul was perplexed within him.

The two warriors now prepared for the combat in which one or both was destined to die. They marked out the lists, and, mounted on their powerful steeds, began the fight by hurling their javelins, and when these were blunted against the steel bucklers, they drew their long Indian swords, and the sparks flew fast as they hacked each other's iron mail, until the massive blades of steel were splintered under the terrific blows. Each was equal to the other, and still unwounded they raised their maces and rained blows until the mail of horses and riders was alike shattered, and each champion was exhausted with the fury of this tremendous combat. By tacit consent they separated and retired to opposite sides of the lists for an interval of repose. Rustem in all his long life of battle had never met a warrior so redoubtable as Sohrab, and for the first time he began to have doubts of the victory.

Once more the champions mounted their chargers and rushed to the mortal fray, beginning with arrows that fall harmless from the iron armor and cuirasses of leopard-hide. All pity and hope now left the heart of each, and a wild fury seized them. They drove their horses together, and Rustem, clutching

Sohrab by the waist-girdle, strove to lift him out of the saddle, as he had done so many other enemies; but he could make no impression on the herculean frame of the youthful hero. Sohrab, on the other hand, quickly seized his mace and smote Rustem on the shoulder, crushing through the mail-armor and bruising the bones. The pain was severe, but Rustem concealed his anguish, while Sohrab mocked him as an old man destined to fall before the power of youth. But they were both exhausted and mutually retired, each seeking relief by leading an attack on the opposing army. But when Rustem saw the havoc that the sword of Sohrab was making in the Persian ranks he rode up to him and induced him to agree to postpone all further fighting until the following day, when the single combat should be resumed. There is no doubt that the result of the fight had been thus far such as to confound the Persians and make them tremble, for never before had the great Rustem been baffled on the field.

Sohrab returned to his camp sorely tired, and yet full of confidence. But Rustem, like a prudent man, gave directions as to his funeral in case he should fall on the morrow. Although not cast down, yet he felt that there is a time for all to die, and he had never been so near his fate as now. But he was nerved also by a thirst for vengeance against the champion who had so nearly reaped the laurels he had won on a hundred fields.

When the sun arose and the black raven was casting its black shadow over the lonely plains, the two champions rode forth once more to try the wager of battle. To prevent the armies from intervening, and in the excitement of the combat falling on each other, they were removed to a distance of several miles apart. Midway between, the champions met in the centre of a lonely, treeless waste, through which coursed a deep, winding river; gray mountain ridges skirted the horizon far away; it was a scene of dreariness and mysterious solitude.

Sohrab rode joyously to meet his implacable foe, and a smile was on his face as he wished him a good-morning and hoped that he had passed the night in refreshing slumber, for he was more than ever convinced in his heart that he had to do with Rustem, and was determined if possible to bring about a reconciliation. He proposed that instead of continuing the combat to a fatal issue, they should now enter into a friendship that would spring from a respect based upon the equal ability they had shown in the test of arms. But Rustem was in no mood to accept such a proposal from a champion so much younger than himself, while the doubtful result of the previous day had made it necessary for him to restore his tottering prestige with the life-blood of his generous but dangerous rival.

This time the combat was renewed on foot. They fastened their steeds to the rocks, and then, clad in complete mail, approached each other stealthily and in diminishing circles, each watching the chance to pounce like a lion on his foe. From morning until afternoon the enemies fought, until by superior agility Sohrab succeeded in felling the great Rustem to the earth, and as he pinned him there, kneeling on the breast of the prostrate champion, he drew a dagger to cleave his head from his shoulders. But Rustem, who was not only strong but also gifted with the craft of one of large experience, had the presence of mind to arrest the arm of Sohrab by saying that it was not the custom in chivalrous warfare to slay a champion in the first fall, but to wait until the second throw, when usage entitled the victor honorably to take the life of the vanquished. Sohrab, as chivalrous as he was brave, immediately removed his grasp from Rustem, and permitting him to rise, departed for the camp. Rustem, scarcely believing himself alive after such an escape, thanked the Almighty for his preservation, and bathed his limbs, covered with dust and blood, in the river. Never before had he been so beset in battle ; never before since the world began had two champions been so evenly matched ; never before had a duel been so long, so desperate, so indecisive.

But when Sohrab related to his army the events of that terrible day, Houman shook his head in sorrow, and bade Sohrab beware when the combat was resumed, for he had no common antagonist, and fortune rarely gives us twice the opportunity to overcome our foes.

After a brief rest the champions came together again, determined to bring this awful struggle to a close ere another night set in. The crisis had evidently come ; ere many hours one or the other would shut his eyes forever on the setting sun. With fresh force Sohrab flew at Rustem ; but he by a supreme effort seized Sohrab around the waist in a grip of iron and hurled him to the ground, and as he lay there panting, before he could struggle to his feet again, Rustem drew his blade quick as lightning and drove it through the bosom of the youthful hero.

With a groan of anguish, Sohrab gasped: "This has come through my own folly; it is destiny that has decided. You are not to blame. My mother described to me the signs by which I might recognize my father, and it is because of my yearning for him that I have met my death. I have searched for him, and for this purpose have sacrificed my life. Alas! I shall never see him; but if you were a fish to lose thyself in the depths, or a star to hide in the heavens, my father will wreak his vengeance on you when he learns my doom. There are those who will report to Rustem, my father, that I was slain while searching to find him."

Rustem, when he heard these words, shook with horror, his mind became confused, a mist passed before his eyes, and he fell in a swoon by the side of his mighty son. When he revived, he asked of Sohrab, in tones of terrible anguish, by what marks he could prove himself to be the son of Rustem, and then he cried out: "For I am Rustem, the son of Zal; would that my name would perish, and that I were dead!" But when Sohrab heard these words, he upbraided his father for slaying him, for had he not that very day pleaded with him to abandon the combat and enter into terms of peace, but Rustem had sternly refused; and he continued: "Unbind my coat of mail, and observe my glowing skin. When the clarions sounded at the gates the hour for departure, my mother ran to me, her eyes filled with tears. And she bound on my arm an onyx, saying it is a memento of thy father, keep it with care till the appointed time has come to need it; but that hour came not until I lay dying before the eyes of my father."

Rustem unlaced the coat of mail and saw the onyx bound to the white arm of Sohrab. Then he rent his clothes and tore out his hair and beat

ANCIENT PERSIAN ARCHITECTURE.

his breast, and lamented: "O my son whom I have slain, my son who art glorious in all lands and among all people!" But Sohrab bade his father do himself no harm, for there was now no remedy; the deed was done and destiny had willed their doom.

When the glowing sun had disappeared below the verge of the desert, and Rustem returned not from the field, Keï Kaoos sent twenty warriors to reconnoitre and learn what had become of the champion of Persia. Seeing from afar that Rustem was not mounted on his horse, they returned and reported that he had yielded at last to the foe. At once great lamentations and cries of alarm arose from the host, and a scout was sent on a fleet dromedary to scour the plains and discover what Sohrab was purposing, for if he were the victor, who was there now in their camp to resist him?

But when Sohrab heard the din, he urged Rustem to show his love for him by permitting the host of Tourân to return unmolested to their country, since it had been out of confidence in Sohrab that they had ventured on this campaign. Rustem in his sorrow could not reply, but flung himself in the saddle and flew to the Persian camp, where all were amazed to see his armor shattered, his garments torn, and his flesh gaping with many wounds. With a wild cry Rustem ordered his army to remain in the camp and on no account to attack the army of Sohrab. He then despatched a trusty chieftain to Houman to inform him of the fall of Sohrab, and to accompany him as a safeguard until the army of Tourân had recrossed the border. Having thus accomplished the last wishes of his son, Rustem returned to him with a litter made comfortable with cushions of silk. But when he reached the spot where Sohrab was lying he found that his brave soul had departed. Amid the lamentations of the father and of the entire army they tenderly bore the corpse of the warrior youth to the camp. While Keï Kaoos and the Persian army returned home, Rustem returned to Seistân with the body of Sohrab, who was buried in the tomb of his fathers far from the land of his birth, and all the land was clad in mourning for him.

When Tehmimèh, the mother of Sohrab, heard of his death, and that he had been slain by the sword of his father, she threw dust on her head, she tore her tresses and her cheeks, she beat her bosom, and declined all food. Then she caused them to bring and set before her the throne of Sohrab and his coronet, and bending over them bathed them with her tears. Thus lamenting she was wasted by grief, and ere many days had elapsed she passed away to rejoin her hero child, Sohrab.

VI.

SIAWUSCH.

It happened on a certain day, when Keï Kaoos was still young in his royal honors, that two of the pehlewans, or warrior nobles, of his stately court departed for the chase. They were accompanied by numerous retainers, falconers with their hooded falcons, and leopards, such as are trained to hunt the gazelle and the wild ass. After a goodly day's sport they came to a vast wood, reaching many leagues. The huntsmen entered the dark recesses of the forest, and to their surprise discovered there a maiden of marvellous beauty, her hair and neck spangled with costly jewels. Excepting her horse, that was nibbling the grass near her, she was entirely alone in this green solitude. To the inquiries of the cavaliers, the lady replied that she was a fugitive from domestic ill-treatment, and was of noble descent, being of the line of Feridoon. There was nothing surprising in this, because the kings of Persia have many wives and concubines and numerous descendants. She expected soon to be overtaken by her father's servants, who, when her flight was discovered, would undoubtedly take every means to trace her path.

The hearts of the warriors warmed towards the

maiden, and Thous said : " It is I who have discovered her, it is on her account that I hastened hither." But Guiv replied : " O servant of the king, you are not equal to me unless backed by an army ; how then shall you claim her ?" A hot discussion arose between them for possession of the maiden, until one of their companions suggested that they conduct her to the presence of the king, and let him decide the question.

When Keï Kaoos beheld the face of the maiden, he smiled and bit his lips, and said to the two noblemen : " You have not been long absent on this hunt ; you have brought back only one gazelle, but a gazelle that belongs only to a king." He then questioned the damsel as to her history, and expressed his satisfaction by gallantly assuring her that she was worthy to recline on cushions broidered with gold, and that he should make her chief of the moon-faced queens in his palace. She replied, without hesitation : " As soon as I beheld you, I selected you as worthiest of all the great." Few women would decline the offer of a king, and in the exchange of compliments at least, she was his equal. Thus neither Thous nor Guiv secured the prize, but the king, while robbing them of a treasure it would have been difficult to award to the satisfaction of both, consoled them by presenting a diadem and ten superb horses to each. But on his new favorite Keï Kaoos showered rubies and pearls.

In due time it was announced to Keï Kaoos that a son was born to him and his fair queen. He was a child of unusual attractions and promise, and the king offered thanks to the Almighty for his gift. But the astrologers foretold for the infant a career of great vicissitude, ending in sorrow. But hope, which ever deludes us into forgetting the inevitable, led Kaoos to disregard these gloomy forebodings, and he entrusted his son to the great Rustem, under whose tutelage it was expected the boy would grow up to be a worthy defendant of the fortunes of Persia. Thus years passed on, until in Seistân with Rustem, Siawusch grew to be a youth of noble proportions, expert in all manly exercises, and with a face radiant with goodness and intelligence. On his return to Persepolis, Siawusch was received by his royal parents with all the rejoicing and splendor of a great court. But in the midst of these festivities the mother of Siawusch fell sick and died. No words can describe the sorrow of the young prince, which only yielded when many days had passed. He learned thus early the sad truth that care makes no distinction, but in one form or another enters palaces and hovels and lays its load alike, on the hearts of peasants and of princes.

Soon after this melancholy event, Siawusch was subjected to a temptation that put his character to the test. Soudabêh, the wife whom Keï Kaoos had brought with him after his Syrian victory, being untrue to her royal spouse, undertook to seduce his handsome son Siawusch from the path of duty, but he ever nobly resisted her advances until her guilty love turned to hate, and with loud outcries she made complaints against Siawusch to the king. The plot devised against the young prince by Soudabêh was so deep that it was impossible for the king to decide as to the guilt or innocence of Siawusch, and between his love for his son and the love he bore to the beautiful woman who voluntarily shared with him the dungeons of Hamaverâm. By the advice of the astrologers, Keï Kaoos reluctantly decided to put Siawusch to the ordeal of fire, to which he willingly consented, conscious of innocence.

Mounted on a black horse, Siawusch rode fearlessly between two immense burning pyres, and came forth harmless, to the great joy of the assembled multitudes. Siawusch being thus proved innocent of the grievous charge, it followed that Soudabêh was guilty of compassing the death of the favorite son of the king for reasons best known to herself. Keï Kaoos, with great reluctance, because of his love for her, which continued in spite of her wickedness, ordered her to be taken to execution.

FIRE ALTAR.

But Siawusch generously pleaded for her life, and his father, glad of the opportunity, freely pardoned her.

About this time, Afrasiab again invaded Persia with a mighty host. The force which Keï Kaoos sent against Afrasiab was placed in command of Siawusch, but Rustem accompanied him to give him the benefit of his experience in war. The king rode a day's journey with his son, and then father and son parted, each with tears in his eyes, for they both had a presentiment that they should never meet again.

Notwithstanding his great defects of character, Keï Kaoos appears to have been a fond husband and father. After three indecisive battles, the Persian army succeeded in shutting up the enemy in Balkh, the capital of Afrasiab, and then carried the city by storm. The proud king of Tourân had an ominous dream after these events, and decided at once to sue for peace. Siawusch and Rustem would only accept the terms on the condition that Afrasiab should give one hundred hostages, nobles and kinsfolk, in token of his sincerity in proposing a cessation of the war. The hostages were delivered. But when Keï Kaoos was informed of the conditions of the peace by Rustem, he drove that chieftain back to Scistân, accusing him of being the author of peace when the war should have been pursued until Afrasiab had been destroyed and Tourân completely subdued. Kaoos then despatched another general to the army in place of Rustem, and ordered Siawusch to bind the hostages and send them to his father Kaoos for execution.

But Siawusch, being a prince of the highest purity and honor, could not be a party to such a disgraceful proceeding. Convinced that Keï Kaoos must be partly instigated in his course by the evil influence of Soudabêh, Siawusch felt that there was only one course that was safe for his life and his honor. The hostages he would not kill, for he said that great as was the authority of Keï Kaoos there was a greater, the law of God ; while if he disobeyed the mandate of his royal father it was wellnigh certain that Keï

Kaoos, in his dangerous capriciousness, would slay him. Siawusch decided to return the hostages to Afrasiab, and to abandon his country and the prospect of a throne rather than yield to dishonor. It was a high resolve, but far different to that which most men would have taken under similar circumstances. In vain the counsellors and generals of his army sought to dissuade him. One strong friend stood by him; his name was Zengueh. Him Siawusch sent to Afrasiab with the hostages to announce the coming of the prince. Siawusch then gave his orders to Bahman to watch the army well until the arrival of the general deputed to take the place of Rustem, and departed for the court of Afrasiab.

The matter of receiving the self-exiled prince was one of difficulty. Afrasiab took counsel with Piran, a venerable and wise chieftain, and decided to welcome Siawusch as a son, and award a palace, and slaves and horses for his comfort, and in every way to treat him as if he were of his own family, and risk whatever results might follow. It must be admitted that Afrasiab was moved to this course not by hospitality or gratitude for the regard the prince had shown for the lives of the hostages. The king of Tourân was aware that Keï Kaoos was old, and liable at any time to leave the throne vacant. If Siawusch were then living in Tourân the possible advantages to Tourân were incalculable.

But whatever selfishness might have entered into the hospitality of Afrasiab, there was none apparent in the reception he accorded Siawusch. After despatching a touching letter to his father, the Persian prince set out at evening with his cortège, and rode until he reached the frontier on the banks of the Gihoon; there he found chieftains and warriors and servants, who escorted him with royal honors to the capital. Every town on the road was decorated, and everywhere the people came forth to give him welcome. At the city of Kafdjak he stopped to rest and was met there by Piran, the first nobleman of Tourân, with one thousand picked warriors. Piran was so overcome by the manly beauty and lofty character of the young prince that from time to time, says the chronicler, he ejaculated the name of God.

When they arrived at Gang, where Afrasiab then held his court, that haughty monarch condescended to show his appreciation towards his distinguished guest by descending from his audience-hall to the palace gates to meet him. When Siawusch beheld him he quickly alighted, and king and prince embraced with every token of friendship. "Henceforth," exclaimed Afrasiab, "war will no longer desolate the earth, and the lion and the leopard will lie down together." The Persian prince was led by his royal host to a magnificent banquet, and when all were satiated with feasting and splendor, Siawusch was conducted to the palace which King Afrasiab had ordered to be prepared for the residence of his guest.

In the meantime a swift messenger bore the letter of Siawusch to Keï Kaoos, who was confounded by its contents. Instead of continuing the war he ordered the army to return home, and abandoned hostilities against Afrasiab.

Siawusch continued to increase in favor with Afrasiab, although in the midst of the honors showered upon him he often longed for home and the friends he had left and was never to see again. By the advice of Piran, Afrasiab gave his daughter, Ferenguiz, to Siawusch, the marriage being celebrated with much splendor, although the astrologers foretold that this alliance would not prove fortunate for the destiny of Afrasiab and Tourân. Soon after this event the king appointed Siawusch governor of one of his largest provinces, and he founded the cities of Siawuschgird and Gang-i-Siawusch, the latter celebrated by the poet Ferdoüsee as one of the most delightful spots in the East. But when the gallant young prince, happy in the lovely wife and the many honors so rapidly bestowed on him, inquired of the astrologers whether this city was destined to add to his happiness, they replied that it did not so promise, and his heart was saddened by their reply. Unhappy prince! who was gifted with every manly virtue, with every physical grace, with every noble accomplishment, who was born heir to a great throne, and was universally beloved; and yet from his cradle destiny seemed to pursue him with misfortune; his virtues even brought him trouble, and the stars predicted

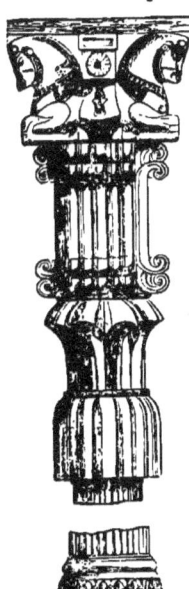

PILLAR BASE, AND CAPITAL, PERSEPOLIS.

unhappiness and doom for one who deserved happiness and success.

During this period Siawusch retained the strong friendship of Piran, who reported to King Afrasiab, with warm praise, all that the Prince of Persia had done to beautify his province. Pleased at what he heard, Afrasiab deputed his brother, Guersiwez, to proceed with many costly gifts and gracious messages to Siawusch. Guersiwez was entertained in a manner worthy of his rank, and athletic games were arranged in his honor. But the amazing strength and skill displayed by Siawusch on this occasion, and the splendor by which he was surrounded, filled Guersiwez with envy, and still more with dread, for he considered Siawusch quite too dangerous to be treated with such honor and confidence by the hereditary enemy of Persia, King Afrasiab. Little did the pure and unsuspicious nature of Siawusch imagine the evil that lurked in the heart of the guest he was entertaining with splendor.

On his return to the court Guersiwez insidiously poisoned the mind of Afrasiab by false tales, in which he accused Siawusch of actually plotting to bring a Persian army into Tourân. At first, receiving these stories with hesitation, Afrasiab at last became furious against his gentle guest, and proceeded against him with an army. A terrible dream had forewarned Siawusch that his doom was at hand; but when he heard of the approach of Afrasiab he entertained not the slightest thought of resistance, but after bidding a touching farewell to his lovely young wife, Ferenguiz, went forth to welcome Afrasiab to the cool bowers of Siawuschgird. But Afrasiab hurled his army on the escort of Siawusch without waiting to confer and to learn the truth, and all were cut to pieces. Siawusch even then disdained to defend himself. Conscious of his innocence, he preferred to die rather than give color to the slanders of his enemies by drawing a sword against his royal host and the father of his bride.

Seized by a hundred cruel hands, the noble youth was bound and thrown into a dungeon of his own palace; from thence he was dragged by the hair of his head to the place of tournaments, and slaughtered by Gerouï, the willing tool of Guersiwez. Not content with this foul deed, this crime against the laws of hospitality, Afrasiab then directed his fury against his daughter, Ferenguiz; she was cast into prison, and the order went forth to slay her likewise, because she was about to become a mother, and the ruthless king of Tourân would have none of the offspring of the murdered Iredj alive in his dominions. During the occurrence of these tragical events the great and good Piran-Wisa was absent from the court. If he had been there, the wisdom of his counsels might have prevailed to turn Afrasiab from his fell purposes. Now when he learned of these events and the terrible fate that awaited Ferenguiz, he flew to his stables and saddling his swiftest steed with his own hands, he dashed over hill and valley, stopping neither to eat nor sleep until he drew rein before the pavilion of King Afrasiab.

With noble courage Piran-Wisa strode into the presence of the cruel king and upbraiding him for his perfidy, foretold a certain retribution when Keï Kaoos and Rustem should learn of the treatment awarded to the pure and high-minded Siawusch. Piran-Wisa pleaded also in lofty tones for the life of Ferenguiz, until Afrasiab hung his head in shame; his soul was seized with remorse, and he ordered his daughter to be released from her chains and given to the care of Piran-Wisa, who promised to be responsible for her child when it should be born.

When a son was given to Ferenguiz she called him Keï Khosroo, in obedience to the wishes of her murdered husband, and again Piran-Wisa interposed to save the infant's life from the executioners. He caused the child to be given to a shepherd, who was to bring him up to the charge of flocks and herds, and carefully to keep concealed from him the fact of his origin from a line of kings. But in the course of years King Afrasiab awoke one night and brooded over the fact that a scion of the royal house of Persia, a son of the murdered Siawusch, still lived and might become the avenger of his father and a scourge to Tourân. Oppressed with these thoughts, Afrasiab sent, ere it was dawn, for Piran-Wisa to confer with him on the subject. On the one hand, the king dreaded to leave the youth alive, and on the other hand, his conscience forbade him to shed more innocent blood in order to ensure the safety of his throne. The fate of the young Keï Khosroo hung in the balance. While he was sleeping on the gray mountains by the side of his flocks, little imagining his destiny, a king was deciding for him the question of life and death.

Again the good Piran-Wisa came to the aid of mercy and justice, and by his cunning succeeded in preserving the shepherd lad for the great destiny that was in store for him. Piran-Wisa represented that there was nothing to fear from a boy who was a mere idiot, without intelligence, although exceedingly handsome. His fears thus quieted, Afrasiab swore a great oath, the oath of kings, by the bright day and the dark night, and God the Creator, that he would never do any harm to Keï Khosroo. Reassured by this tremendous oath, Piran-Wisa went to the mountains and sought out the royal shepherd boy and brought him before the king, having first carefully instructed him to act the part of an idiot. When he entered the palace of Afrasiab strong men wept as they thought of the fate of his father, and even the hard-hearted king condescended to shed a tear when he gazed on his grandson for the first time. But Piran-Wisa shook with dread when he beheld the defenceless youth standing in the presence of the terrible king.

For a long time Afrasiab gazed on Keï Khosroo, while pity and hate, the remembrance of his vow, and the dread of the house of Feridoon, shook his bosom with conflicting emotions. At length his better nature prevailed, and he addressed the youth with pleasant words, asking him such questions as he thought would prove whether Piran-Wisa had told him the truth in regard to his idiocy. Keï Khosroo answered so cunningly that Afrasiab was convinced that his mind was indeed weak and that there was no cause to fear aught from him in the future.

Greatly pleased, Afrasiab ordered Piran-Wisa to carry Keï Khosroo to Siawuschgird and leave him in the care of his mother, Ferenguiz.

But while these events were occurring in Tourân, tidings of the fate of Siawusch reached Persia. Great was the rage of Keï Kaoos and Rustem; deep was the remorse of Keï Kaoos for the conduct which had driven his son from him and deprived Persia of so noble an heir to the throne, while universal lamentation filled the hearts of all the people. When the great Rustem heard the sad tidings, he called to mind the days when Siawusch, while yet a mere youth, had studied the art of war with him in Seistân. He arose and vowed not to rest until he had wreaked vengeance on the king of Tourân. Then he journeyed to the capital, and in the presence of Keï Kaoos himself, accused Soudabêh of being the wicked cause of a catastrophe which had reft Persia of one who promised to be the pride and glory of that ancient monarchy. He offered his aid to crush Afrasiab, on condition that Soudabêh be sacrificed for her crimes, and then proceeded from the audience-hall of Keï Kaoos to the apartments of the women and seized Soudabêh. The shrieks and entreaties of the unhappy queen were of no avail when she was at last in the terrible grasp of Rustem. He dragged her forth into the outer court and plunged a poignard into her heart.

From all parts of Persia a vast army was now gradually assembled, which with slow but steady march proceeded towards the frontier and invaded the territory of King Afrasiab. The uneasy con-

RELIEF AT BEHISTOON.

science of that treacherous monarch and the redoubtable arm of Rustem brought about the complete overthrow of Afrasiab, who was forced to seek refuge far in the East with the king of China, and Rustem was appointed Viceroy.

When Afrasiab fled towards the far East he caused Ferenguiz and Keï Khosroo to be driven into a hidden nook distant in Central Asia, where for a long time all traces of them were lost. But at last Guiv, one of the heroes of the court of Keï Kaoos, succeeded in finding them, and after many thrilling adventures brought them to Ispahan, where Keï Khosroo was received with much joy by his grandfather, Keï Kaoos, who was now very old. Indeed Keï Kaoos was drawing near the end of his long and disturbed reign, and he had scarcely named Keï Khosroo for his successor, than he felt the hand of death lie heavily upon him.

After Keï Kaoos had gone, his old enemy Afrasiab made a final effort to recover his throne. Rustem being also of great age and desirous of ending his days in Seistân, left Tourân. Afrasiab seized this opportunity to collect a large army, and at first met with some success. But Keï Khosroo, whom he had so justly dreaded, was now in the bloom of early manhood, at the opening of a long and glorious career. He had also the task of avenging the murder of his father, Siawusch, and he entered therefore on this his first campaign with great ardor. In his last struggle, Afrasiab displayed ability and fought with the force of despair. But he fought in vain; and a career which had for many years been sullied with blood, and wrought so much evil to Persia, was at last destined to close in defeat.

But the victory of Keï Khosroo was not an easy one; the armies of Tourân had never fought with such obstinacy and courage; repeatedly was a truce agreed on to allow both armies to rest. At length the good Piran-Wisa was slain. He had always been the friend of Siawusch. To him Keï Khosroo owed his life on several occasions; but when Piran-Wisa saw that war was inevitable, he could do no less than fight for his country, even if in doing so he opposed Keï Khosroo. Once he was taken prisoner, but was released at the intercession of Ferenguiz. And when, at last, in a later conflict, he fell covered with wounds in honorable battle, the glorious veteran was mourned by both armies, and Keï Khosroo caused a sumptuous tomb to be erected over his grave. But when the treacherous Guersiwez, who had betrayed the father of Keï Khosroo, fell into the hands of the Persians, he was executed with the treatment he had so richly deserved. In the end Afrasiab himself was slain by the terrible arm of Keï Khosroo, and the hosts of Persia filed victorious through the fallen palaces of her greatest foe. In the words of the Persian bard: "The spider hath woven his web in the imperial palace; and the owl hath sung her watch-song on the towers of Afrasiab."

VII.

KEI KHOSROO, OR CYRUS.

HITHERTO we have been considering episodes in the legendary history of Persia. Although scarcely alluded to in the Greek and Roman accounts of Persia, yet they have great value among the Persians themselves, and are undoubtedly founded upon actual events that occurred before the period of which the Greeks began their accounts of Oriental history. In narrating the history of Persia from the commencement of Keï Khosroo, or Kur, as the Persians call him, or Kuros, according to the Greeks and Romans, and Cyrus in our language, we find it often difficult to distinguish between what is true and what is false, for there is great diversity in the records of Persia, as given by her own historians and those of Greece. This is especially the case in the rendering of proper names, of which a striking example is seen in the various ways of expressing the name of Cyrus. In general, a comparison of the two records seems to indicate that greater reliance can be placed upon the statements of the Greek historians, although, doubtless, often exaggerated. But the Persian method of giving Persian proper names is, on the other hand, far more correct; to adopt it, however, in this volume in the case of names already familiar to us under other forms, seems in the present case unadvisable, and thus we shall say Cyrus instead of Keï Khosroo, and Darius Hystaspes instead of Dara Gushtasp, and Artaxerxes instead of Ardesheer, and, of course, Alexander instead of Iskender.

Nor is it expedient in a volume of this size to go into a discussion concerning the discrepancies or historic difficulties that exist between the records of the Persian and the Greek or classic historians. But the writer will give a simple statement of the facts which appear to him most likely to be the true ones, and generally those which European scholars have accepted as belonging most correctly to the history of Persia since the commencement of the reign of Cyrus.

At the time of the birth of Cyrus the territory of Persia appears to have included the provinces of Fars or Pars, and Irân or Irâk, which is now the centre of present Persia, and was called from it by the Persians themselves Irân,* evidently another way of pronouncing Aryan. Besides this, it extended to the shores of the Persian Gulf, and probably over part of Assyria and Arabia on the south, and in the east over part if not all of the country now called Afghanistan. In the northwest, Media and Armenia and the adjacent provinces of Asia Minor formed the kingdom of Media, with the capital at Ecbatana, now called Hamadan. Media seems to

* This word is spelled thus in this volume in accordance with accepted usage ; but it is pronounced by Persians, Erâu.

have held close relations with Persia, but was practically independent, and at that time was ruled by Astyages. Directly north of Iran was the mountainous region of the Elborz, called by the Greeks Hyrcania, which was only partially subdued by and in a constant state of insurrection against Persia. On the northeast was the vast region called by the Persians Tourân, of whose wars with Iran so much has been related on the previous pages. It is probable that the beginnings of the Persian empire were partly in that region; the early legends suggest this. The Touranians were Tartars or Turks, whose mounted hosts many times since then have invaded and devastated the territories of Iran, although such has been the vitality of the Persian race that it has proved impossible for the Touranians to remain long as conquerors on the soil of Iran. By the Greeks the Touranians were called Scythians, Massagetæ, and Saccæ.

Such was the condition of Central Asia at the time when Keï Khosroo, or Cyrus, called the Elder, was born. In the previous chapter we have learned the Persian account of the parentage and early life of Cyrus. Greek historians state that he was the grandson of Astyages, while Persians record that his grandfather was Afrasiab. Both accounts resemble each other in the particulars of his infancy and youth, and for this reason it seems preferable to believe that in boyhood Cyrus led a humble life among the mountains with shepherds, although modern historians are inclined to reject entirely the stories about his infancy, as fictitious.

TOMB OF CYRUS.

By Greek historians, as well as modern writers, it has been the custom to regard Cyrus as the founder of the Persian empire. This is only measurably true. That the Persian people, as one of the great representative branches of the so-called Aryan race, had existed as a distinct nation for ages before the coming of Cyrus, there is no sound reason for doubting.

But at the same time, as indicated above, another branch of the Aryan race, called the Medes, had established themselves northwest of Persis, or the original seat of the subsequent Persian empire, which is now partially represented by the province of Fars. At the birth of Cyrus the Medes had already reached a good degree of civilization and power. Their capital of Ecbatana, now called Hamadan, was surrounded by seven walls, and contained magnificent palaces. Cyaxares, a Median king,* carried his arms as far west as the Mediterranean, and although obliged to retire in consequence of a total eclipse, 580 B.C., which threw his army into confusion, yet he made such an impression on the minds of the Greeks, that for centuries later they called all Persians alike, by the name of Medes. It is recorded of Cyaxares that he was the first Asiatic monarch to introduce a regular organization in the conduct of war, dividing his troops into distinct battalions according to the arms they bore, and also making the infantry an important branch of the service. It seems that previous to that period the vast desert uplands of Cen-

* There is little question that the Cyaxares of the Greek historians is the Kei Kaoos of Persian legend.

tral Asia had suggested the use only of mounted troops. We may infer from this fact also that at this time those parts of Asia began to be traversed by made roads, facilitating the movements of trade and war.

It was during the reign of Cyaxares, and while he was absent invading Assyria, that the Touranians made one of their frequent invasions into Persia, and for a time held Media under a tyranny so galling that Cyaxares was at last impelled to destroy them by a stratagem that was peculiarly Oriental. He ordained a grand banquet in the pleasure halls of Ecbatana, for it appears that the Touranians had imprudently permitted him not only to survive his subjection to their power, but also left him some semblance of wealth and authority. To this banquet were invited the Touranian chieftains, where they were plied with wine until intoxicated; while they were in this state Cyaxares gave the signal, and a troop of warriors issued from a place of concealment and cut them to pieces. This tragedy was followed by a general rising of the Medes and the expulsion of their Touranian tyrants.

It was among the Medes that the famous sect of the fire-worshippers first took root in the Persian race. This religion is said by some to have originated in Atropatene, now represented by the northwest province of modern Persia, called Azerbaijân. But this is probably an error, as the peculiar doctrines of the sect seem to have previously existed far in the East, in Bactria or beyond. But as there is no doubt that Zoroaster or Zerdusht was the founder of this religion in Persia, and as he was a native of Atropatene, it may be inferred that he travelled in the Bactria, and brought thence the ideas on which he built a religious system which continues to exist to our time and is acknowledged to be one of the great fundamental religions of the world. While the fire-worshippers made fire the symbol of the Almighty, yet it would be an error to conclude that this was all that was included in their creed; for Zoroaster laid down many rules of morality, and in the commentaries he either wrote or collected, suggested profound theories about the All Ruler of the universe and the destiny of man. The priesthood of this sect were called mobeds or magi, and formed a distinct community who had great influence and power.

But while Media and Persis had thus side by side represented the Aryan race for ages, yet Cyrus may perhaps be justly considered the founder of the Persian monarchy of the great Achemenian line, as he, being the fourth in descent from Achemenes, or of a prominent chief of that name, succeeded in uniting the Median and the Persian branches of the Aryan race under one sceptre, and gave to the now united empire the name of his own country. There is reason to believe that Cyrus succeeded in overcoming Astyages, the king of the Medes, by the treachery of Harpagus, a Median dignitary of high rank. After their union with Persia, the Medians in turn instructed their conquerors in the arts of civilization.

Greek historians have ascribed many noble qualities to Cyrus, which a wider knowledge of Oriental history than they possessed leads us to consider as impossible in an Eastern monarch. The exaggerated statements of classic historians regarding Cyrus are due quite as much to the fact that he was the first Persian king with whom the Greeks came into direct collision as to his real greatness. For the same reason we learn from the Greeks far more of Cyrus and his successors than of the Persian kings whom modern historians speak of as legendary, of whom so much has been recorded on previous pages of this volume. It is as decided a mistake to consider the Persian nation to have begun with Cyrus as to commence the history of England with William the Conqueror.

But while saying this much in favor of the importance of that portion of the history of Persia which the Greek historians neglected to notice, we may well grant that Cyrus was undoubtedly a monarch of unusual ability, and a conqueror whose exploits have justly merited immortality. The reign of Cyrus seems to have begun about the year 558 B.C., and to have continued thirty years. Having subdued the kingdom of Media, Cyrus turned his attention to the Touranians, and this may have been the war to which Persian historians refer, which he undertook, according to their legends, in order to avenge the death of his father. It was after this that Cyrus undertook the great war against the Greek colonial states along the western shores of Asia Minor previously threatened by Cyaxares, thus for the first time bringing the two civilizations of Europe and Asia into direct contact, for these Ionians, Dorians, and Lydians of Asia Minor had brought their arts and customs from Greece, and in their character were Europeans rather than Asiatics. Crœsus, King of Lydia, was at this time ruler of Asia Minor west of the river Halys, having united all the Greek colonies in that region under one sceptre. He seems to have been a man of uncommon ability, as well as ambition. The rising greatness of Cyrus began to arouse the attention of Crœsus, and he consulted the famous oracle at Delphi for guidance in this crisis of his affairs; crisis it was indeed, for the boundaries of Persia and Lydia were gradually drawing nearer, and the ambition of two such restless monarchs foretold a conflict between them.

Although Crœsus paid large sums of gold out of his almost fabulous treasures in order to draw a favorable reply from the oracle, the crafty pythoness or priestess of Apollo would pronounce nothing more definite than that if Crœsus made war on Persia he would destroy a great empire. This was sufficiently vague, but Crœsus assuming it meant that the empire to suffer would be that of Cyrus, instead of reflecting that possibly it might be his own, declared war and invaded the dominions of Cyrus. After an indecisive campaign, Crœsus was preparing to obtain auxiliaries from Egypt; but it was here that Cyrus displayed military genius; for he followed his antagonist so closely, although still his equal in the field, that Crœsus was forced to fight a great battle at Thymbra, where he was defeated and shut up in Sardis, his capital. At the end of fourteen days Sardis surrendered and was burned; and the Greek colonies came under the rule of Persia, to which they continued subject for centuries. Cyrus seems to have shown greatness of soul in his treatment of Crœsus, who although taken to Persia was treated with kindness and distinction until his death at a great age. Such was the varied career of a king whose wealth was so vast even for a monarch, that it has passed into a proverb.

The next exploit of Cyrus, which probably contributed more than any other since the origin of Persia to elevate its civilization and give it a permanent character, was the capture of Babylon, the ancient capital of the consolidated empire of Babylon and Assyria. This great metropolis is recorded to have covered an area of seventy square miles on each side of the river Euphrates. It is probable, judging from the character of most Oriental cities, that much of this space was covered with extensive gardens, either for orchards and grazing fields or pleasure grounds around the extensive mansions of the nobles as well as of the palaces of the sovereign. But, in any case, there can be no question that Babylon contained a vast population and was decorated with many superb palaces and sumptuous temples, of which the most prominent was the famous tower of Bel, or Belus, the god, which was reputed to be one of the seven wonders of the world. It was constructed in eight separate towers, one over the other; and the topmost was the chamber of the god, containing furniture of solid gold.

The city was surrounded by the most extraordinary walls of defence the world has seen. They were constructed of bricks, cemented with bitumen instead of mortar, and were of enormous height and thickness, and surrounded by a deep ditch. Against the military engines of those times the fortifications of Babylon were impregnable. All the streets leading to the river-banks were also closed with gates of brass. The great gardens of the city were capable of raising provisions to enable the city to resist a siege for an indefinite period.

Stratagem was the only way to capture this great city. In this instance Cyrus was aided in his plans by the sense of security which caused the besieged to relax their vigilance; and it is also likely that treachery, so common a vice among Asiatics, came to the aid of the designs of Cyrus. The Persian king had besieged Babylon for nearly two years, and seemed no nearer the attainment of his object than when he sat down before its gates with a vast army. To storm the walls was out of the question; to starve the garrison was hopeless; but to retire from the siege was for Persia to confess that she had reached the limit of her conquests.

Again it was genius that assisted Cyrus; to an ordinary general the plan he now devised for the capture of Babylon could not have occurred. His scheme was to turn the course of the Euphrates and enter the city by marching along the bed of the river on a night when it was the custom for all Babylon to abandon itself annually to revelry, from the king to the lowest soldier. Such is the size of the Euphrates, that only a genius of the most daring character could have dreamed of such an enterprise and successfully achieved it. There was a lake in the vicinity of Babylon which had been excavated by Nebuchadnezzar to contain the waters of the river, while he was facing the banks within the walls with bricks. Between the lake and river was a canal; both lake and canal were probably dry at this time, and the river was prevented from entering them by a high broad embankment. As soon as night set in,

DARIUS HUNTS.

probably a long night in winter, Cyrus ordered a large division of his host to break down the dam. The size of his army may be inferred from the fact that while there were enough present to open a passage for the Euphrates into the lake by midnight, large divisions were stationed where the river entered and left the city, with orders to march up the dry bed into the heart of the capital. Even after proceeding thus far, this desperate enterprise might have failed, and the Persian army been utterly destroyed, if the brass gates of the streets leading to the river had been closed. Notwithstanding the general revelry that reigned throughout the city, it is too much to believe that all these gates were left open. It is more probable that one or two only were carelessly neglected, or that Cyrus had succeeded in bribing some of the garrison.

Belshazzar, the king of Babylon, was in his palace surrounded by his wives and the nobles of the empire. The pillared halls were lit by the glare of myriad lights, and the splendor of the occasion was increased by the gleam of vessels of silver and gold, by jewels accumulated for ages, and the responsive flash of eyes more glorious than the diamonds of Ind. The beat of timbrels, the songs of dancing girls, rang before the couch where the voluptuous monarch reposed, little imagining that he was flinging away the treasures, the power, the crown, and the life inherited from a long dynasty of kings.

At that moment, as the sacred Scriptures record, Belshazzar was struck dumb by a vision of strange and awful portent. On the wall of his palace he beheld emblazoned in letters of fire the mysterious words, "mene, mene, tekel, upharsin." When the king could recover his speech, he hoarsely commanded the astrologers and wise men of Babylon to be summoned into his presence and promised that he among them who should rightly interpret those words should have a chain of gold and be promoted to the highest office in the gift of the king.

The words were Chaldæan and easily understood; the question was to interpret what was their application on this occasion. It is probable that the interpretation was understood by all the wise men, but only one dared incur the terrible wrath of an Eastern king by repeating the interpretation to Belshazzar. That man was Daniel, who declared that the mysterious words foretold the approaching downfall and death of Belshazzar himself. To the honor of the haughty monarch, instead of ordering Daniel to be slain for so fearlessly pronouncing his doom, he kept the promise he had made. This remarkable scene is not mentioned by other historical writers, but there is no good reason for doubting that Belshazzar, perhaps in a drunken frenzy, beheld before his mind's eye a wild vision, whose interpretation he demanded of the astrologers. Such an event is quite in accordance with the general tenor of Oriental history.

But while these scenes were transpiring in the banqueting-halls of the imperial palace, platoons of Persian troops were marching along the dry bed of the Euphrates and stealthily approaching the royal abode. When at last the fearful cry ran forth over the city, that the foe was within the very walls of Babylon itself, the capital was already doomed. Resistance was in vain. From street to street, from hall to hall, the Persians swarmed sword in hand. The revellers fled in all directions for safety, and everywhere encountered the enemy fierce and irresistible. Belshazzar was slain on the steps of his throne, and his wives were carried into captivity.

This great event occurred 538 B.C. When we consider the condition of the art of war in those times, the character of the defences of Babylon, and the superiority of her civilization over that of Persia at that period, we must conclude that the capture of Babylon was one of the most remarkable military achievements of all ages, and that Cyrus must be awarded a position among the greatest generals in history.

After these events Cyrus was engaged in fresh wars with the hereditary enemies of Persia in the north and east, and seems to have extended his arms as far as India. The accounts of his death are conflicting. But it is generally accepted that he was killed in a great battle with the Touranians. Some historians call the people with whom he was engaged at the time, the Massagetæ; others, the Derbices or the Saccæ. In either case it was undoubtedly one of the numerous tribes of Tourân. Persian legends confirm this statement of the death of Cyrus, for they say that towards the close of his life he resigned the throne and mysteriously disappeared into philosophic retirement in the north. As the Persian historians, according to their custom, would be inclined to say little that would be against one of their favorite heroes, this is evidently the way they have taken to explain his defeat and death.

But the battle, whether a defeat or indecisive for the Persians, does not appear to have been so overwhelming an overthrow as to prevent them from bringing back the body of the great warrior and king to be buried in his native land. That Cyrus was buried at Passargadæ, his capital, there is no doubt, for a marble tomb is still standing there in the plain of Murgab, which has in all ages been reputed to be the last resting-place of Cyrus. We also know that Passargad, or Passargadæ, as the Greeks called it, was the capital of Persia during his reign, notwithstanding that some historians state that after the capture of Babylon Cyrus removed his court to Susa or Sushan, near the Euphrates. But as Persepolis, which was also in the plain of Murgab, was, until the conquest of Alexander, the real capital of Persia, Susa was probably only one of the numerous resorts which it continues to be the custom of the kings of Persia to establish in various parts of their dominions, and embellish them with sumptuous palaces and gardens.

It is interesting to learn from the Greek historians who accompanied Alexander the Great to Persepolis, that in their time the tomb of Cyrus was still in good preservation, surrounded by shade trees. On entering the tomb they found the body of the conqueror in a coffin of gold, guarded by magi, or priests. Around it were a golden couch, a table with dishes, embroidered robes, and costly swords. On the tomb was inscribed: "O, man, I am Cyrus, who won dominion for the Persians, and was King of Asia. Grudge not this monument then to me."

VIII.

FROM CYRUS TO DARIUS I.

WHEN one turns over the records of history, and studies the career of the men and women who alternately inspire admiration or disgust, love or aversion, there is no fact that becomes more impressed on the mind than the great contrasts that constantly occur in the characters of those to whom, as rulers, has been entrusted the happiness and welfare of men. The greatest monarchs, they who have been most prominent as benefactors, have often been succeeded by sons who have been monsters, revelling in injustice and blood. Marcus Aurelius Antoninus, the best of all the emperors of Rome, the purest and noblest of heathen kings, was followed by Commodus, one of the most ignorant and brutal tyrants that has cursed the earth. In like manner Cyrus, who was undoubtedly one of the most beneficent of Oriental sovereigns, was succeeded by his son Cambyses, whose extraordinary career presents a marvel of human folly and wickedness.

He found Persia entering upon a period of rare prosperity, but requiring to be for a time at rest, in order to consolidate the vast conquests of Cyrus. Cambyses seems, however, to have had his reason

affected by coming into possession of such power. He began his reign by organizing an immense armament of armies and fleets against Egypt. The Egyptians were defeated in a great battle at Pelusium, the gate to their country, and Psammetticus, the king of this unhappy people, was cruelly slain, after Cambyses entered the capital. We say unhappy in speaking of the Egyptians, for no people were ever more harshly treated by a conqueror than they were when the hosts of Persia encamped on the banks of the Nile and profaned the majestic temples of Thebes.

Having entirely subjugated the country, Cambyses pushed his conquests far to the south, among the burning plains of Nubia, called in those times Æthiopia; the objective point of the expedition was the Temple of Jupiter Ammon, in the southwest, and Æthiopia, in the south, the latter division being under the charge of Cambyses himself. He penetrated as far as Meroë. The former army vanished in the desert, victims to thirst and the deadly simôôm. The latter division was also overcome by hunger, and forced to return. The hardships of this expedition seemed to increase the caprice and cruelty of Cambyses. There was no people so superstitious, so addicted to the most minute religious ceremonies, so absorbed in a profound veneration for the gods or the sacred symbols, as the Egyptians. Cambyses left no means untried to outrage every object they considered sacred. When the people of Memphis were engaged in rejoicing at the appearance of the bull they worshipped as Apis, Cambyses himself slew that sacred animal with a stroke of his poignard. He also gave himself up to the most brutal excesses.

In the midst of this career of unbridled debauchery, the tyrant dreamed that his brother Smerdis had conspired against him in his absence from Persia, and seized the throne. Without any confirmation of his dream, Cambyses sent Prexaspis, one of his near

GATEWAY OF XERXES (PERSEPOLIS).

officers, to Persepolis, who, without trial or examination, caused the unfortunate Smerdis to be secretly beheaded. When Atossa, the sister and wife of Cambyses, heard of this atrocious deed, she upbraided her husband for his wickedness. He only replied by kicking her so violently in the stomach that she died. Deciding to return at once to Persia,

Cambyses in turn received a mortal wound from his naked sword while in the act of mounting his horse.

Thus the empire of Persia, in a critical period of its existence, was left without a king or any direct heir to the sceptre. But when the news of the death of Cambyses reached Persia, an extraordinary event occurred. Although a state secret, yet the death of Smerdis appears to have been known to some of the magi. One of them bore a striking resemblance to the murdered brother of Cambyses, and he now usurped the throne, and for over a year succeeded in avoiding suspicion. But the false Smerdis, for a reason which was afterwards revealed, kept himself so closely in the ark or citadel of the capital, that Otanes, a Persian nobleman, had his suspicions aroused. Aware that there was a magian who resembled Smerdis, it occurred to Otanes that perhaps Smerdis had been made away with by a conspiracy of the magi, who had thus got the power into their own hands. If this were so then the false Smerdis could be detected, because he had been deprived of his ears. Phædyma, a daughter of Otanes, had been one of the wives of Cambyses. When the false Smerdis usurped the throne, he also, according to custom, married the wives of the late king. At the request of her father, Phædyma felt of the head of the usurper when he was asleep. She thus obtained convincing proof of the true character of him who had so boldly aspired to sit on the throne of Cyrus and Djemsheed.

After this revelation a conspiracy of seven nobles connected with leading families of Persia was formed, who speedily murdered the false Smerdis. Persia was again without a ruler. The crisis was desperate. Here was a vast empire composed of many opposing elements and ready to fall to pieces on the first opportunity; while those magnates of the empire who were best fitted to be selected to succeed to the crown were naturally ambitious to grasp the opportunity themselves, and so jealous of their rivals that a civil war, attended with the most disastrous results, seemed exceedingly probable. The difficulty was avoided by a device as ingenious as it was creditable. The seven conspirators agreed to select one from their own number to be possessor of Persia. Various accounts are given of the way in which the election was made. Some records state that they decided to meet at sunrise, and he whose horse should neigh first should be adjudged the winner. Owing to the cunning of the groom of Darius, his horse first gave the auspicious signal, and thus raised him in a moment from a mere subject to absolute ruler of one of the largest of the world's empires. But as Darius was distantly connected with the Achemenian line, the only one of the seven in whose veins coursed the blood royal, it is more likely that the other six preferred to settle the succession on him rather than allow such a prize to one of merely equal rank with themselves.

Whatever the cause which led to the selection of Darius,[*] the result of this event proved of great ad-

[*] In the original Persian this name is spelled Darayavalm. Most of the ancient Persian names have come down to us through Greek and Latin sources, and are often very unlike the original.

vantage to Persia. The young king, for he was at this time only about thirty years of age, showed himself at once to be a born ruler of men, a great soldier, and an administrator of vast capacity. He was also a man whose ambition seems to have been tempered with patriotism, and, unlike many Oriental monarchs, he did not allow his unlimited power to degenerate into reckless and ruthless cruelty.

Darius found the great empire which had come into his hands torn by dissensions, or falling apart for lack of a strong arm to hold its various inharmonious elements together. He set to work with amazing vigor and ability to restore peace and order, and left behind him a record which stamps him as one of the greatest sovereigns in history, if not the most remarkable ruler who has sat on the throne of Persia.

For a knowledge of many of the exploits and successes of Darius we are indebted to an inscription which he caused to be engraved on a tablet, or smooth surface, on the famous rock of Behistoon. From this inscription we learn that Darius had to encounter and suppress revolts in Sardis, Susiana, and Babylonia, Arachosia and Media, Parthia and Hyrcania, and even in Persia, the original seat of the empire. But one after another they were subdued by the herculean grasp and genius of Darius, who did not hesitate at the same time to order the execution of Intaphernes and all his family. Intaphernes was one of the six confederates who had elevated Darius to the throne; for this reason he seems to have thought he could treat him with less respect. But Darius, who well knew that an Oriental king can only hold power by exacting every iota of respect and subservience that is due to him, soon showed the great Persian nobleman the fatal error he had made, by condemning him and his kinsfolk to instant death. The custom which has so widely prevailed in the East, of making the innocent members of the family of a criminal suffer punishment with him, may have been based on good reasons suggested by a pitiless expediency. One reason may have been that by exterminating an entire family no survivor was left to avenge the fate of the chief offender. A more solid reason probably lay in the fact that, as Oriental families are organized, the head of it rarely took any important steps or entered into a conspiracy without consulting with most of the members of his family, who perhaps not only approved, but also instigated him to pursue such a perilous path, and were therefore practically participants in the offence.

After reducing the entire empire once more to subjection, Darius devoted himself like a patriotic ruler to the improvement of the condition of his people. He organized the numerous provinces of Persia under governors called khshathrapavan, which the Greeks shortened to satrap. These satraps lived with great pomp and wielded much power. They were permitted to command the armed contingents of their respective provinces, but the fortresses were invariably held by troops of the king. Reports were regularly rendered to the sovereign by officers specially commissioned by him, and thus while apparently independent rulers, the satraps were held in check. The system was the most complete that had yet been seen in Asia. Darius also introduced a more careful method of taxation than what had previously existed in Persia. Each province was obliged to render a fixed portion of its revenue to the crown. For most of these facts we are indebted to the celebrated rock chronicle of Behistoon.

After reorganizing the great empire of Persia, the soaring genius of Darius was not satisfied to remain idle. His energies were such that the stated business of his position was insufficient to occupy his mind and he entered upon a series of foreign expeditions and conquests. He extended the boundaries of his empire eastward as far as the Indus. After this he undertook to subdue the vast wastes now called Russia in Europe, which went by the name of Scythia with classic writers. A bridge of boats was built across the Thracian Bosphorus. Darius conducted the expedition in person. The Scythians, wild hordes mounted on horses as wild as themselves, fled before the hosts of Persia. But if Darius had been less ignorant of the inclemency of the climate and the worthlessness of those steppes that seemed to extend without end towards the North Star, he would not have undertaken such a barren conquest. He was forced to return, rather ingloriously it must be confessed ; but it was nature and not man that brought about this result; it was the wild climate, that, in later ages wrecked the fortunes of Charles IX. and Napoleon, which drove the great king of Persia back to the shores of the Euxine. More fortunate than they, however, he was able to return unmolested to Thrace, which he not only subdued, but reduced all the Greek colonies on the northern shores of the Ægean, and obliged the king of Macedonia to yield allegiance to him. Thus, while baffled in Scythia, Darius was yet able at the close of this expedition to boast sovereignty from the Nile to the Oxus, and from Macedonia to India.

HEAD OF DARIUS.

A glance at the map will indicate the vastness of the territory commanded by the skilled brain of Darius of Persia.

If Darius had been content to rest on his laurels after this, he might well be considered one of the few men who have been specially favored by destiny. But few are they who know when they have reached the limit of success—nor was he an exception. Still, in the expedition which he now launched against Greece, it must be said in his favor that up to this time he had been able to cope successfully with the Greeks. Even on the sea, where Asiatics in all ages have been inferior to mariners of European races, Darius had proved victorious. The great naval battle of Ladé, to which the Greeks led three hundred and fifty-three galleys, was decided so decisively in his favor, that he was able to place at his feet all the revolted Greek states of the western coast and isles of Asia Minor. The city of Miletus was captured after a long siege, and the inhabitants were sold into slavery.

The evil genius of Darius was the great and ambitious noble Mardonius, a man of brilliant abilities, who urged the king to continue his war against the Greeks, by sending an army of invasion across the Ægean, to attack the plucky little states that held the purple crags of Greece on their own soil—states that had grown strong by frequent wars among themselves. It is impossible for one to consider the character of the Greeks at that time without enthusiasm. No one who has in him a spark of poetry, of sentiment, of romance, or who is capable of admiring freedom and heroism, can avoid a thrill of pleasure as he pores over the history of Greece at the period when she crossed arms with the glittering hosts of Central Asia. Nor were the armies of Persia, in the time of Darius, unworthy of the Titanic conflict which was now about to begin. If the Persian generals depended upon numbers to win, more than upon military discipline and intricate knowledge of the art of war, yet no braver men than they existed, and the valiant hosts they led deserved to conquer, if victory be the invariable reward of courage. That the Persians were unable to maintain themselves in Greece was due to the fact that their smaller numbers had made it easy for the Greeks to reach a high order of military training, together with the fact that the invaders met them on their native soil, defending it with the desperation of lions driven to bay. It must be remembered, also, that in the account of these wars between Persia and Greece we are obliged to depend almost entirely upon the statements of the Greek historians, who quite likely exaggerated, perhaps unconsciously, the merit of their own side, and the numbers to which they were opposed.

According to Herodotus, and other Greek writers, the expedition which Darius sent against Greece, in the year 490 B.C., was commanded by Datis and Artaphernes, and numbered 100,000 men. Doubtless the army which was actually landed at Marathon was considerably less, for thousands must be subtracted as mariners and rowers of the fleet, besides the servants of the officers. On the whole, it seems to the writer very improbable that the army which the Greeks fought at Marathon was over 50,000 men, and probably less than that; for the number of Persians who fell in the battle was only about 6,000 men, which was a very small proportion for a defeated army of 100,000 to lose in the bloody conflicts of those times.

The Greek army numbered at least 10,000, massively clad in brass and steel, and commanded by a hero named Miltiades. It was a weakness of the Athenian military organization that their armies were often under the lead of several generals, who took command on alternate days. It was fortunate for Greece that on this decisive day Miltiades was in command. His little army was deployed in one long line with the cliffs behind them, and the Persian fleet drawn up on the beach in front of them. Before the Persians had fairly deployed their platoons on the sea-shore, Miltiades gave the order to charge. Singing the pæan of victory, the Greeks rushed across the narrow interval between the two armies. Brave as they were, the Persians were unable to withstand the serried spears that bore them to the ground. They were thrown back on the fleet, and all was now confusion and dismay. With loud appeals, the generals vainly sought to rally the flying masses of fugitive Persians, while the mariners strove

PERSIAN ARCHITECTURE.—FROM THE TOMB OF DARIUS I.

to force the galleys into the water before the Greeks could burn them with the torches they hurled through the air on the decks. Many of the Greeks were slain, and a brother of Æschylus, the poet, lost a hand as he grasped the gunwale of one of the ships. In the end, the Persians were able to withdraw with most of the fleet and the army.

A wounded messenger started from Marathon to carry the news to Athens, where wives and children were anxiously awaiting tidings of the battle, on which hung the fate of their homes. He ran the entire distance without stopping, until in the marketplace of Athens, he cried to the waiting throng: "The day is ours!" and fell dead.

As we look back over the ages that have come and gone since that glorious event, we are better able to judge of its importance in shaping the world's progress than were they who were actors in the great drama of Marathon. For Darius was a man of far superior force than Xerxes, and if he had succeeded in mastering Greece at a time when Persia was at the zenith of her glory, his genius might have entirely transformed the destiny of Greece at a critical period of her intellectual development. Æschylus, who participated in the battle, and composed a magnificent drama founded on the conflict of Marathon, pays a very high tribute of admiration to the genius of Darius, notwithstanding that the Persian monarch had threatened the liberty of Greece.

The remaining years of Darius the First seem to have been devoted to the arts of peace. He survived the battle of Marathon about eleven years, and in that time must have done much to promote the prosperity of his vast dominions. If Darius did not found the magnificent palace at Persepolis, whose ruins are to this day one of the marvels of the ages, it is highly probable that he did much to enlarge and beautify its noble terraces and colonnades. The clemency of his disposition and the ability he displayed in the choice of the high functionaries who ruled under him, must have done much to add to the repose which Persia enjoyed during the closing years of the great king. He died in 479 B.C., in the fortieth year of his reign, and was buried in the elaborate rock tomb which he had caused to be excavated in the steep hillsides that overlooked the superb palaces where he had gathered the spoils of a long career of conquest and glory.

IX.

XERXES.

DARIUS I. left a son named Xerxes, or, as the Persians pronounced the word, Khshayarsha. He was a son of Atossa, daughter of Cyrus the Great, and as such was doubly heir to the throne. But he was a degenerate scion of a noble line. Perhaps the great contrast between him and his father might have been less apparent, in history at least, if he had been content to follow a career suited to his moderate ability and enervated character. The vast enterprise that has rendered his name famous does not, however, altogether prove, as some undertake to show, that he was utterly unworthy to succeed to the throne, for foreign conquest had become the policy of Persia, and it was only natural that he should undertake to follow in the steps of his distinguished predecessors. The failure of Darius, a far greater man than Xerxes, in the invasion of Greece, showed that the ill success of Xerxes in his expedition against Greece was due as much to the desperate character of such a tremendous undertaking, as to his own lack of ability to conduct a great foreign war at a long distance from his capital. It must also be admitted that Xerxes exhibited some talent in selecting the officers suited to command his forces. It seems proper to say this much in his favor, because history appears to have been a little inclined to be too severe in its judgment of the character of this unfortunate monarch. Some of the absurdities with which he is charged are also palliated by the superstitions and beliefs of the age in which he lived. Certainly the Greek historians who believed that nymphs dwelt in the rivers and dryads in the woods, and that Jupiter and Venus and Neptune were actual beings, could not afford to laugh at a king who, according to their statements, whipped the sea when it proved unruly.

Xerxes appears to have been a man of visionary and ambitious temperament rather than one of a character depraved beyond that of most Oriental monarchs. His brain was fired by the thought of the vast enterprises he meditated. For years before the death of Darius, that monarch had been making steady preparations for a renewal of the invasion of Greece. The vast armaments that were gathered, and the perpetual discussion of an event upon which such calculations and hopes were based, naturally had their effect on the mind of such a character as Xerxes. This is shown by the dreams that haunted him and aroused his apprehensions regarding the issue of the coming expedition. In personal bearing Xerxes is said by Herodotus to have been in the highest degree imperial; in stature he exceeded all his subjects; his features were handsome, his eye keen and penetrating, but his disposition was inclined to cruelty. Xerxes is generally considered to have been the Ahasuerus, whose magnificence and peculiarly Oriental caprice are so strikingly suggested in the Book of Esther.

Such was the monarch who succeeded Darius Hystaspes on the throne of Persia. At the very outset of his reign he found himself confronted by a formidable revolt: Egypt had taken up arms and sought to throw off the Persian yoke. Xerxes himself led an army into Egypt and, although the Egyptians were good fighters, he succeeded in crushing the rebellion. This event appears to indicate that he was not as destitute of ability as some historians have undertaken to prove.

On his return from Egypt, Xerxes put his vast army into motion upon the greatest military enterprise recorded in history. Herodotus states that the land and sea forces of this prodigious host, which had been gathered from every province of Persia's heterogeneous empire, numbered 2,641,000 men, while the sailors, muleteers, and servants amounted fully to the same number, making a total of over five millions of men. Herodotus says that the number was ascertained by building an enclosure at Doriscus which could contain ten thousand men. Through this the host defiled; every time it was filled ten thousand men were thus told off. We think that the Greek chronicler was probably misinformed on this point. But there is no question that the army of Xerxes was the largest that has ever been collected.

Provisions and supplies for no less than three years had been gathered at depots along the line of march; but the difficulty of feeding such an army must have been a prodigious task. That a host like that was transported so great a distance without apparently suffering from lack of supplies shows what a degree of executive ability had been infused into the complicated machinery of the government of such a vast empire, composed as it was of various races and kindreds and tongues.

Another important work had been accomplished previous to the starting of the expedition. In those times navigation was slow and cautious. Instead of avoiding the land, sailors then hugged the shore, being without the compass, and depended for motive power as much on oars as sails. Galleys and even entire fleets, instead of coming to an anchor, generally lay on the beach when in port. As the tides of the Mediterranean rise only a few inches, this process must have entailed great labor when the ships had to be launched to put to sea. In view of this system of navigation the difficulty of taking a fleet of 1,200 galleys across the Ægean Sea was very great, even although land was always in sight. But the ports of the Greek isles were generally not sufficiently large to hold such a fleet. The ships of Xerxes appear to have sailed from the Hellespont for Greece, skirting the northern shores of the Ægean, which then formed part of the Persian empire. But midway in the course, a small peninsula, crowned by a lofty, bold headland, over 6,000 feet high, called Mt. Athos, impeded the progress of the fleet, unless the Persian admirals were willing to row around this lowering cape. It was deemed more prudent, however, to dig a canal across the peninsula.

This canal was one mile and a half in length. No fact could more clearly indicate the cautious timidity of the mariners of a period which in other respects had made such strides in civilization.

The events of the great Perso-Hellenic war have been related in detail in another volume of this series, but we may be permitted to give a sketch of the leading movements which resulted in arresting the further progress westward of the empire of Iran. The vast army of Xerxes kept company with his fleet along the shore, traversing Thrace, Macedonia, and Thessaly without meeting opposition. If Greece had been a level country, there is good reason to believe that the prodigious multitude of Asiatics would have completely overrun it like a cloud of locusts descending on a field and devouring every thing, for the Greeks, with all their courage, were too few in number to be able to offer successful resistance at once to millions of armed men.

But Greece is one of the most rugged and mountainous countries in the world, and its shores are everywhere indented with deep bays and retired ports. A small army of patriots, fierce, with a passion for defending their homes, and knowing every inch of their territory, was equal here to an invading force far exceeding it in numbers. At Thermopylæ the Greeks decided to make their first stand. It was a narrow pass on the edge of a mountain, the cliffs on one side and the sea on the other. Leonidas and ten thousand Spartans were stationed there to hold the pass. Thousands of Persians fell in attempting to force a passage. It was essential to the Persian plans to move the army through Thermopylæ. But it is not likely they would have succeeded in the attempt, if they had not found a shepherd who was willing to sell his country for gold. Treachery is quite too common a trait of the Greek character, as it is of the Asiatic. This shepherd knew of a goat-path over the mountain ridge by which Xerxes could send a body of men, single file, to attack the Greeks in the rear. When Leonidas saw that the Persians had turned the pass he dismissed his army, unwilling that Greece should lose so many valiant defenders. He reserved three hundred picked men, heroes who were willing to sell their lives for the immortal glory they were to win at Thermopylæ. Calmly the three hundred bathed themselves and combed their long hair and readjusted their helmets and coats of mail. On the morrow they all fell before the irresistible tide of the Persian host. On the hillock where the last of the immortal three hundred died, the Greeks in later ages erected a lion of marble, overlooking the blue Ægean and the white sails that bore the fame of Greece to every land.

On the same day the Persian and the Greek fleets met at Artemisium, and fought two battles with desperate courage on both sides. In the first the Greeks were victorious, but in the second the victory inclined to the Persians.

On the approach of the army of Xerxes to Athens the greatest consternation prevailed. The city of Athens was abandoned, and in obedience to the oracle, which declared that the safety of Greece lay in her wooden walls, the people embarked on the fleet, interpreting the meaning of the oracle to be the wooden sides of their fleets. From the decks of the ships they saw the smoke of their burning homes and temples rising to the heavens. It was a dark day for Greece, but no days are hopelessly dark while the heart is warmed with hope and nerved with courage.

The combined fleet of the Greeks was collected in the bay formed by Salamis, Ægina, and the mainland. And hither it was followed by the vast fleet of Xerxes, numbering nearly one thousand ships. So terrible was the crisis that the allies of the Athenians lost heart and were disposed to withdraw their contingent, in order to protect the Peloponnesus, or southern half of Greece, and leave Athens to her fate. Such was the question mooted the night before the battle, when the captains were in council. It is not strange that they hesitated to hazard the fate of all Greece upon a single blow, for doubtless if Xerxes had won at Salamis the whole country would have been at his feet.

At this critical hour, Themistocles, the chief captain of the Athenians, stole away from the council and secretly despatched a messenger to Xerxes to inform him of the proposed flight of half the Greek fleet. On learning of this, Xerxes did exactly what Themistocles had expected. He ordered a portion of his fleet to be drawn in a line across the mouth of the strait, thus effectually closing the passage by which the allies intended to withdraw their ships. On learning of the manœuvre of the enemy, the Greeks saw that they were in a trap, and that the only thing left for them to do was to fight.

XERXES' SEAT AT SALAMIS.

The battle was of the most desperate character. Although inferior in numbers, the Greeks made up for the disparity by superior discipline and skill. On the side of the Persians, was Artemisia, Queen of Caria, who commanded her own fleet, and greatly distinguished herself by her courage and superior ability in manœuvring. When her galley was chased by the Greeks, and on the point of capture, this heroine, with great presence of mind, ordered the helmsman to steer directly into a Persian ship and run it down with the iron beak of her own ship. When the Greek captains saw this, they imagined that they were pursuing one of their own ships and stopped the chase. The Persians were encouraged by the circumstance that they were fighting under the gaze of their king, who would not hesitate to flay alive every coward, for Xerxes beheld the battle from a silver throne he had caused to be placed on the rocky promontory of Mount Ægialus. But neither the numbers nor the courage of the Persians availed against the desperation and military genius of the Greeks. His vast navy was broken; hundreds of galleys were sunk or captured, and the remainder which escaped, only escaped to encounter further disasters.

Well might Byron sing:

> "A king sat on the rocky brow
>   Which looks o'er sea-born Salamis;
> And men by nations lay below,
>   And ships by thousands—all were his.
> He counted them at break of day,
> And when the sun set where were they!"

The battle of Salamis occurred 430 years B.C., or two thousand three hundred and sixteen years ago; and Persia still exists as an independent nation, even though shorn of some of her vast dominions. Great empires have risen and fallen since the day of Salamis, and yet Persia lives. If she was unable to conquer Greece, she had yet in her people a vitality and an intellectual force that could only belong to a race of a very high order. The fact is, that the Persians of that day, as in our times, were comparatively few in number; but they had great organizing and executive ability, and were able to make others contribute to the success of their arms. The Persians furnished the brains which built up and have maintained their empire to the present century. A power of inferior quality would have fallen to pieces after the failure of an expedition which demanded such stupendous efforts.

Xerxes showed less courage in defeat than one would expect from a man of such ambition. He turned his face towards Persia, and finding the bridge of boats he had built over the Hellespont shattered by the waves, he crossed in a ship. But before leaving Greece so ingloriously, he granted the prayer of Mardonius, who petitioned that he might be permitted to continue the war on Greek soil. The remainder of the army accompanied Xerxes to Persia. Mardonius was a hero, and by his courage deserved a better fate than destiny awarded him. He knew not what we now see, that he was fighting in a hopeless cause, as it had been ordained that Europe should never belong to the races of Asia.

After considerable manœuvring, the opposing forces met on the plains of Platæa. Greece has never before nor since, on any one field, mustered such an army as she drew up at Platæa. It numbered 110,000 men. The place of honor, on the left, was awarded to the Athenians. The Persian army amounted to 300,000, according to the statements of Herodotus. For several days the two armies faced each other, anxiously consulting the auguries, which from day to day proved unpropitious.

The inevitable conflict was finally precipitated, it is said, by Mardonius, in spite of the auguries of the soothsayers. It is more likely that the demand for water and supplies to sustain his large army forced him either to fight or retreat; in the former there was hope, but in the latter, ruin for the Persian host, and therefore Mardonius chose the former course.

Once more fortune came to the aid of Greece. The battle was long and obstinate. The Persians fought with courage equal to that of the foe. But they were out-generalled. It should be recorded, however, that the plans of Mardonius were betrayed by his ally, the king of the Macedonians, the night before the battle, which gave the Greeks a very great advantage. Mardonius was slain, and the greater part of his vast army fell on the field. We cannot, however, accept the statement of the Greek historians that only a few hundred of the Greeks were killed in this tremendous conflict. To believe this is to assume that the Persians were cowards and offered no resistance, whereas those historians themselves concede to them at least the merit of heroic valor.

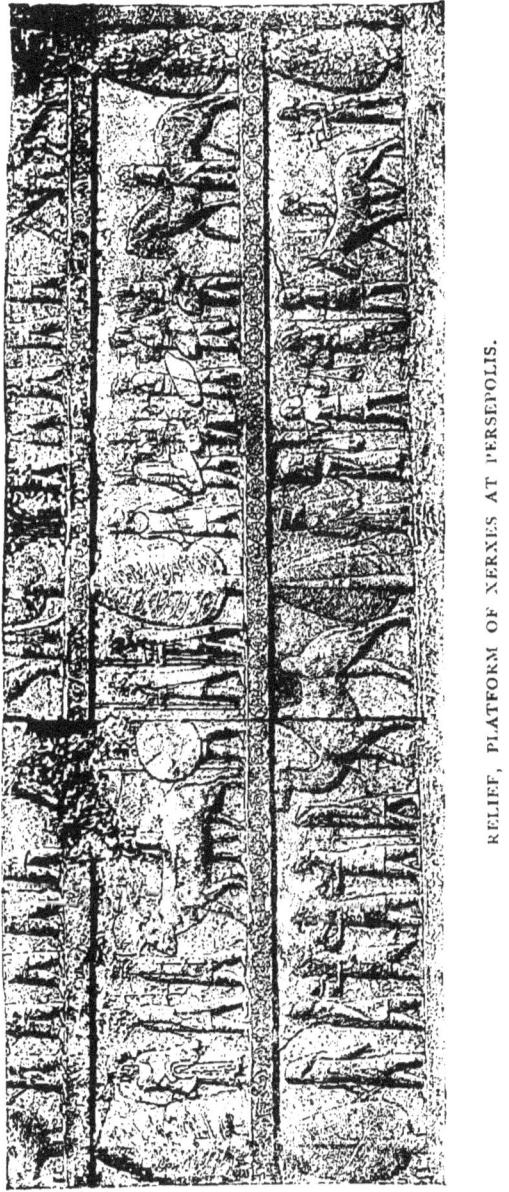

RELIEF, PLATFORM OF XERXES AT PERSEPOLIS.

On the same day the Persians were defeated at Mycalé, on the coast of Asia Minor, by a Greek fleet, and soon after, by the loss of Abydos, Persia was stripped of all the possessions which had been won in Europe by Darius. Well might the Greek dramatist, in the stirring strophes of his great tragedy,[*] which was inspired by these events, make Atossa and her attendants wail in these wild words of woe over the vast calamities which befell the best blood of Persia when Xerxes invaded Greece:

> "Wo to the towns through Asia's peopled realms!
> Wo to the land of Persia, once the post
> Of boundless wealth, how is thy glorious state
> Vanished at once, and all thy spreading honors
> Fall'n, lost! Ah me! unhappy is his task
> That bears unhappy tidings; but constraint
> Compels me to relate this tale of wo.
> Persians, the whole barbaric host is fall'n.
> "O horror, horror! What a baleful train
> Of recent ills! Ah, Persians, as he speaks
> Of ruin, let your tears stream to the earth.
> "It is even so, all ruin; and myself
> Beheld the ruin which my tongue would utter.
> "Wo, wo is me! Then has the iron storm,
> That darkened from the realms of Asia, poured
> In vain its arrowy shower on sacred Greece.
> "In heaps the unhappy dead lie on the strand
> Of Salamis, and all the neighboring shores.
> "Unhappy friends, sunk, perished in the sea;
> Their bodies, 'mid the wreck of shattered ships,
> Mangled and rotting on th' encumbered waves!
> * * * * * * *
> "Raise the funereal cry, with dismal notes
> Wailing the wretched Persians. Oh, how ill
> They planned their measures, all their army perished!

[*] "The Persians," by Æschylus.

> " O Salamis, how hateful is thy name!
> And groans burst from me when I think of Athens.
> " How dreadful to her foes! Call to remembrance
> How many Persian dames, wedded in vain,
> Hath Athens of their noble husbands widowed?
>
> * * * * * * *
>
> " Griefs like these exceed
> The power of speech or question; yet even such,
> Inflicted by the gods, must mortal man,
> Constrained by hard necessity, endure."

Xerxes does not appear to have entered into any other important enterprises after his return to Persia, where he reigned for some time after that event, although hostilities between Persia and Greece did not actually cease for some time. It may be inferred that he aroused indignation and unpopularity in certain quarters, for he was assassinated in the twentieth year of his reign by Artabanus, the captain of the royal body-guard.

X.

PERSIA UNTIL THE INVASION OF ALEXANDER.

XERXES left two sons, Darius and Artaxerxes. The former, as the eldest, was the natural heir; but Artaxerxes formed a conspiracy with the murderer of his father, Artabanus, and in turn caused Darius to be slain, and usurped the throne. It was a natural sequel to this series of atrocities, that when Artaxerxes felt himself firmly established in power he should order Artabanus, the author of these crimes, to suffer the death he had so richly merited.

Artaxerxes was surnamed Longimanus, or the Long-handed, for what reason does not distinctly appear. At the very outset of his reign he had to encounter a formidable uprising in Egypt, which during so many years had been subjected to the Persian rule. The rebellion was led by Inarus, son of Psammeticus. The Egyptians called the Athenians to their aid, who sent them a fleet of two hundred sail. In the end, however, the Persians, conducted by Megabyzus, were successful in once more reducing Egypt to subjection, and the Athenians were obliged to retire with little glory and considerable loss. One result of this event was the final settlement of a peace between Persia and Greece, which seems to have been advantageous to the former country. For while Persia agreed to allow her rival to enjoy unmolested sway and navigation in the Western Mediterranean, Greece, on the other hand, consented to allow Persia to retain undisputed possession of all the territories she had conquered on the eastern shores of the Mediterranean from the Hellespont to Egypt, although in many parts the population was composed chiefly of Greeks.

After the Egyptian revolt Artaxerxes was disturbed by the rebellion of Megabyzus himself, who had quelled the insurrection. Megabyzus aspired to nothing less than the throne of Persia. He succeeded in maintaining an independent position in Syria for several years, aided very likely by the Jews; for it seems probable that it was at this time, about the year 445 B.C., that the destruction of Jerusalem occurred, which is bewailed by the prophet Nehemiah. It is a fact remarkable in Oriental history, that Megabyzus received a full pardon and was permitted to return to the court of Artaxerxes, where he continued to reside unmolested. Although probably due in part to the influence of Amestris, wife of the king and mother-in-law of Megabyzus, yet such clemency on the part of an Eastern monarch towards a subject who had sought to dethrone him, was an event so extraordinary as to require especial comment.

Artaxerxes the Long-handed died in 424 B.C., after a reign of forty years. He appears to have been of a mild if not weak disposition, humane, and unambitious. Like his father, Xerxes, he was of tall and commanding presence, and in his love for the chase resembled many of his line.

Xerxes II., who succeeded to the throne was murdered within a month and a half by his brother, Sogdianus, who in turn was defeated and slain by Ochus, another son of Artaxerxes, who took the name of Darius II., with the surname of Nothus. The person who possessed the most influence during this reign was Parysatis, the sister and wife of Darius. If not distinctly authorized by the religious laws of Zoroaster, the practice of marriage between brothers and sisters was not considered a crime in Persia in those days, and was often followed by the sovereigns of that country. Parysatis was a woman of strong will, fierce passions, and unprincipled character; her hold over the mind of Darius was imperious, and many of the dark intrigues and acts of blood which stain the pages of Persian history must be charged to this beautiful but wicked woman. The power which such women as Parysatis have frequently obtained in the East is a sufficient proof that the system of seclusion to which Oriental women have been subjected in all ages does not appear to have much effect in reducing the influence of their charms.

The reign of Darius Nothus is distinguished by the loss of Egypt, which for one hundred and fifteen years had been one of the most brilliant ornaments of the Persian crown. The Egyptians were too intelligent and active a people to allow themselves to be permanently absorbed into another government, while as a people who were profoundly religious, they could never forget nor forgive the frequent affronts offered to their gods by the haughty satraps set over them by the Persian monarchs. Amyrtæus, a descendant of the royal line of Egypt, assumed the reigns of government and succeeded in expelling the Persians from the banks of the Nile.

The degeneracy into which the Persian monarchy was rapidly falling during the reigns of the successors of Darius became clearly apparent during the reign of Darius Nothus; and also the cupidity of the Greeks, a trait which has unfortunately been too prominent a blemish of the Greek character in all ages. Even the Spartans, whose strict discipline and laws had made Spartan simplicity proverbial, now showed that their boasted virtue was not proof against Persian gold. Not only were the Greeks willing to sell their services as mercenaries, but many of their chief men, such as Pausanias and Themistocles, and Lysander and Alcibiades, engaged in dark intrigues with the Persian satraps, and more especially that craftiest of the crafty, Tissaphernes, satrap of Sardis.

The aim of these intrigues was generally to give advantages to each in the attainment of power, the Persians being able to furnish unlimited supplies of money, and the Greeks soldiers, whose valor and discipline were superior to that of the Persian troops which these satraps, when intending to revolt, had to encounter. The Greek leaders who engaged in these mischievous plots also sought to win for themselves in turn supreme power in Greece at the expense of the liberties of their countrymen. So far as the Greeks were concerned, all the leaders engaged in these ambitious schemes came to a disgraceful end one after another, and such also was the case with the Persian conspirators in due time; but unfortunately not until they had done infinite evil to their respective countries.

One of the most important events in the world's history, the invasion of Persia by Alexander the Great, resulted indirectly from these secret and unscrupulous negotiations, as will be apparent in the sequel.

Darius II. was succeeded by his oldest son, who took the name of Artaxerxes II. He had a brother named Cyrus the younger. Parysatis was the mother of both. The brothers, although very different in character, were equally under the influence of this powerful woman, but Cyrus, in ambition and will, appears most to have resembled their mother. On learning of the approaching death of their father, Cyrus left his satrapy and came to the capital attended by a military escort which included three hundred Greek mercenaries. It was his intention to seize the throne. But he arrived too late, for Darius II. had already expired, and Artaxerxes Memnon was master of the crown. Cyrus, however, conscious of superior talents and popularity, still meditated treason, hoping by intrigue to dethrone his brother.

At this juncture his designs were betrayed by a celebrated Persian grandee named Tissaphernes, whom he had befriended, and who professed to be zealously attached to his cause. But through the influence of Parysatis Cyrus was pardoned and sent back to his province in Asia Minor. When one con-

TOMB OF ESTHER AND MORDECAI, AT HAMADAN.

siders that in later and, we might suppose, more enlightened ages, the sovereigns of Persia often executed or blinded all their male kinsmen before they had even attempted conspiracies, lest they might plot against the king, it must be admitted that the monarchs of the Achemenian line were often remarkably lenient towards their brothers.

But Cyrus the Younger was not content to have so narrowly escaped death. He was of an ardent temperament, and from what we can learn was not only a man of superior intelligence, but also possessed of certain lofty qualities not too common among Persians of rank at that period, and certainly scarcely to be looked for in a son of such a woman as Parysatis, a woman who had married her own brother, who had, among many other crimes, poisoned her own daughter-in-law Statira and induced her son Artaxerxes to marry his own daughter Atossa. That Cyrus was ambitious to the point of rising against his king and brother, is no more than could be expected from any Oriental prince conscious of possessing especial genius for government.

Cyrus showed his intelligence by purchasing the services of thirteen thousand Greek mercenaries, who were commanded by Clearchus. He well knew what they were capable of accomplishing in the desperate enterprise toward which he was now turning all the energy of his restless soul. It is hardly likely that he would have ventured on the attempt without the aid of these well-disciplined auxiliaries. Besides them he took with him over a hundred thousand Persian troops.

Cyrus had marched as far east as Cunaxa (about fifty miles from Babylon) before he received any certain information that his brother Artaxerxes intended to offer resistance. This is a curious illustration of the simple methods which characterized the movements of armies in those times. Xenophon, in his account of this expedition, in a few brief but vivid sentences, describes the sudden discovery of a vast army approaching over the plains at early morning, amid clouds of dust in which might be discerned the flash of helmets and spears.

The army of the king far overlapped the lines of the prince. But a vigorous attack of the insurgent army on one of the wings crushed it back on the centre, and would have resulted in a victory for Cyrus if Clearchus had moved his mercenaries with sufficient activity to support the prince, who fiercely cut his way through to the chariot which bore Artaxerxes. When the king saw his brother approaching, he showed the greatest consternation, and Cyrus had actually wounded Artaxerxes when he was borne down by numbers coming to the rescue. Having in his haste entered the field only half-clad in armor, he was speedily despatched. Thus in a few moments an enterprise which had been in preparation for years, and which might have altered the destinies of Persia, came to an untimely end.

The shining qualities of Cyrus the Younger would alone have perpetuated the fame of him who fell at Cunaxa. But, as if to give emphasis to these events, they are handed down to us by the pen of one of the greatest historians of ancient times, who was himself an important actor in the scenes he describes in such matchless style. We refer to Xenophon, an Athenian who was one of the officers of the Greek contingent which accompanied the expedition of Cyrus.

After the fall of Cyrus, Clearchus called off his troops and collected them upon a slight eminence, to await an attack from the vast host of the king. But Tissaphernes, the royal general, had no idea of wasting his men by hurling them against a few thousand Greeks, who, though now reduced to little over ten thousand, were desperate and disciplined and prepared to sell their lives dearly. He preferred to resort to the Persian tactics of treachery and intrigue, well aware that so small a body of men, one thousand miles from home, surrounded by hungry mountains and desert plains in the heart of an enemy's country, must soon perish.

Clearchus and his associate commanders should, as Greeks, have been sufficiently shrewd not to fall into the snares of treachery. Yet this is exactly what happened. Wily as a fox, Tissaphernes lured them into his tent on the pretence of arranging terms by which they should be permitted to return unmolested to Greece. They were never seen again alive. But when the Greek troops learned from the heralds sent to them by Tissaphernes that through the loss of their generals they were in a most desperate position, instead of surrendering to Tissaphernes in compliance with his demands, they at once proceeded to elect generals to conduct them on their homeward march. Among those selected for this forlorn hope was Xenophon, whose abilities soon made him virtually sole commander.

The route selected by Xenophon for the famous retreat of the Ten Thousand lay in a northerly direction. Although it led over steep mountains and among fierce and barbarous tribes, yet, after getting into the mountain regions, the Greeks would be less troubled by the Persian troops and would be able to embark at a Greek port on reaching the Euxine.

The difficulties encountered on this long and harassing march could hardly be exaggerated. Only the skill of Xenophon and the heroic endurance of his troops availed to escape the wiles of the Persians and the perpetual attacks of the Carduchi, who in our time are called Kurds. After six months of fighting and travel the Greeks at last beheld the blue sea, those in advance announcing it by loud cries of "The sea, the sea!" It was at Trapezus, now called Trebizond, that Xenophon found ships which transported his army to Greece.

One result, and that a very important one, of this famous passage of so small a body of Greeks across the Persian empire, was to show the low condition to which that empire had fallen through the inefficiency of its later rulers. The authority of the king hung loosely on many of the provinces. The inefficiency of the government had been communicated to the army, which was therefore far less able to resist invasion than when Cyrus and Darius held the reins of empire with a firm hand. It was a knowledge of these facts which in time led Philip of Macedon to make preparations to invade the Persian empire; but he was assassinated before he could undertake this enterprise, which was then carried to a successful issue by Alexander the Great.

Artaxerxes Memnon had many other revolts to occupy his attention besides that of his brother Cyrus. The satraps Mausolus and Datames appear to have given him the most trouble. Although by the energy of Ariobarzanes and other skilful generals, these insurrections were generally put down, yet they indicated that the great empire founded by Cyrus must soon crumble from the weakness of its monarchs and the corruption of its governors and subordinate officers, unless a strong brain and arm should arise to revive its decaying vitality. Such a man appeared on the death of Artaxerxes after a mild but ruinous reign of forty-six years.

Artaxerxes II. was succeeded by his son Ochus, who took the name of Artaxerxes III. He proved to be a man quite the opposite in character to his father, possessed of unusual energy and great determination. He found the Persian empire ready to fall asunder; on all hands the satraps were in revolt, and the various races which had been held subject by the superior intellect of the Iranian race were preparing to proclaim their independence. The Athenians, ever ready to war against their hereditary enemies, the Persians, whom they haughtily styled barbarians, extended aid to Artabazus, satrap of Phrygia. But the threats of Artaxerxes to carry hostilities into Greece brought them to their senses, and Theban mercenaries at the same time came to the assistance of the Persian monarch,

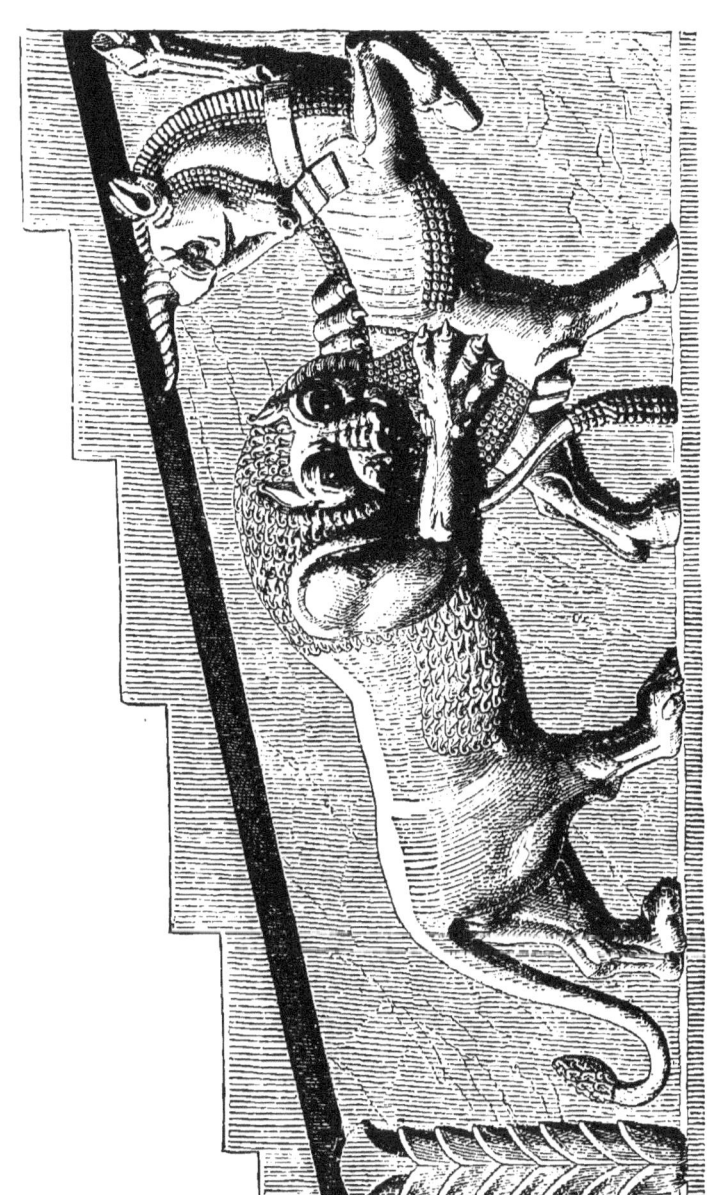

RELIEF ON THE STEPS OF XERXES, AT PERSEPOLIS.

Artabazus was forced to fly for refuge to Macedonia, which appears to have been at that time an asylum for the enemies of Persia.

About the year 353 B.C., Artaxerxes III. gave further evidence of the vigor of his character by actually planning another invasion of Greece, and the great Athenian orator and statesman, Demosthenes, warned his countrymen to act with caution in order that they might not afford Artaxerxes a desired pretext for once more inundating the soil of Greece with the hordes of Central Asia.

Artaxerxes was, however, diverted from undertaking this invasion by renewed hostilities with Egypt, and by the revolt of Cyprus, Judæa, and Phœnicia. After a period of complete independence, Egypt was again reduced to be a vassal of Persia. Artaxerxes overran the country and subjected the gods of Egypt to insults equal to those of Cambyses. Mentor, the victorious general who conducted the Egyptian campaign, received the highest tokens of his sovereign's appreciation. It was the turn of Cyprus next, and she too learned to her cost that a man of genius was again wielding the sceptre of Persia.

Artaxerxes Ochus himself conducted the war against Judæa and Phœnicia, and laid siege to Sidon. This is one of the most remarkable sieges in history. It lasted for many months, and no less than 400,000 people perished when Sidon was stormed and burned, B.C. 351.

The extraordinary ability of Artaxerxes now led him to act in the affairs of Greece in a manner quite the reverse of that followed by his predecessors. Philip of Macedon was threatening the liberties of the numerous small but active republics of Greece. His great ability and ambition had awakened the keenest alarm. In this crisis the Athenians turned for aid to the country which had so often threatened their very existence, and formed an alliance with Artaxerxes III. There seems good reason to believe that a man of his shrewd intellect perceived the danger to Persia, if all Greece should be at the beck of a commanding will like that of Philip of Macedon. At any rate, Artaxerxes furnished money and troops to the Greeks, and probably intended to proceed in person with a large army to Greece. But before he could accomplish that design Philip succeeded in defeating the united forces of Greece at Chæronæa, 338 B.C., a conflict, which, in view of its vast results, may be considered one of the decisive battles of the world.

It was at this critical time that Artaxerxes III. was murdered by the eunuch Bagoas. It requires but a little reflection to judge how much apparently depended upon the continued reign of such a man as Artaxerxes. A soldier and statesman of his stamp might have prevented Alexander from entering on his expedition against Persia, or at least greatly hindered the career of conquest which enabled Alexander to change the map of the world for ages.

Bagoas placed Arses the youngest son of Artaxerxes on the throne; but when Arses was planning to punish the eunuch for the death of his father, Bagoas caused the young king and his entire family to be slain, and elevated in his place Darius Codomanus, called Darius III., who was a great-grandson of Darius II. Bagoas now suffered his deserts; he had played the part of king-maker with rare success, having put two kings out of the way, and placed two on the throne. But it was a dangerous precedent to allow so powerful a subject to live, and Darius ordered him to execution. Bagoas affords an example of the great influence and power which have often been acquired in past ages by men of the unfortunate class to which he belonged.

XI.

DARIUS CODOMANUS AND ALEXANDER.

PERSIA had arisen, as it were, from her ashes. The genius of Artaxerxes Ochus had renewed her splendor and power, and given the empire a new lease of life, which would have insured its continuance for ages if he had been succeeded, as was Cyrus the Great, by rulers of similar talents. But destiny had willed otherwise, and when Persia had to meet in the field one of the greatest generals in history, her fate was confided by Providence to one of the most incompetent sovereigns who ever sat on a throne. Darius Codomanus may not have committed as many crimes as some of his predecessors, but neither was he impelled by their energy and genius. He had the spirit of a coward, and a weakness amounting nearly to imbecility. The successes of Alexander the Great lose in merit, when one considers what an unworthy foe he was to encounter when he passed his army across the Hellespont to conquer Asia in the spring of 334 B.C.

At the river Granicus Alexander, not without difficulty, utterly routed a Persian army which far outnumbered his own. Alexander after this event pushed his advance southward along the western coast of Asia Minor, where the large number of Greeks made conquest easy. Sardis might have offered a long resistance; but the Persian general in command, with a pusillanimity at that day uncommon among Persians, surrendered without a blow, and with his garrison went over to Alexander.

While the Macedonians were manœuvring in this direction, Memnon, the ablest of the captains of Darius, was busy planning movements which might have effectually checked the advance of the invaders. With the Persian fleets Memnon swept the Ægean, taking isle after isle; at the same time he was massing a large force which was intended to be transported to Greece, and combining there with an allied army of the Greek republics to invade Macedonia. If this movement had been carried out Alexander would doubtless have been obliged to return in all haste to defend his native dominions. But once more destiny came to the aid of him whom she had chosen to execute her designs. Memnon died in the midst of his plans. With him died the last hope of saving Persia from the redoubtable phalanx of Macedonia.

At Issus Darius again attempted to resist the victorious march of the Macedonian legions, but with the usual result. He made a poor selection of a field suited for the manœuvring of a large army, and Alexander was able to beat the Persians in detail. He then proceeded to reduce Phœnicia, in order to rob Persia of the last ports in which she could concentrate her fleets. Tyre, garrisoned by Persians, resisted Alexander seven months, and bitterly did she rue the obstinate resistance she offered.

In the year 331 the Macedonian hero finally turned directly towards Persia itself—the heart of the great empire he was attempting to overthrow. Once more Darius had gathered a vast host to make

DARIUS AT ISSUS.—FROM MURAL PAINTING AT POMPEII.

a last stand. On the plains of Arbela or Gaugamela Alexander's magnificent generalship dispersed an army which, if rightly led, might have swept his own little army of veterans out of existence. In later ages we have examples of how bravely the Persians could fight when in smaller numbers, but more ably commanded, even against such soldiers as the veterans of Rome. It was not lack of valor, but inefficiency and corruption on the part of her rulers which cost Persia her independence when invaded by the Macedonians. If Persia should ever fall again into the power of a foreign invader, it will be due, in part at least, to similar causes. The Persian people are brave and intelligent, but, like all Asiatics, their destiny is in the hands of their rulers.

Babylon and Susa and Persepolis and Passargadæ* fell into his hands successively, with scarcely any resistance, except what was heroically offered by the mountain tribes called Huxians, who may have been the same as the Loories and Bachtiarees of the present day. Vast wealth and treasure fell into the hands of the conquerors, the opulence which had been reaped for ages from many a province and kingdom, and had administered to the luxury of monarchs whose power was wellnigh limitless, and whose love of luxury had been as great as their power to gratify it.

The entry of Alexander into Persepolis is rendered doubly memorable by the conflagration which followed soon after and reduced one of the most magnificent of the world's capitals to ashes. We may judge of what Persepolis must have been by the grandeur and beauty of the few ruins which yet remain to remind us of the glory of Darius and of the

* As I have intimated on a previous page, Persepolis is merely a Greek translation of a Persian word, and means the city of the Persians. I am strongly inclined to consider Persepolis and Passargadæ as one and the same place, Pars, Pers, and Fers all meaning Persia in the native tongue, and the final "æ" being purely a Greek terminative; or, one might have been a suburb of the other.

ruthlessness of war when her torch is in the hand of one like Alexander.

According to the usual accounts, the burning of Persepolis was the result of the fierce orgies to which the victors abandoned themselves in the hour of triumph. Flushed with wine quaffed out of the golden and jewelled goblets of Persian kings, Alexander listened to the wild songs of Thaïs, a courtesan who had accompanied him from Greece. She bade him immortalize his name by applying the torch to the palaces of Persia. Their flames would emblazon his name with letters of fire on the scrolls of time. Dryden has recorded this incident in one of the finest odes in the English language, entitled "Alexander's Feast." But in his famous lyric the poet takes what is probably the rational view of this great calamity, which it certainly was to the history of architecture. Dryden represents the king of Macedon fired at a banquet in the halls of Persepolis by the strophes of Timotheus, the bard, who recited the wrongs which Greece had suffered at the hands of Persia, and summoned them to take a vengeance that should ring down all succeeding ages.

> "Revenge, revenge, Timotheus cries,
>   See the Furies arise;
>   See the snakes that they rear,
>   How they hiss in their hair,
>   And the sparkles that flash from their eyes!
>   Behold a ghastly band,
>   Each a torch in his hand!
> Those are Grecian ghosts, that in battle were slain,
>   And unburied remain
>   Inglorious on the plain;

> Give the vengeance due
>   To the gallant crew.
> Behold how they toss their torches on high,
>   How they point to the Persian abodes,
> And glittering temples of their hostile gods.
> The princes applaud with a furious joy,
> And the king seized a flambeau with zeal to destroy ;
>   Thaïs led the way,
>   To light him to his prey,
> And, like another Helen, fired another Troy."

The burning of Persepolis was a mistake, whether done in a moment of wild frenzy, or as an act of profound policy. He who wars against the arts, wars not against nations, but against mankind.

After the defeat at Arbela, Darius Codomanus, still accompanied by a large army, including the contingent of Greek mercenaries who remained by him to the last, fled to the northeast. Another monarch or general, with the least spirit and with such forces operating in his own country, might easily have continued to offer such resistance to Alexander and his moderate-sized army that might have at last brought them to ruin. But Darius was of the stuff of which they are made who throw away what their fathers have accumulated. The founders and the losers of great empires are cast in different moulds. In Bactria, Darius at last met his fate ; he was assassinated by Bessus, a satrap of that province, and the dynasty of the Achemenidæ established by Cyrus the First came to an end.

Although Alexander had conquered this vast empire in what seemed a very easy manner, yet his difficulties were not yet over. His little army, which probably never numbered at any one time over fifty thousand men, was in the heart of a hostile country. Of course it had met with many losses, which had to be constantly repaired. by recruits brought from home. But Greece, including Macedonia, was a small country with a meagre population; garrisons had to be placed in many of the captured cities, and sooner or later the supply of Greeks for his army would be exhausted. The situation was one requiring no less ability to overcome than the invasion which had just been accomplished. It is one thing to invade and conquer a hostile country; it is quite another affair to reduce it to permanent submission. The problem was made the more difficult because Alexander proposed to continue his conquests towards India and Central Asia, and it was of the last importance to have the country in his rear tranquil and submissive.

In this emergency, Alexander adopted two measures, the only ones, perhaps, that were available. The first was to fill vacancies in his regiments with Persian troops, who, under good command could be depended on to fight well, provided their fidelity could be as sure as their valor. The other measure was for the Macedonians to intermarry with Persian women in the hope that such alliances would have the double effect of reconciling the conquered to the rule of the invader, and of making the Greeks willing to forget the homes they had left behind them beyond the blue Ægean. Alexander set the example by marrying Roxana, the daughter of a Bactrian prince, but afterwards, to still further orientalize himself and secure the affection of the Persians, accepted the system of polygamy, contrary to Greek usages, and took to wife Statira, daughter of Darius and Parysatis, the daughter of Artaxerxes Ochus. Ten thousand of the Macedonian soldiers, besides nearly a hundred of the higher officers also, married Persian women. Alexander, after this, went a step further, and actually organized a separate corps, composed entirely of Persians, armed and disciplined like the Greeks, to the number of 30,000.

After arranging these affairs in Iran itself, the hero of Macedon started to reduce the north and eastern provinces of Persia, where Bessus, the slayer of Darius, of blood-royal himself, had set up his authority and undertook to assert himself as king of Persia. In his progress, Alexander is said by the Persian legends to have come to a famous plane-tree which grew near Damghan. This tree was in two parts, or trunks—the one male, the other female. The former spoke by day, and the other by night, uttering oracular sayings. Alexander took counsel with these mystic plane-trees, which, like so many of their species in Persia, stand in lonely spots overlooking vast and arid table-lands. The trees gave forth a boding voice to him as they whispered that he was to die while yet in his prime, and others should reap the fruits of his victories. The prediction of the plane-trees does not appear to have in the least dampened the warrior's ardor for conquests. For he continued on his marvellous career until his cavalry watered their horses in the waters of the Indus.

Alexander on his return from India fixed his capital at Babylon. There, in the short time that remained before his death caused by the excesses in which he indulged, he proceeded to organize the immense empire which now acknowledged his sway. The old satrapies or governments into which the empire had been divided were in general continued, and in many cases Persians were appointed to them, which tended to conciliate the people. The central and western provinces seem gradually to have accepted the situation in good faith. But the eastern and northern provinces, such as Sogdiana, Bactria, and India, were ever rebellious and gave Alexander much trouble. When one considers of what incoherent materials the vast empire of Persia was composed, one is surprised that it held together at all after his death; for the Macedonian rule introduced yet another element of discord.

The reader will remember that Philip of Macedon had subjugated the Greek republics and brought them under the rule of Macedon. The Macedonians were allied by race with other Greeks, and yet, on account of their intermixture with other races, together with their inferior civilization, the Macedonians had always been regarded by the Greeks, and especially the Athenians and Spartans, as aliens. The Greek republics had not been beaten by reason of military inferiority, but because they were rent by dissensions and the jealousies and small political intrigues seemingly inseparable from republics, as well as the fact that Philip of Macedon was a man of unusual genius, who to this added the power of buying up some of the leading men of Greece.

When Alexander the Great entered upon his Persian campaign his army was composed not only of Macedonians; it was reinforced as well by recruits from all parts of Greece. Macedonians and Greeks fought side by side in his battles, and this mutual rivalry perhaps aided to stimulate their courage.

But when Alexander came to found cities and colonize them with Greeks who had no especial sympathy with his cause, or placed entire provinces under their control, then the smouldering fires of jealousy, and the hate against the Macedonians found expression. After his death this feeling burst forth in various quarters, and was one of the causes which in the end brought about the ruin of Macedonian and Greek rule in Asia. Alexander founded more than seventy cities in which he implanted Greek and Macedonian colonies. By this military network he proposed that he and his successors should hold in unbroken form the empire which had reached its utmost limits under Darius I.

But when, in the year 323 B.C., the news flew from India to the Nile that Alexander, he who had proclaimed descent from the gods, was dead, then dissension broke forth in every quarter. For over forty years the unhappy people of this vast region were rent with discord, and the sod was drenched with blood. The generals of Alexander fought for the throne. Perdiccas, who as regent at Babylon during the minority of Alexander's son, naturally claimed the regency, if not the sovereignty, of the whole empire, was soon assassinated, and his power was claimed by Pitho, satrap of Media; but he was displaced by a conspiracy of the other satraps, who united in electing Eumenes to occupy the throne of Alexander, at Susa, in 316. But Eumenes was betrayed into the hands of Antigonus, another great Macedonian general. Antigonus in turn was obliged to yield to Seleucus, one of the Alexandrian generals, who took possession of Babylon and may be said to have founded, about the year 312 B.C., the great dynasty of the Seleucidæ. During these fierce civil wars Persis or Iran, the real seat of the Persian empire, seems to have suffered but little, being as it were in an eddy at one side, while the tide of war surged wildly over Media, Babylonia, and Parthia.

Seleucus Nicator founded the city of Seleucia on the Tigris, which he made the capital of the Persian or rather the Greco-Persian empire. Those who look at the condition of the East Indies in this century, where a population of two hundred and forty millions is governed by scarcely one hundred and fifty thousand Englishmen, may form an idea of the condition of Persia and its provinces under the reign of Seleucus Nicator and his successors. The Macedonians with their Greek troops were probably at first less numerous even than the English in India, and quite as different in habits and character from the subject races.

But the Macedonian rulers had two elements to contend with, which greatly complicated the difficulties of their position, and was one of the causes which in the end brought about the fall of their dominion in Asia. One of these was the dissension which grew up between the cavalry and the infantry of the Macedonian forces. The former had in some way united in considering that the first object for them to accomplish was to preserve the empire in the form which Alexander had left it, and to place that object before the question of Macedonian supremacy; if necessary, they were even willing to sacrifice the authority of Macedonia, if expedient to do so in order to keep the Persian empire intact. But the infantry considered that at all hazards the strong arm of Macedonian power should rule in Asia over both Greeks and Persians, and that rather than yield that point the empire might be allowed to fall to pieces. It was a "rule or ruin" policy.

The other element of discord, which grew in part out of the former, was the distinction which the Macedonians proposed to preserve between themselves and the citizens of the subject republics of Greece who had aided them in the conquest of Persia. One way in which this was shown was by the appointment of Macedonian governors and generals over the satrapies and over the garrisons which manned the one hundred and fifty cities founded by Alexander and Seleucus Nicator.

The Greeks resented such treatment, and after Alexander's death the dissatisfaction found vent in open rebellion and many a bloody conflict. One of the most terrible of these tragedies occurred when the Greeks in Northeastern Persia heard of the death of Alexander. What cared they to remain away from their homes now that the soldier was dead who had forced them to march over the wilds and wastes of Asia to crown with laurels the son of him who

ALEXANDER VISITING THE FAMILY OF DARIUS AFTER THE BATTLE OF ARBELA.

had robbed them of their liberty? An army of Greeks to the number of twenty-three thousand undertook to fight their way back to Greece. It is probable that they would have accomplished their purpose but for the treachery of one of their generals, who sold them to Pitho, the Macedonian satrap of Media. Having thus got them in his power, Pitho agreed to allow them to risk the chances of the journey home if they would lay down their arms. But the Macedonians under his command were furious at the action of their general, and after the Greeks had in good faith surrendered they fell upon the poor wretches and slaughtered them to a man. It is easy to see that such an atrocious calamity only tended to increase the hate which had been only half subdued while the iron hand of Alexander held this incongruous army together.

The Greek colonists in Bactria, the extreme northeast satrapy of Persia, also revolted and were put down with difficulty by Seleucus Nicator. But the disaffection continued, and in the reign of Antiochus II., Diodatus, satrap of Bactria, arose against the authority of the Seleucidæ, about the year 240 B.C., and founded a separate Greek state in the heart of Central Asia. The kingdom of Bactria presents one of the most singular episodes in history. A small colony of foreigners and aliens, many hundred miles from the sea, entirely isolated, and numbering probably not over thirty-five thousand, not only maintained their independence one hundred years in a strange land, but extended their conquests to the Ganges and included one thousand populous cities in their dominions.

So entirely alone were the Greeks of Bactria, so completely were they separated from the mother-country beyond the seas, and so completely have all vestiges of their race and civilization disappeared, that it is only by roundabout ways we are able to trace the progress of the state which was founded by Diodatus. For a knowledge of the facts relating to the later years of its existence we are almost altogether dependent on the coins which are found from time to time in that region, and the records of Chinese historians. China was at that period beginning to extend her commerce and arms in a westerly direction, and thus it is to that country that we are indebted for much of the little we know about the Greek colonies in Central Asia.

Another curious fact connected with the history of Bactria, is the circumstance that the establishment of that kingdom as an independent power incidentally furnished the cause of its final extinction, for it led to the founding of the Parthian empire, which overthrew the power of Bactria. It came about in the following manner: When the Greeks settled in Bactria, they found it peopled by tribes of mountaineers and shepherds, who, like the modern Turkomans, added to these pursuits the love of adventure and the practice of brigandage. The rising of an independent government that ruled with intelligence and with a firm hand reduced the population to order, was little to the liking of the free-roving tribes of the Bactrian deserts. A tribe of these nomads called the Parni, probably of the same Aryan stock as the Persians, not feeling strong enough to expel the Greeks from Bactria, decided to expatriate themselves and in new pastures to seek their lost freedom. Therefore they moved westward and settled in Parthia, a large satrapy of Persia, now represented by the great province of Khorassan and the adjacent districts. The head chiefs of the Parni were two brothers, Arsaces and Tiridates by name.

Parthia was held at that time for the Macedonians by the satrap Phericles. The small number of Greeks and Macedonians in the Persian empire may be inferred from the ease with which the Macedonian rule was abolished in Parthia by a small tribe of nomads who had but recently settled within its borders. Phericles evidently thought there was little to fear from these shepherds; for he wantonly insulted Tiridates, the younger of the two chieftains. He must have been surprised indeed when he found that they dared to attack him in his stronghold. But this was not all; for the revolt was so successful that Phericles was slain and the rule of Macedon ceased from Northern Persia forever. Arsaces assumed the throne 250 B.C. and founded the great Parthian monarchy, whose dynasty took from him the name of Arsacidæ. Ever since the accession of Arsaces I., the Parnians have been called Parthians, although they were not in any sense entitled to that name. Is it not a curious example of the contradictions of destiny that a tribe which exiled itself from home in order to escape from the precise laws of a regulated government should within a very few years establish a similar government as a direct result of the action it had taken to escape from such rule?

The capital of the Arsacidæ was, at least in the earlier reigns, at Rhages, now called Rheï, near Teherân, the modern capital of Persia. It is now in ruins which are yet sufficiently numerous and widespread to show that a very large city once stood on that spot. Some writers assume that the capital of Parthia was at the place now called Shahr-i-Veramin; ruins still exist there, of which the oldest and most important is an immense low mound, square-shaped, with the remains of a parapet that shows it to have been a fortress at some remote period, perhaps the citadel of a capital. It is quite possible that the Parthians first established themselves at that place, but finding it to be unhealthy, removed the seat of government to Rhages, which had already gained importance as a large city.

XII.

THE PARTHIANS.

The founding of the Parthian monarchy marks the opening of another great era in the story of Persia. We have thus far been following the history of that empire during three important periods, the legendary age, the period of the Achemenian dynasty, and that of Alexander and his successors. We now have before us the rise and fall of the Parthians as rulers of the empire founded by Cyrus the Great, the historical successor of the legendary kings of Persia.

While it is doubtless true that the successors of Alexander continued their authority over large portions of his empire for ages after the Parthians entered the field as rivals, and repeatedly defeated them, yet the fact remains that from the time Arsaces I. was proclaimed king of Parthia, the Seleucidæ began to lose ground in the distinctively Persian provinces of their dominions until they were entirely expelled by the Parthians.

For some reasons it is not easy to see why the Parthian dynasty should not be considered and called Persian. The Parthians, if inferior in refinement and quickness of mind to the lively and brilliant race which had sprung up in Persia, and given birth to Cyrus and Darius, was probably a branch of the same stock. It was originally a nomadic tribe similar to those which now roam in Persia with their flocks. In religion also the Parthians, like the Persians, were at first devoted followers of the doctrines of the great Zoroaster. But historians have agreed to consider Persia as under subjection during the rule of the Parthians, because Persis or Irân, which gave birth to Cyrus and the men who helped him establish the Persian empire, was not the ruling province during the Parthian period.

The Parthians also had customs which were so peculiar to themselves that they never intermingled much with the people of the subject provinces. The king had under him a few hundred nobles, who were free, except as to their allegiance to him. All the other Parthians were serfs, who were bound either to the domains of the sovereign or were distributed among the nobles, each of whom was practically a large slave-holder. When Parthia went to war the leading officers of the army were chosen from the body of grandees, and all under their command were slaves so submissive that they never seemed to have thought of rising and securing their freedom.

The Parthians were great horsemen, and their armies were composed entirely of cavalry, completely clad in chain armor and riding without saddles. Their method of fighting was remarkable. They charged furiously at the enemy, hurling javelins and arrows into their ranks, then wheeling suddenly appeared to fly in confusion, but shot arrows by turning as their steeds flew over the plain. If the enemy mistook this movement for flight and imprudently pursued them, they suddenly wheeled and threw them into terrible confusion, too often ending in defeat.

Such were the people whom we now see looming up above the horizon of history. They left few records; indeed, we really know very little of the internal history of the Parthians, and would have known still less but for the frequent wars between them and the Greeks and Romans. It is to the historians of the latter that we are indebted for almost all reliable history until the Dark Ages. Oriental people have shown much quickness in the arts and in the composition of poetry, but in the statements of facts, such as history or science, they have always been far behind the races of Europe. The Oriental mind can hardly be considered inferior to that of Europe, but it belongs to quite another type.

The Parthians also struck a great many coins, of which numbers are still found in Northern Persia; these coins have been of great value to the historian who, thousands of years later, has tried to put together the disjointed history of the Parthian dynasty.

Amid the faint and confused outlines which alone remain to record the career of the powerful Parthian race that for over four hundred years ruled in Persia with a rod of iron, and a force that over and over again hurled back the mailed and veteran legions of Rome shattered and dismayed, we are able to discern two or three grand forms and several events that will live as long as the world lives.

Of these heroes of Parthia the most important was Mithridates the Great, who not only repaired the losses the empire had sustained during several reigns in warfare with the Seleucidæ, but carried the conquests of Parthia as far as India in the east, and to the banks of the Euphrates in the west. And now for the first time the Parthians and Romans met, not in this case for war, but by means of embassadors, who arranged a treaty of peace between the two great powers of that age. Soon after this event Demetrius III., king of the Seleucid dynasty, was forced to surrender, with his entire army, to Mithridates, and ended his days in captivity. Armenia also fell under the Parthian rule during the reign of Mithridates.

COIN OF MITHRIDATES I.

The coins of Mithridates are very numerous and clearly cut; the design shows the portrait of that monarch, a man with a full beard and strongly marked but pleasing features.

The immediate successors of the great Mithridates were men of entirely different stamp, and Tigranes, King of Armenia, was able therefore not only to revolt, but to rob Parthia of some of her western provinces. But in time Phraortes succeeded to the throne of the Arsacidæ, and by calling for aid from the Romans caused the overthrow of Tigranes. But the haughty republic of the west granted its assistance to Phraortes with such ill-concealed insults, that a hatred was aroused that could only be wiped out in blood.

Phraortes was murdered by his two sons. Orodes as the Latins called him, but Huraodha, according to the Zend or Perso-Parthian tongue, mounted the throne; but to avoid dissension it was agreed that his brother, Mithridates, should rule over Media as an independent king. It was not long before civil war broke out between the brothers, and in the end Mithridates was taken and executed before the very eyes of his brother Orodes.

It was now the year 54 B.C. The civil wars in Rome had ceased for a while, and Crassus, who with Cæsar and Pompey shared the authority in the republic, assumed the charge of the Roman armies in Asia. Rome in that age always had one war (generally two or three) on her hands, and was rapidly growing wealthy and luxurious with the spoils of the nations that she was constantly leading in chains at her triumphal car. Crassus required but the merest pretext to invade and attack Parthia. The easy victories of Pompey in Armenia led him to imagine that he had but to reach the borders of that empire to have it fall helpless into his grasp. He was a brave man, and he led sixty thousand of the best troops in the world. But his contempt of the enemy and the greed of gold, for which he was notorious, caused him to fall into a terrible catastrophe.

The chief general of Orodes was Surenas, the first nobleman of the empire and, as it appears, a man of great ability, who had rendered very valuable services in securing Orodes on the throne. It was on the 6th of June, just nineteen hundred and forty years ago, that the Romans and the Parthians of Persia first crossed their swords in battle, at Charræ, near the sources of the Euphrates.

Surenas concealed the mass of his army behind the hills, allowing the Romans to see at first only the heavily armed cavalry. Little suspecting what was the actual force of the enemy, Publius Crassus, son of Crassus, charged them at the head of the Roman cavalry. The Parthians, following their usual tactics, broke and fled as if in dismay. When they had drawn the Romans far enough from the main body, the entire army of Surenas deployed, and surrounding them, cut them to pieces. After this success, the Parthians hovered around the flanks of the Roman infantry, galling them with spears and arrows, while themselves suffering only trifling loss.

The heat, the thirst, the dust, completed the discomfiture of the Romans, who, when the sun set on the plains quivering with mirage, were powerless. But, according to their custom, the Parthians withdrew at the close of the day to renew the attack on the following morning. Under the shades of night the Romans fled, having suffered immense losses, and leaving their wounded on the field. But such was the rout and consternation of the remnants of the iron legions of Rome, that on the morrow Crassus was fain to accept the proposals made by Surenas. On descending into the plain to confer with the Parthian general, the Roman general soon perceived that his fate had come. On a slight pretext the conference came to blows, and Crassus was immediately despatched. His head was sent to Orodes, who caused the mouth to be stuffed with gold, saying mockingly : " Be satisfied now with thy life's desire ! " Of the great army that Crassus led into Asia not twenty thousand remained alive ; ten thousand of the survivors were captives, who were settled by Orodes in Margiana.

Surenas, the hero of the greatest victory won over a Roman army since the immortal campaigns of Hannibal, was ill rewarded for the remarkable services he had rendered his country. Orodes, in the true spirit of an Oriental despot, was unable to allow so powerful a subject to live, and Surenas paid for his victory with his life. But Orodes expiated his crimes in a horrible manner, for after a long reign, which carried Parthia to her highest pinnacle of power, he was strangled in his eightieth year by his son Phraates. Orodes first among the Parthian kings assumed the title of king of kings.

Phraates removed the seat of government from the north of the empire to Taisefoon or, as the Greeks called it, Ctesiphon, a suburb of Seleucia, which continued after this to be the capital until the Mohammedan conquest, more than six hundred years later. Hatra, in that vicinity, also acquired importance under the Parthian kings, who caused a splendid palace to be erected there. Phraates was eminently successful in his military operations, although steeped in crime ; besides murdering his father, he had caused all his near relations to be sacrificed, in order to ensure his position on the throne. Phraates, however, was not destitute of ability. The common saying that cruelty and cowardice go together is not always true, and certainly not in the case of Orientals. And it must be said that the peculiar form of government which has always existed in Asiatic states tends to make rulers wary, and often obliges them to act with quick decision and great apparent cruelty; for Oriental kings live a lonely life, with few friends and surrounded by

RUINS OF PALACE AT HATRA.

many, often of their own household, conspiring for power. It was somewhat the same in Europe before the rising of the people from time to time forced kings to give up much of their authority and allow the people to have a voice in the government.

Phraates soon had another Roman war on his hands. Before the death of Orodes, that monarch had associated with him his son Pacorus, a soldier and statesman, who conquered Syria and ruled both there and in Palestine, with a mildness that contrasted agreeably with the stern authority of the Roman governors, whom he had expelled. But Pacorus was finally defeated and killed by the Roman consul, Ventidius, and the territories he had captured on the coast of the Mediterranean were lost to Parthia.

The victory of Ventidius encouraged the celebrated Mark Antony to enter himself, in the year 33 B.C., on a campaign against the Parthians, whom the Romans could never forgive for the crushing defeat of Crassus, while as long as Parthia continued so powerful, she presented an impregnable barrier against the advance of the Roman eagles into Central Asia. Antony made far greater preparations than Crassus; he was determined that this time Parthia should be humbled. His army numbered one hundred thousand men including no less than forty thousand cavalry, who were intended to cope with the invincible horsemen of Parthia. The army was also abundantly provided with baggage and siege trains. Antony himself was a general of unusual military qualifications; he further strengthened his position by deluding the Parthians into the idea that his intentions were peaceful, and it was not until the Roman host was near at hand, that Phraates became aware that Parthia was threatened by the most formidable invasion she had yet encountered.

To oppose this great peril, Phraates could only hastily collect forty thousand cavalry; but he was equal to the emergency; and immediately began operations by surprising the baggage trains of the enemy, and putting the attending escort of seven thousand five hundred men to the sword. Antony was at the time engaged in besieging Phraaspa. He was obliged to abandon the siege, but the pursuit of the Parthians was so vigorous that it was the greatest difficulty that the Roman general was able to reach the frontier of Armenia after a loss of thirty thousand of his best troops. This disaster proved decisive. For one hundred years after this, Rome dared not again attack Parthia; and when, in later ages, her legions repeated the attempts to penetrate to the heart of Persia, they always failed. Rome, in every other quarter successful, uniformly found that the frontiers of Persia formed an impervious barrier to the advance of her legions into Central Asia. It is not a little thing to record on the pages of history, that of all the people of antiquity, the only races that checked the advance of Rome were those which sprung on Persian soil.

COIN OF ORODES.

Phraates, subsequent to these events, was dethroned by a conspiracy of his brother Tiridates. He fled to Tourân, or Scythia, of which we hear so often in the legendary history of Persia. There he succeeded in raising an immense army of Tartars, and hurling the usurper from power, forced him to fly for an asylum to Rome, where he endeavored to induce the Romans to grant him assistance, promising important concessions in return for such aid. But they cautiously declined. Rome had no more hunger for war with the tremendous mounted squadrons of Parthia and the eagle-eyed generals who manœuvred the veterans of Crassus and Antony out of existence.

Up to this time there had been one decided advantage to Parthia in her wars with Rome ; she was forced by this formidable foe to keep up the vigor of her armies and preserve a degree of internal peace. The long period of tranquillity that now followed between the two empires proved most disastrous to the Asiatic state ; it gave abundant opportunity for discord and civil war ; king after king arose and fell ; the capital was filled with the blood of brothers killing brothers ; and the strength of a once powerful dynasty was hopelessly wasted. Amid this record of strife and confusion we perceive here and there a hero or a sovereign who, by exceptional virtues, relieved the monotony of these dreary events. Among them, one of the most notable was Vologeses I., who distinguished himself by rare mildness and benevolence toward all the members of his family, and in the year 63 A.D. conducted a war with Rome which, with varying success, left the final results in favor of Parthia. Later on the great Roman emperor, Vespasian and Vologeses I. cultivated a friendship as honorable as it was rare in those troublous times.

Half a century later Trajan, the distinguished general and emperor of Rome, invaded the western territories of Parthia, and although that empire was now rapidly going to decay, he won no glory in the contest, and retired with the conviction that the true frontier of Rome in the East must ever be limited by the Euphrates River. Vologeses II. is memorable both for his death in 148 A.D., at the great age of ninety-six, and the fact that he had reigned for the almost unexampled period of seventy-one years.

During the reign of Vologeses III. her western territories were invaded by Cassius, the Roman consul. Vologeses was defeated in a great battle, and Cassius penetrated as far as the province of Babylonia, of which the capital was Seleucia. This was a most flourishing city, teeming with commerce and riches and numbering a population of over four hundred thousand. Cassius wantonly gave up this city to fire and sword and wiped it out of existence. The destruction of Seleucia is one of those inexcusable deeds which must be branded to all time as gigantic crimes.

Parthia never recovered from the results of her last war with Rome; not that Rome had become more strong herself, but because, in the very nature of the case, the dynasty which had founded the greatness of the Parthian empire had been enervated by its successes: it was crumbling to pieces through the sheer weakness produced by luxury, corruption, intrigue, and civil war. It is a curious and extraordinary illustration of the irony of fate that when almost in the last throes of dissolution the great dynasty founded by Arsaces four centuries earlier dealt its most tremendous blow at Rome, the hereditary foe. One of the last of the descendants of Arsaces who sat on the throne was Artabanus, who usurped the sceptre from his brother in the year 213 A.D. He proved to be a man of such force that, coming earlier, he might have prolonged the existence of the Parthian dynasty several ages. In the year 216 the oft-repeated war with Rome was renewed. Artabanus had tested his strength by crushing several rivals and reducing the greater part of the empire into his power. Macrinus, the Roman emperor, suffered two crushing defeats from Artabanus and was obliged to purchase peace by actually paying an indemnity of 50,000,000 denarii, equal to $9,000,000, to the great rival of Rome almost in the very hour when the doom of Parthia was sounding on the great bell of time. The hero who wrested a war indemnity from a Roman emperor was also the last of his line. Is there any event more dramatic in the record of the nations!

XIII.

THE HOUSE OF SASSÂN.

WE now enter upon a new and most important era in the history of Persia. Six centuries have come and gone since Alexander the Great overthrew the Achemenian dynasty and undertook the prodigious task of establishing a Greco-Persian empire. When his successors, to whom he had bequeathed the duty of perpetuating his empire, began to lose ground and there was hope that Persia might resume her independence, the Parthians, in a most unexpected manner, as we have seen, established an empire so firm and vigorous, that the original division of the Persian empire, the province of Persis or Fars, was forced to continue under subjection. Thus, while undoubtedly Persians fought in the armies of the Seleucidæ and assisted the Parthians in their foreign wars, yet for a space of six centuries they had formed merely one of many provinces of an empire which indirectly owed its birth to them.

During this long interval we hear but very little of Persia proper. We may gather, however, from the records that the Parthians treated the Persians with moderation and allowed them to be governed by satraps of their own people connected with the

Achemenid dynasty. In these centuries of comparative repose the Persians did not forget the glory of their ancestors, nor the national religion; and they gradually gained new strength, which would be required when the decisive hour arrived for them to throw off the Parthian yoke. The yearning for independence increased as the years went on, for the contrast between the coarse Parthians and the intellectual and refined Persians became constantly more evident and galling. With such a history behind them, a proud people like the Persians could not well endure the rule of those they considered their inferiors, even though the chains of the oppressor were laid on lightly.

Another cause arose, as the years went on, which increased their hatred of the Parthians. The latter were at first followers of Zoroaster, and Vologeses I. had ordered a careful collection to be made of the writings and precepts of the great prophet of the religion of fire worship. But latterly the Parthians had fallen away from the strict practice and belief in that faith, and had become idolaters, one of the forms of this idolatry being a religious reverence paid to the early monarchs of the Arsacidæ. The Persians, being naturally fanatical regarding the religion they profess, took offence at the religious practices of the Parthians; this was probably one of the reasons that led them finally to revolt.

The rise of the Neo-Persian or new Persian power, as it is sometimes called, was brought about by Artaxerxes,* the son of Pabêk. To judge from the

* In the Zend or Persian tongue this name is Ardeshir.

most reliable authorities, he was the hereditary satrap of Persia, and descended from Sassân, who was a scion of the Achemenian dynasty. There is nothing incredible in this statement, although some modern historians profess to consider it very unlikely that the record of such descent could have been kept through so many centuries. But Orientals give much attention to this very subject of lineage, and sometimes extend the record to the lineage of their favorite horses.

It is said that Artaxerxes, when he discerned the weakness of Parthia and the impatience of the Persians, was fortified in his purpose by secretly hearing that Artabanus, the king of Parthia, had discovered by divination the approaching downfall of his dynasty.

COIN OF ARDESHIR I.

The insurrection began by declaring the independence of Persis. Artaxerxes then proceeded to the conquest of Carmania, now called Kermân, and gradually carried his arms into Media. Artabanus was at last aroused by these movements to offer determined resistance. He was defeated in two battles. Parthia was not, however, so reduced but that she could bring another large army into the field. The decisive conflict occurred, by previous appointment, it is said, at Hormuz, in the southwestern part of the present kingdom of Persia, May 28th of the year 227 A.D. The contest was doubtful, and was finally decided in favor of Artaxerxes by the defection of the Persians who were in the Parthian army. Artabanus was slain, and Persia became once more a great and commanding power in the world.

Artaxerxes, or Ardeshir, found himself engaged in the beginning of his reign in a war with Rome, which now discovered that by the transfer of the sceptre of Western and Central Asia from the Parthians to the Persians she was farther than ever from pushing her conquests eastward, or even holding the possessions she already claimed beyond the Mediterranean. Nothing impresses one more in considering the rise of dynasties and kingdoms in Persia than the amazing energy and ability displayed by their founders, and often by their immediate successors. We find a counterpart to it in Europe only rarely, as in the case of Charlemagne or Napoleon.

Alexander Severus, the Roman emperor, was obliged to retire in disgrace before the armies of the new Asiatic power. Armenia, which had sought aid from Rome and was ruled by Chosroës, of the Parthian line, was brought under subjection, and Artaxerxes now found himself at the head of an empire equal to that of the Parthians in their prime.

Feeling firmly established on the throne, Artaxerxes devoted his attention to the reformation and strengthening of the national religion. He caused the idols of the Parthians to be destroyed, and ordered a general restoration of the doctrines of Zoroaster throughout the empire. The more readily to accomplish this purpose, the king col-

lected the magi or priesthood of Zoroastrianism at
Persepolis, or Ishtakr, once more the capital of
Persia. The magi formed a large and distinct class.
They assembled on this occasion to the number of
forty thousand, it is said. They were required to
choose from their number the most worthy; they
in turn selected the wisest and most learned and
the most pious, until the number was reduced from
four thousand to four hundred, from four hundred
to forty, and from forty to seven. The seven decided that Ardâ
Virâf, a young priest
of high repute for
sanctity, was above
them all as the representative of their
religion.

Ardâ Virâf now
bathed himself in
the most careful
manner, and after
drinking a powerful
narcotic, laid down to sleep wrapped in pure white
linen. Seven of the first nobles of the land watched
beside him while he slept. At the end of seven days
and nights he awoke and began to recite his interpretation of the faith of Oromasdao, or Ormuzd.

ORMUZD.

This is the record given by Persian historians of
the way by which the books of the Zendavesta
were reduced to writing.

Although, perhaps, this account is highly colored
in the Oriental style, yet it is certain that in the time

and by the order of Artaxerxes, the founder of the Sassanian dynasty, the Zendavesta was published in written form by Ardâ Virâf, the high priest of Persia. Although but few of the followers of this religion now remain, yet the very fact of their existence to the present time as a small but highly intelligent and respectable sect, both in Persia and India, gives very great interest to the question of what is the faith established by Zoroaster nearly three thousand years ago.

The Zendavesta was originally composed in the pure Persian tongue called the Zend, a branch of the Sanscrit. But at that time the Persian language had gone through the changes which affect all tongues with the lapse of ages. The difference we see between the English language of the present day and that of so recent a period as that of Chaucer, affords a familiar example. When Persia resumed her independence, the Zend had become incomprehensible except to scholars, and the name then given to the spoken language of Persia was Pehlevee. Artaxerxes therefore caused a translation of the Zendavesta to be made into Pehlevee. It may be added that the ceremonial duties connected with Zoroastrianism were numerous, and to any but an Oriental people exceedingly burdensome.

In order more thoroughly to carry out one of the purposes which Artaxerxes had in view in throwing off the Parthian yoke, the re-establishment of the religion of Zoroaster, he now distinctly associated the clergy with the government. Never has the combination of church and state been more emphatically and authoritatively laid down as a principle. Persecution of those who opposed the magi and their teachings was not only permitted, but proclaimed as one of the arms of Persian law. In a very short period the edicts of Artaxerxes against any other than the state religion resulted in the closing of every place of worship in his dominions, except those of the fire-worshippers. It must, we fear, be admitted that the example of the Christians of the early church acts as a palliation of this intolerance of the Zoroastrians; for almost from the outset, intolerance of any belief but their own has been the practice of the various Christian sects, enforced, as we know, for many ages by fire and torture and the sword. Human nature seems to be pretty much the same everywhere, in spite of the teachings of religion. Doubtless in the early periods of a nation's career religious intolerance added to the association of church and state is an element of strength; but in the end nothing more surely saps the vigor of a state and brings it to premature decay.

In order still further to display the religious character of the Persian revolution, Artaxerxes caused an altar with fires to be stamped on the reverse side of his coins, with a priest standing on each side. This design was continued on all the future coinage of the Sassanian dynasty.

Artaxerxes continued the general form of government which had been established by Darius the First, and which has been perpetuated with little change to the present day. The provinces were under the rule of satraps. When a separate people, as in the case of Armenia, had a royal house of its own, he permitted it to continue in power, although tributary to Persia and furnishing troops and money. It was the latter circumstance which caused a Persian monarch to style himself king of kings. Artaxerxes also established a regular army. It was a saying of his: "There can be no power without an army, no army without money, no money without agriculture, and no agriculture without justice." On the whole the founder of the Neo-Persian monarchy was a man of large sense and far-sighted views.

Some of the last words of Artaxerxes to his son Sapor, were: " Never forget that as a king you are the protector of your religion and your country . . . You should be an example of piety and virtue, but without pride or ostentation. . . . Remember, my son, that the fate of the nation depends on the conduct of the individual who sits on the throne. . . . Learn to meet the frowns of destiny with courage and fortitude, and to receive her smiles with moderation and wisdom. . . . May your administration be such as to bring the blessings of those whom God has confided to our parental care." *

According to the records of Persian historians, Artaxerxes delegated the government to his son some time before his death, and sought in retirement repose and opportunity for religious reflection. There is a sculpture design on the rocks at Tacht-i-Bostân which seems to confirm this fact, for it represents Artaxerxes presenting the royal diadem to Sapor, while Ormuzd, the benevolent ruler of the universe, looks on approvingly.

* This translation is quoted from Rawlinson.

RUINS OF A CASTLE OF THE FIRE-WORSHIPPERS IN THE SOUTH OF PERSIA.

XIV.

SAPOR I.

ARTAXERXES, the first of the Sassanians, died in 240 A.D. He was succeeded by Shapooree, or, as he is known through the Latin and Greek historians, Sapor. He was a worthy scion of a great father, and by his administrative and military talents left a name that ranks with the foremost sovereigns of the East. It must be allowed that, like most of the monarchs of that age and country, some of his actions would perhaps not be approved in our day. But every land and age has its own standard, and it is only fair to judge of all by the code of morality under which they have been reared.

At the outset of his reign Sapor was forced to take up arms in order to quell the rebellion of the city and province of Hatra, between the Euphrates and Tigris. The city was practically impregnable, as well by the character of its inhabitants as the tremendous strength of its walls. Manizen, the chieftain of Hatra, had a daughter, urged by a violent ambition,—a dangerous thing in a woman without high moral character. She intimated to Sapor that to be queen of Persia she would betray her father into his hands. She carried out her side of the compact; but when

Sapor came into possession of Hatra, instead of marrying the traitoress he ordered her to be executed.

About the year 241 Sapor decided that a convenient time had come to renew hostilities with Rome. Gordian was at this time emperor. The chief object of Sapor was to strengthen his western frontier, or, according to modern diplomatic phrase, "to rectify his frontier," by the seizure of several important fortified cities. Of these, Nisibis was perhaps the chief, affording to Rome a key by which she could enter the territories of Persia. The first movement of the Persian campaign was to lay siege to this fortress. The Persians, in most respects admirable soldiers in their best days, were deficient in a knowledge of siege operations, and Nisibis made an obstinate resistance. At last a breach was effected, and the place surrendered.

But the Romans were not idle, and Gordian was assisted by Timesitheus, who defeated Sapor in a great battle at Resaina, and recovered Nisibis. The untimely death of Timesitheus and the murder of Gordian once more turned the tide, and a peace was concluded giving equal advantages to both contestants. During part of the interval of fourteen years which followed, Sapor was engaged in wars with the hereditary foes in Tourân; and Bactria, which had been subdued by the Arsacidæ, revolted, and seems to have permanently secured its independence.

In the year 258 the Persian king felt that he could best counterbalance his losses in the East by taking advantage of the disturbances which for some time had racked the Roman empire, and once more the diamond-studded leathern apron of the blacksmith was placed at the head of a Persian host marching to attack the strongholds and mailed legions of Rome. The two great fortresses of Edessa and Nisibis fell. Valerian was emperor when Persia renewed hostilities. Whether treachery brought about the final result is uncertain, but, at any rate, Sapor succeeded in forcing Valerian into a position where he was obliged to surrender with his entire army.

This tremendous event is one of the most remarkable in the long history of Persia, which is emblazoned with so many brilliant deeds. It was followed by the capture of Antioch and Cæsarea Mazaca, the most important city in Asia Minor. Sapor overran all the Roman possessions in Asia, and like the "scourge of God," marked the path of his army with fire and blood. The return of the victorious army was, however, harassed by the flying squadrons of Odenathus, the king of Palmyra and husband of the famous Zenobia. Odenathus had under his command the trained horsemen of the desert, and for a time was able to maintain Palmyra as an independent government. But after his death the emperor, Aurelian, besieged the superb capital of the desert, and Zenobia was led a captive to Rome. The ranks of columns which still rise above the plains, called Tadmor in the Desert, attest in our time to the splendor of the brief-lived kingdom of Palmyra.

Valerian was taken a prisoner to Persia, where he remained until he died. There is no good reason to doubt that he was treated with clemency and a certain degree of honor during his captivity. But after his death his skin was removed and preserved as a trophy. The Romans made no serious attempt to avenge the terrible disaster of Valerian.

The remaining years of Sapor were devoted to cultivating the arts of peace and promoting the welfare of his empire. He founded a great city in Fars or Persis, which was named after him,—Shapoor. The ruins which still remain there, suggest its grandeur, as well as the progress made by Persia at this period in the arts. The ruins of Persepolis indicate clearly that in the Achemenian period Persia had reached a high degree of excellence in architecture and sculpture, and most likely in other arts as well. But during the Parthian rule little seems to have been done to develop the great artistic genius of the Persian race.

HEAD OF SAPOR I.—
FROM A GEM.

The rise once more of a genuine Aryo-Persian dynasty again offered the opportunity for the expression of the native taste for the beautiful. It is probably to this period that we may assign the commencement of the school of architecture and decoration which, borrowed from the Persians at a later date by the Arabs, and by them carried to Syria, Egypt, and Spain, has been called by Europeans Saracenic. According to a usage common in all ages to the monarchs of Persia, Sapor illustrated and recorded some of the chief incidents of his reign by rock sculptures.

One of the most interesting of these colossal historic sculptures represents Sapor and the conquest of Valerian. Sapor is on horseback; kneeling before him is the captive emperor, and the Roman army is typified by seventeen figures ranged behind him on foot. The Persian monarch is supported by ten horsemen, representing the terrible cavalry that was instrumental in winning the victories of Persia. Another most impressive sculpture commemorating the same important event includes not less than ninety-seven colossal figures. Many other historic sculptures were set up by Sapor at Persepolis, Darabgerd, and elsewhere in Southern Persia. These sculptures are sometimes accompanied by inscriptive tablets in Greek and Pehlevee. Sapor still further illustrated his genius by the construction of numerous public works, intended to add to the improvement of the country. Of these, one of the most important, which is still in existence, was a great dyke across the river Karoon, at Shuster, no less than twenty feet wide and twelve hundred feet long. It is built of solid hewn masonry.

The arts of Persia received great impulse during the reign of Sapor from a remarkable source. The Persian race from the earliest period to the present day has been inclined to mysticism and speculation in matters of philosophy and religion. Whatever be the prevailing creed of the country, it has been assailed by numerous sects differing from it in more or less degree. During the reign of the first Sassanidæ, the early Christian church extended its influence in all directions, and made many converts in the Persian dominions. This, of course, tended to increase the great intellectual activity of Persia in that period, and added to the problems which Sapor was forced to consider. The introduction of Christianity into the empire at a time when every effort was exerted to revive and reform the worship of the fire creed, was a serious question. Matters were not improved when a third element of discord was introduced by a prophet who set himself up as the founder of a new religion, which, after its founder, has been called "Manichæism."

Mance was born in Persia about the year 240 A.D. He had a broad, unprejudiced mind, strong force of character, and great versatility, qualities which led him to formulate a religious system which not only aroused apprehension among the followers of Zoroaster, but convulsed the entire Christian world. His views were looked on as dangerous and impossible at that period, but in our time a wider tolerance and a truer insight into the relative value of the world's creeds and religions, leads us to admire the grandeur of the religious system of Mance, even if we are unable to accept it as practical while men continue to be what they are.

Mance had profoundly studied the Magian doctrines of Ormuzd and Ahrimân, the Levitical ordinances of the Jews, the mysterious question of the Christian Trinity, and the remarkable system of Sakya Moonee, called Buddhism. For a time Mance accepted Christianity and received holy orders. But the nature of his mind made it difficult to subscribe to any one creed. He saw that all the great religions of the world contained a share of truth mixed with error, and that the principles of morality were common to all. It occurred to him to combine in one universal creed the essential truths of these leading religions. So far the scheme showed good sense, and was in harmony with the tendency of our time to abolish sectarianism and at least to acknowledge the element of truth which is common to the great religions of the world.

But Manee went a step further. He avowed himself to be the Paraclete or Comforter foretold by the Saviour, and composed a gospel which he called the Ertang, which was illustrated by pictures drawn by his own hand; he claimed that the Ertang should take precedence of the New Testament. It was this false move that really led to the violent opposition which the Christian church displayed towards the Persian prophet. The plausibility of his doctrines proved so fascinating, however, both to Zoroastrians and Christians, that Sapor was impelled by the Magians to expel him from Persia, on pain of the extreme penalties which the laws of that country then visited upon those who attempted to proselyte the fire-worshippers.

Manee, being forced to fly, proceeded as far as China, where he remained for a number of years. Finding no field for the spread of his religious doctrines among the people of the Celestial Kingdom, he devoted his attention to cultivating another side of his versatile nature. Manee was possessed of

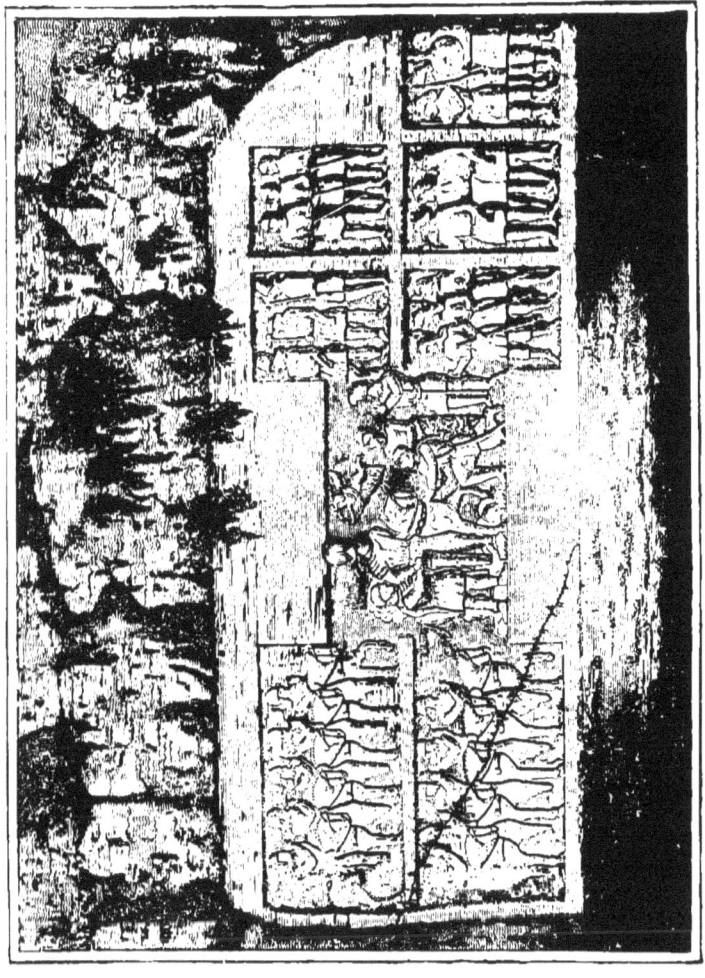

ROCK SCULPTURE NEAR SHAPOOR, REPRESENTING THE CAPTURE OF VALERIAN.

a strong love for the fine arts, and he now gave careful attention to the study of Chinese art, which at that early period had already exhibited the originality and beauty which we associate with it; it is what is called decorative art, and is particularly rich in the rendering of effects of color. We have no means of knowing what were the artistic talents of Manee; but we do know that he was able to appreciate whatever was beautiful in art, and when, after some years, he ventured to return to his native land, he brought with him numerous examples of the art of China. But he did not long survive his return, for he fell a victim to the intolerance of the age, and was put to death by the command of Varahnes I.

Manee must always live in remembrance, however, not only as the founder of a great religious sect, but as one to whom Persia owes a great debt for the vast impulse he imparted to the progress of the arts in that country when he returned from China. The Persians, like all great races, know how to borrow ideas, or at least gain intellectual inspiration, from the arts of other art races. The Greeks and the Romans did the same—in fact, it will be found that nearly all national arts were first inspired by foreign ideas. But, like the Greeks, the Persians had such artistic talent of their own that they very soon gave a national character to what they had borrowed; just as when their victorious kings put their own stamp upon the gold that they captured from the enemy. The impulse given to Persian art by Manee, at a period when the government was ready to encourage its growth, was incalculable, and may be said to be felt even to the present day. We know that soon after occurred a great revival in the decorative arts of embroidery in Persia, and that carpets of silk and of wool, of great beauty of design and exquisite texture, were made in that country, which has ever since that period been famous for its textile fabrics and fine needle-work. Sapor, as a patron of art, aided the impulse given to it by Mance, by importing artists from Greece and Byzantium.

Sapor I. died in 271, after a reign of thirty-one years. He is said to have been a man of handsome presence and great personal courage. What we do know is that he was an excellent soldier, and a patriotic sovereign who left behind him the record of being a benefactor to his people, and one of the ablest monarchs who has occupied the throne of Persia.

SAPOR I.—FROM A PERSIAN SCULPTURE.

XV.

PERSIA UNTIL THE REIGN OF SAPOR II.

THE energies of the Sassanian dynasty seemed for a time to reach their limit after the death of Sapor I. His successors for several reigns were either weak and unfortunate or men of merely average ability. The corruption and reaction which follow after great effort combined with the gain of wealth and power now showed itself for several generations in the character of the sovereigns of Persia. Hormisdas, or Hormuz, a son of Sapor, succeeded his father, and seems to have been a man of amiable disposition. During his reign Mance returned to Persia, and was at first received graciously. A castle was presented to him, and there he proceeded to organize a great sect, called after him Manichæan. But when, in the year 272, Varahnes I., or Bahrâm, came to the throne he caused Mance to be seized and flayed alive. The skin of the unfortunate prophet was suspended, stuffed with straw, over a gate in the city of Shapoor, a warning to all who dared to promulgate doctrines differing from those of the established religion of Persia.

It is singular that there is no clear record of the entire period that elapsed between the death of

Sapor I. and the reign of Sapor II. For example, we may infer, but have no precise proof, that Hormisdas II. had a son who incurred the resentment of the nobles and was by them imprisoned on the death of his father and deprived of the succession. The election of a monarch by the nobles is a form which has existed in that country, although in most cases it has been only a form, by which the people seem to approve the succession of the crown prince. But in this instance the nobles of Persia showed their power, by combining to exclude the oldest son of Hormisdas and give the crown to an infant son of that monarch born several months after the death of his father.

Immediately on his birth the infant was elected king with the name of Sapor II. He was born in the year 309, and reigned from the cradle to the grave, over a period of seventy-two years. During this long space of three quarters of a century ten emperors succeeded each other as rulers of the Roman empire.

When we consider the circumstances surrounding the early years of Sapor II. and what obstacles he overcame during his long career, we are bound to allow that he was a man possessed of extraordinary ability for government and war. A succession of feeble monarchs had weakened the power bequeathed them by the founders of the Sassanian dynasty. The fact that a boy was king, counselled by a regency of nobles of very ordinary talents, only aggravated the condition of the empire. Insurrections at home and frequent invasions over the border devoured the resources of Persia, and it seemed only a question of time when the great empire would fall to pieces from the lack of a strong arm to guide its destinies.

As if conscious of the career that was before him, the youthful king early devoted himself to athletic exercises, in which he excelled, and to study of the arts of governing and of war. As he approached manhood he seized the reins of government with a vigor that soon informed his vassals and enemies that a master hand was again at the helm. At the age of sixteen Sapor II. freed himself from the dictation of the regency and took personal command of his armies. From the first, victory attended his arms, invaders were driven back, and the foes who had preyed on the vitals of Persia soon learned to quail before the terrible and irresistible genius of a mere youth. It is rare indeed that such examples of precociousness are found on record, followed as it was by a vigor that never failed until death quenched its fire.

At the age of twenty-eight Sapor had restored the Persian empire to its wonted state of tranquillity and power. He had tested the force of his genius and was ready to renew hostilities with the Roman empire. A pretext for proclaiming war he found in the haughty remonstrances of Constantine the Great, who had embraced Christianity and zealously sought to protect the Christian subjects of Persia from the fierce persecution waged against them by Sapor II., who, whatever his other virtues, was of a stern and sanguinary disposition.

The great war which now opened between the

rival empires lasted for twenty-seven years. While fortune, with her proverbial caprice, perched sometimes on one banner and sometimes on the other, yet, on the whole, the results were largely in favor of Persia; while often defeating the enemy, and causing the death of a Roman emperor in battle, Sapor, when commanding in person, never lost a battle during the entire war. The chief events of this protracted conflict were the three sieges of Nisibis, which failed, although Sapor obtained it finally by the negotiations following the overthrow of Julian; the great victory of Singara, won over the Roman army commanded by the Emperor Constantine; the capture of Armida; the defeat of the Emperor Julian; and the disgraceful peace by which Jovian, his successor, purchased the escape of the Roman legions from the grip of the Persian host commanded by Sapor. In all these operations we discover in this military monarch immense determination, fortitude and courage, daring tempered by caution, skill in conducting a campaign and manœuvring an army on the battle-field, and a cruelty tempered by good faith in the keeping of compacts with the enemy—altogether a character to command our respect and often our admiration.

The event for which Sapor II. will probably be most remembered by Christian nations was the overthrow of Julian. This emperor won the abhorrence of Christians for abandoning Christianity, and endeavoring to restore the Paganism of the Greeks after it had been officially abolished by the conversion of Constantine. By the Christians Julian received the hateful epithet of Apostate. But an impartial examination into his case enables us more easily to render justice to a man who, if mistaken in his efforts to restore the dead past, was at least sincere, and deserves praise for his lofty character and genius.

It was, perhaps, too much to expect that one who had been steeped in the learning of the Greeks, and who had studied their paganism in the elevated pages of Homer and Socrates, Plato and Aristotle, should accept, as a matter of course, the doctrines of Christianity, which were until recently unacceptable to a very large number of his subjects. Julian was a scholar and a philosopher; he was also a great general who would have gained a permanent place in history even if he had never undertaken to supplant the cross by a revival of a refined paganism. Until recently Christian historians have failed to render justice to the emperor Julian.

After conducting several severe campaigns with great success in the north of Europe, Julian was called to the throne of the Roman empire, and immediately made preparations on a colossal scale for the invasion of Persia.

The dispositions made by Sapor to meet the most formidable expedition which had yet been undertaken against Persia, were of a nature to indicate the hand of a master, showing courage tempered by caution, a clear knowledge of the danger which threatened him, and careful preparations to meet it successfully. When Julian was at Antioch massing his forces for the campaign, the Persian king sent an embassy suggesting in respectful terms that a peace be concluded, leaving to each state the limits it then occupied. Julian haughtily replied that Sapor might have saved himself the trouble of sending an embassy, as he proposed to treat with him in person in a short time. The Roman emperor, while well aware of the power of his rival, overestimated his own qualifica-

PERSIAN CAVALRYMAN.—FROM AN ANCIENT SCULPTURE.

tions; the same arrogance, which was born of a desire to imitate Alexander the Great, led him also to offend Arsaces, King of Armenia, who was an ally of Rome. The Armenians, newly converted to Christianity, were deeply affronted by the insults offered to their religion by the Roman emperor, while their sovereign resented the lofty tone with which Julian commanded him to furnish thirty thousand troops for the expedition. As the plan of the campaign made it necessary for Julian to preserve the friendship of Armenia, the course taken by him was imprudent in the highest degree.

On the other hand, Sapor, although victorious in so many conflicts with the Romans, and sure of the veterans who composed his army, acted with the greatest prudence, holding himself in check and calmly waiting for events to develop a course of action. Only a general whom experience had made justly confident of his own powers would have ventured upon the plans which Sapor adopted for resisting the advance of such an army and general as were now steadily aiming at the overthrow of the Persian empire.

Julian set out from Antioch for the Euphrates in the early spring. His army numbered at least ninety-five thousand men, of whom many had become inured to war under his own eye, in four years of desperate fighting against the martial tribes of Germany. A body of eighteen thousand men was detached to manœuvre in Northern Media with an auxiliary force of thirty thousand Armenians, distracting the attention of Sapor by an invasion of his dominions in the northwest, and then, marching along the line of the Tigris, rejoin the main army.

The point which Julian intended to reach first was Southern Mesopotamia, whence the heart of Persia could be easily approached. By looking at the map the reader may easily follow the course selected by Julian for carrying out his purpose. A fleet of over eleven hundred galleys, probably small flat-bottomed boats, was in readiness on the Euphrates to transport the siege trains, the baggage, and the provisions. Fifty of these vessels were so constructed as to serve also as pontoons for bridging. As the fleet floated down the tawny river the legions of Rome marched proudly along the right bank of the Euphrates. The disposition of this army on the march was skilfully made to protect it on all sides from any unforeseen attacks of the enemy. At Zaitha Julian addressed his troops in an eloquent speech, in which he encouraged them by relating the past successes of Rome, and foretold an easy victory over a weak and timid enemy.

A number of small but well-fortified places along the line of march were left unmolested, on agreeing to preserve neutrality, as Julian was impatient of allowing any sieges or assaults to interfere with the march or reduce the size of his army. In this he committed a military blunder. At Hit the Romans found that all the male population had fled, leaving the women and children behind, supposing that they would be safe. But Julian permitted his soldiers to massacre them all. Such a deed as this tends to withdraw our sympathy from an emperor who had loudly proclaimed himself as a reformer and philosopher.

At Hit the Romans entered on the rich alluvial lowlands of Babylonia, frequently intersected by broad canals. Up to this time the Persians had offered no resistance to the Roman advance. But now they changed their tactics, and flying squadrons of cavalry constantly hovered on the flank of the invading army or threatened it in front, cutting off small detachments and stragglers. The result was greatly to harass the Romans and sometimes actually to check the onward march of the heavy-armed legions. On arriving before the walls of Peri Sabor, or, as the Persians called it, Firooz Shapoor, Julian found that the place was too important to leave in his rear, having, as it did, a large population and powerful garrison. The resistance was exceedingly obstinate, and the place was finally surrendered only after Julian had caused an immense moving tower to be constructed which overtopped the walls, and laid bridges across the ramparts. Even then he was obliged to permit the entire population to retire with clothes and money.

Proceeding thence southwest, Julian at last succeeded in transporting his fleet and army from the Euphrates to the Tigris through a canal which joined the two rivers, and found himself opposite to Ctesiphon. This city, the last capital of Parthia, and still a most important resort of the court of Persia, was the strategic point at which the Roman emperor directed his plans. With Ctesiphon in his hands the campaign would be a success even if he proceeded no farther; to retire without besieging it would be to return baffled if not disgraced. But a large Persian army with elephants and chariots defended the passage of the Tigris. Julian at this juncture displayed both ability and courage. He succeeded in forcing the passage with the aid of his ships, and put the Persian army to flight. And now commenced a race for the possession of Ctesiphon, which must have been most exciting. The Persians flew for refuge within the walls, while the Romans pursued in order to enter the gates with the fugitives. But the Persians were in first, and the gates were firmly closed as the enemy's troops dashed up to the drawbridges. Julian had lost the prize that at one moment seemed in his grasp, and from that hour the star of his fortune began to decline.

Admirably fortified, well garrisoned, and victualled for a long siege, it was evident that Julian would be obliged to make a formal investment of Ctesiphon and perhaps spend months without its walls. This would have been sufficiently trying in that hot and malarious climate, even if he could count on being left unmolested to carry on the tedious operations of a siege. But this was exactly what could not be expected. While it was true that Julian had defeated one Persian army, he well knew that a much larger force, under the command of the great king himself, was in the neighborhood, awaiting the critical hour when it could swoop down on the jaded legions of the invader, and perhaps under the eagle eye of their redoubtable sovereign wrest still another triumph from the hosts of Rome.

It was a trying moment for the proud and haughty emperor. After his vaunted boasts it was doubly hard to think of giving the order to retire. But, like a prudent general, he allowed himself to be guided by expediency, and reluctantly decided to retreat. A greater captain might perhaps have made the very desperateness of the situation minister to victory, for even retreat had now become dangerous.

Having made his decision, Julian commanded the entire fleet to be burned, with the exception of the pontoon ships, as he proposed to return by the line of the Tigris instead of the Euphrates. This plan would lead the army through a country at once more healthy and abounding in provisions, and enable him to form a junction with the corps under Procopius. But, on the other hand, this course made pursuit by the Persians more easy. A retreating general is always forced to make a choice of evils.

But before the retreat began, Sapor, wily as well as skilful, and keeping a careful watch on the movements of the enemy, sought to gain time and still further entangle his antagonist in difficulties by once more sending an embassy to Julian with proposals of peace. It would have been fortunate for Julian if he had accepted these negotiations, both for himself and for Rome.

No sooner had the Roman army broken up its camp and turned its face homewards than a cloud of dust began to rise up above the horizon. It grew rapidly, and erelong the spears and breastplates glittering through the dust betokened the approach of the army of the "Great King." Sapor had been lying in wait for his opportunity to spring on the enemy, and now it had come. The Persian vanguard made a violent attack on the rear of the retreating army. True to the training they had received, the Roman veterans stood their ground and repulsed the attack. This was no more than Sapor had expected, and although for the moment calling off his troops, he closely followed the enemy, watching every opportunity to harass them, and burning the forage on which Julian in taking this route had calculated to subsist his army.

The march of the Romans was greatly impeded, and the troops were worn and disheartened by the obstinate persistence of the foe, as well as the scarcity of food which was now beginning to be felt. The hardy horsemen of Persia, well armed and nimble, were able to endure, and now here, now there, never rested from the policy of constant attack which Sapor adopted. The emperor himself began at last to yield under the distressing circumstances which surrounded him. At night in his tent he fancied that he saw the Genius of Rome sadly stealing past him with her emblems of power depressed. To add to the horror of the situation, the soothsayers declared the omens of sacrifice to be adverse, and warned him to avoid active hostilities. But yet, what could he do but fight, for the constant attacks of the Persians obliged the emperor to be ever on the alert and repel the enemy with open force; likewise no food could be obtained without fighting.

On the tenth day after the retreat began, the Romans struck their tents with the hope that the enemy had at last desisted from the pursuit that was fast wasting away their strength. Far as the eye could see, the plains were clear of any appearance of the army of Sapor. But near Samarah the country became hilly, and as the Romans entered on this stage of the march, they were suddenly surprised by a tremendous attack delivered by the Persian army, which, from the covert of the hills, dashed from all sides against the Roman legions. The critical moment had come which demanded every energy, or the Roman army was lost. But half-armed, Julian rushed from his tent to rally his lines; in the heat of the conflict his side was pierced by a Persian spear, and he was borne to the ground mortally wounded.

The fury of the Romans at the fate of their commander, instead of causing a rout, nerved them to revenge, and a terrible conflict raged until night. Both armies suffered heavily, but the advantage lay with the Persians, because they had voluntarily retired, prepared to renew the attack on the morrow; while the invaders had lost their general, and without provisions or reinforcements, could only foresee ultimate destruction.

Julian died in his pavilion at midnight. A council of generals was immediately summoned to elect a general and emperor in his stead. Unwillingness on the part of several to accept such a responsible post, jealousy on the part of others, prevented the election of the fittest, and the choice finally fell upon Jovian, who was immediately inaugurated, and thus achieved a place in history as a Cæsar, which his moderate abilities never could otherwise have won.

The Persians, on the following day, renewed the attack on the retreating army. Nerved by desperation, the Romans repelled their assailants, but only with very severe losses to themselves, and continued the retreat for four days more. Then the astute king of Persia considered that the time had come when the Romans would be willing to purchase their escape by advantageous terms of peace, and he again renewed negotiations. He rightly judged the temper of the enemy. Jovian commissioned two generals to treat with the commissioners of the "Great King." Never since the foundation of Rome, had she been forced to listen to such rigorous terms; but every day increased the peril of the invaders, and Jovian reluctantly accepted and ratified the treaty proposed by Sapor. It was stipulated that the peace now concluded should last for thirty years, and the Romans be permitted to return unmolested across the river. Rome, on the other hand, ceded the provinces she surrendered to Persia without delay, withdrawing her garrisons from the important fortresses she abandoned. Both sides honorably respected the compact, and Sapor furnished the survivors of the Roman army with provisions.

Rome never rallied from this blow in the East. Often did she renew the contest in later ages, but she never recovered the prestige nor the provinces ravished from her when Julian fell on the field of Samarah.

It is impossible to consider the conduct of Sapor, without profound admiration. For twenty-seven years he waged war with Rome; he had never lost a battle where he commanded in person. He had vanquished three Roman emperors, and closed this relentless war by wresting from the iron grip of Rome, some of her fairest provinces and most impregnable strongholds. In the course of his long military career, he displayed the qualities which make a great commander.*

It has been the custom of Western writers to assume that Orientals, including the Persians, are inferior in mettle to Europeans. It may be granted that Eastern soldiers are more dependent than European troops on leadership, and with the loss of their general are more easily routed. But properly led, there are no better fighters than some Asiatic races, and foremost among them are the Persians. The frequent wars of Persia with Europeans prove this fact. If Darius the Great had led the Persians against the Greeks in person, there is no doubt that their victory would have been more uncertain. The conquests of Alexander were rendered easy by the character of the Persian monarch he had to overcome. But when the Persians were led by the genius of the Arsacidæ and the Sassanians we see of what they were capable.

No greater soldiers have lived than the tremendous legions with which Rome vanquished the Carthaginians, the Gauls, and finally the redoubtable phalanxes of Macedonia. Until she attacked Persia, Rome had been invincible. For five centuries such generals as Crassus and Antony, Trajan and Julian, had dashed

* One cannot avoid drawing a comparison here between the campaign of Julian against Persia and the invasion of Russia by Napoleon Bonaparte. The tactics of resistance employed by Sapor and the Russian generals possess many points of resemblance. It is greatly to be regretted, for the glory of Napoleon, he did not, like Julian, close his career on the battle-field, instead of in exile on a lonely isle of the sea.

SCULPTURE AT TACHT-I-BOSTÂN, REPRESENTING ARTAXERXES TRANSFERRING THE CROWN TO SAPOR I.

their armies against the frontiers of Persia in vain; for five centuries of hostilities Rome had made no impression on the Asiatics beyond the Euphrates. Army after army was shattered before the military genius and invincible cavalry of the Persian empire. Emperors were captured or slain, and disgraceful treaties concluded, but in all that period not one army of Persia surrendered to Rome—not one sovereign of Persia was led at the triumphal car of a Roman consul. And yet in her thousand years of conquest and war, Rome attacked no country with such pomp and preparation, or such formidable armies and armaments, as she hurled against Persia. In view of these facts, we are perfectly safe in assuming that, when properly led, the world has produced no greater soldiers than the Asiatics who leaped to battle at the command of Sapor and Chosroës.

XVI.

FROM SAPOR II. TO CHOSROËS I.

Sapor II. died in the year 380 A.D., old and clothed with renown. Never, since the death of Darius I., had Persia reached such a pinnacle of power. But the repose which Sapor had won for his country was followed by civil wars and dissensions, such as occur in the history of all nations, and he was succeeded by sovereigns whose incapacity was in marked contrast with the genius he had displayed.

One hundred and fifty years went by. They may be dismissed with a few rapid paragraphs in the condensed pages of history; yet in that long and comparatively obscure period the Persian empire was steadily pursuing its career; monarchs were crowned and died; the intrigues of the luxurious court went on as ever; births and marriages continued in the land; the merchant in the bazaar, the cobbler at his bench, the artist with his pencil, the priest at his altar, pursued their avocations as they do now, thinking their own lives and times of more importance than all that had preceded, or than were to come, when they too had joined the nations beyond the tomb.

Long intervals of peace were broken by insurrections in the subject provinces, or wars were renewed with the hereditary enemy—Rome. But during those five generations few men or events call for especial record here. Among these we may note the high character of Isdigerd I., who appears to have borne such an excellent repute, that the Emperor Arcadius on his death-bed bequeathed his youthful son, Theodosius, to the care of Isdigerd. The Persian king accepted the trust in the spirit in which it was given. He deputed a high officer of his court to instruct the young prince, and assisted him to mount the throne. Ever after Isdigerd remained on friendly terms with the emperor, who had been his ward, and refrained from hostilities with Rome.

When we consider the excellent character of some of the monarchs who in Europe have achieved an unenviable notoriety for the fierceness of their religious persecutions, we are not surprised to learn that Isdigerd, notwithstanding his honorable course towards Theodosius, was one of the most cruel persecutors the world has seen. At first he inclined to Christianity during his relations with the Romans of Constantinople, and at the instigation of Christian bishops,—we regret to record it,—persecuted the fire-worshippers. But repenting later on of his Christian leanings, he became a most bigoted magian, and ordered all the Christians in Persia to be exterminated with cruel tortures. It is not singular that all classes of his subjects having suffered from this sanguinary and inconsistent conduct,

Isdigerd should have left a name but little loved; they branded him with the epithet *Al-Athim*—the Wicked.

When the throne became vacant, Bahrâm or Varahran, the eldest son of Isdigerd I. and the rightful heir, was in Mesopotamia with the Arabs, who were dependent on Persia. For some reason, not stated, he had been sent there in boyhood and received his education among the fierce horsemen and hunters of the desert. It was believed that he possessed the harsh and violent character of his father. His brother, Sapor, in turn, had made himself obnoxious to his countrymen by his ill-timed ambition. In order to seize the throne he had abandoned his satrapy in Armenia at a critical time, and the Armenians had revolted.

COIN OF SAPOR II.

The nobles therefore decided to allow the succession to neither of the brothers; they selected and crowned Chosroës, a descendant of Artaxerxes I., who was but distantly connected with Isdigerd I.

But Varahran was not of a temper to permit his rights to be stripped from him so easily. He had the address to induce the Arabs to furnish him with a large army, and swooped down on Ctesiphon with such irresistible energy that Chosroës, the nobles, and the magi accepted him as the rightful sovereign of Persia without a struggle. Chosroës retired again to private life, and it is to the credit of Varahran that he does not appear to have in any way molested that prince for usurping a position to which he had no legal right.

Varahran V. was crowned 420 A.D. Perhaps as a matter of policy, he at once sided strongly with the magians, and vigorously persecuted the Christians in his dominions. So far did he carry his measures against them, that he peremptorily demanded the surrender of Christians who had fled for refuge to Constantinople. When Theodosius, the emperor, rejected the demand, Varahran declared war. Hostilities continued only a short time, and peace was concluded in 422. No events of importance characterized the two campaigns during which it lasted; neither side showed much spirit in maintaining it, and the advantages were nearly evenly balanced.

Varahran was the more willing to conclude a peace because of the disturbed state of Armenia. A peculiar condition of things existed in that province. The Armenians were and are still a people very tenacious of the national feeling; they have clung together with great firmness, and have obstinately resisted all who have ruled over them. And yet since their first appearance in history they have rarely been independent, even when their rulers or kings have been of their own race. At the period of which we write, the Armenians were Christians, and yet were divided on the question of rulers. Artaxerxes, their king, who was a feudatory to Persia, was a Christian, and a descendant of the Arsacidæ, to whom the Armenians were attached. But he was a man of the worst character, and the nobles therefore preferred, instead of continuing under such a prince, to have him dethroned and to request Varahran V. to make Armenia a simple province of the Persian empire. But the patriarch or primate of the Armenian clergy opposed this measure, arguing, strangely, as it appears to us, that a Christian ruler was preferable, even if desperately wicked, to a pagan prince. In the end the nobles carried their point; the patriarch was deposed from office, Artaxerxes was dethroned, and Armenia, henceforth called Persarmenia, ceased to be independent in any sense, and received Persian governors. We think it must be admitted that Varahran acted with moderation and wisdom in these transactions.

During the reign of this prince Persia first began to be molested by the fierce inroads of an obscure numerous horde, who came from the steppes on the east of the Caspian Sea.

HOUSEHOLD FIRE-ALTAR.

Persian writers call them Haïathelch. The Greek historians speak of them as Ephthalites and White Huns. It is very possible they were the original Turks from whom proceeded the Ottoman Turks at a later period. In any case, they were a brave and formidable people, and when it was whispered at Ctesiphon that their khakhân, or chief, had burst over the northeast border of Persia with a vast host, great alarm was aroused. It was expected that Varahran would take immediate and sufficient measures to repel this formidable invasion. But to the consternation of his people he took the matter very coolly, and announced his intention of going on one of the hunting expeditions for which he had a passion. For this purpose he named his brother, Narses, regent during his absence, and left the capital.

The course taken by Varahran, when such a crisis was threatening, led all to conclude that his mind was disordered; and by the advice of the nobles, Narses sent an embassy to patch up a hasty peace with the Ephthalites, before they could overrun the whole of Persia. The terms offered by the embassadors were so humiliating, including as they did the payment of a tribute by Persia, that the king of the Ephthalites accepted them and promised to abandon the Persian territory as soon as the first instalment of the tribute had been paid.

In the meantime nothing was heard from Varahran; he had mysteriously disappeared, and no news came to indicate his movements. All was in suspense at the capital, when a swift herald suddenly dashed into the city, on a panting steed covered with foam and dust, and alighted at the palace gates. He announced great tidings: the complete overthrow of the Ephthalites, the death of their king, the capture of his wife, the seizure of vast plunder, and the pursuit of the flying and scattered foe towards the Oxus.

It seems that with a secrecy and celerity that show very unusual ability, Varahran had made his way to Adiarbene with a few picked horsemen. Arriving there he collected an additional force of light cavalry and pushed eastward along the narrow alluvial plain between the Caspian and the Elborz mountains, travelling cautiously but swiftly by night, and taking every precaution to conceal his movements. By this means he arrived in the vicinity of Merv, where the host of the Ephthalites was encamped awaiting the tribute money. Varahran aided his preparations for an attack by filling the dried skins of oxen with loose pebbles, and attaching them to the necks of horses. When night came on, and the enemy, little suspecting danger, were asleep, he sounded the charge and fell upon the slumbering camp like a thunderbolt. The rattling noise of the pebbles in the skins increased the terror that ensued, and the Persian cavalry drove irresistibly over the Ephthalite host. In the awful confusion that ensued a vast number of the barbarians were slaughtered, including their king, and the remainder were put to flight and pursued without mercy for many a league.

Having achieved this great victory, Varahran sent a detachment across the Oxus which administered another crushing defeat to the White Huns; they sued for peace, and Varahran set up a pillar to mark the future boundary between the two countries. He returned to his capital overwhelmed with the admiring plaudits of his subjects. It is said by Persian historians that he proposed next to invade India, adding a province or two in that quarter to his dominions, and introducing Indian musicians into Persia. Although this expedition is doubted by some modern historians, the writer is inclined to think the account is based on fact, although perhaps exaggerated by the somewhat partial historians of that period.

There is a characteristic story related of Varahran V. by Persian writers. It is said that one day he was seated with his favorite mistress in an upper pavilion overlooking a plain. They were looking out of a window when two wild asses appeared. The king drew his bow, and, being a man of great strength and skilled in the chase, shot an arrow with such force that it transfixed both animals. Proud of the strength and skill displayed, Varahran turned to the lady for the words of praise to which he was accustomed. But she airily answered, "Practice makes perfect." The king was so incensed by such apparent indifference, that he ordered her to immediate execution. The next moment he repented of his rage, and contented himself by banishing her from the palace.

Years went by; quite likely the haughty king thought sometimes of the fair lady whom he had treated so harshly, but perhaps his pride would not permit him to send for her, and all trace of her was lost. Then it happened that he went hunting, and towards evening he saw a sight that not only attracted his attention, but also his curiosity, to a remarkable degree. He saw a woman carrying a cow on her shoulders up and down the stairs of a country house. He sent for her, and inquired how she was able to perform such a feat of strength. She quietly replied, perhaps with a twinkle in her eye as she dropped her veil, "Practice makes per-

VARAHRAN V. IN BATTLE—FROM SCULPTURE AT TACHT-I-BOSTÁN.

fect." The king recognized the lady, no longer young, but still fair and attractive, whom he had driven so cruelly from his presence. She had shrewdly planned this feat of skill with the hope that she might sometime win back her royal lover. She began with a small calf, taking it up the steps each day, and gaining strength in proportion as the calf grew. It is needless to say that Varahran was so overjoyed to see her that he invited the lady to become once more an inmate of his palace. There is nothing improbable in this story, as it is quite in accordance with Oriental character, except as regards the size and weight of the cow. In Persia, however, cows are small, and perhaps the tale in its first form meant a gazelle rather than a cow.

Varahran lost his life in a manner highly characteristic of his vigorous, impetuous, but eccentric career. He was called by the Persians Bahram Goor, or Bahram the Wild Ass, because of his passion for hunting that swift but graceful animal.[*] In the twentieth year of his reign this talented sovereign was chasing a wild ass heedless of all but the nimble-footed beast he sought to make his quarry. Without warning, the king's horse plunged into one of the dry quicksands which are found on the plains of Persia, and in an instant the king was swallowed out of sight.[†]

[*] The onager or wild ass is still seen on the desert plains of Persia; it is of a handsome sorrel hue and incredibly fleet.

[†] A friend of the writer came on one of these quaking quicksands near Teheran, in his carriage; but it was less dangerous than the one which swallowed Bahram Goor. The writer's horse also floundered in a quagmire at the base of the cone of Demavend, and he escaped

Varahran was a monarch whose character was such as to make him popular and to leave a mark in history. His faults were chiefly those of his education and country. While his energy, originality, and courage were popular qualities that would attract the admiration and love of his subjects, indicating, as they did, a strong and breezy individuality, and giving a tinge of romance to his reign, as an administrator and a soldier he favorably disappointed the fears of the Persians, and enlarged and strengthened the empire he inherited.

The reign of Perozes was remarkable for unfortunate wars with the vassal kingdom of Armenia and with the Ephthalites, a tribe of Tartar warriors on the northern shores of the Caspian, descendants of the Turanians, who had so often sorely beset Persia from the northeast. This reign was also marked by a terrible drought which lasted seven years, accompanied by pestilence. Many thousands perished in Persia at that time. The Ephthalites succeeded in so badly defeating Perozes that he made peace on condition of not passing a pillar which was set up to mark the frontier. Feeling bitterly the disgrace to which he had been subjected, he broke the terms of the treaty and marched once more against the Ephthalites. By a stratagem the entire Persian army fell into their power, and the king himself lost his life. Perozes was a man of good disposition, with few vices and great personal courage; but he was deficient as a commander in the field.

only by grasping a bush and throwing himself off the saddle, while the horse was dragged out by bridle and tail just in time.

Perozes was followed by Balas, or Valasgash, his brother, who reigned only four years, but proved to be a wise and good prince, who in that brief period did much to repair the disasters of Perozes. He pacified the Ephthalites, who threatened to overrun Persia, by agreeing to pay them a small tribute; in return for this concession they restored the wife and daughter of Perozes, and refused to assist the sons of that king in their claims to the throne of Persia. Balas also reduced Armenia from the state of enmity to become a willing vassal who was ever after true in her allegiance to Persia. He conciliated her by wisely revoking the edicts against Christianity issued by Isdigerd I., and permitting the Armenians in turn to destroy the altars of Zoroaster, and expel all fire-worshippers from their dominion. We find from the earliest periods that religious liberty with Christians no less than pagans meant simply the liberty to practise their own beliefs; all united alike in denouncing and fiercely persecuting those who believed any other creed within their territory. More than three fourths of the world's population, including many Christians, even at the present have no other notion of the principles of religious liberty. Balas, towards the close of his short reign, appears to have refused to continue the tribute to the Ephthalites, and hostilities were about to be renewed when he died, and was succeeded by his nephew Kobâd, a younger son of Perozes.

Kobâd was enabled to secure himself on the throne against all pretenders, by the aid of a contingent furnished by his friend Kush-newaz, king of the

Ephthalites, to whom the young king appears to have continued the tribute, until at least he had so strengthened himself and his country as to be able to hold them in defiance. Kobâd was soon involved in a war with the Khazars. They were fierce barbarians who dwelt between the Don and the Volga, and as they grew in numbers and strength made terrible plundering incursions through the passes of the Caucasus mountains and ravaged the northern portions of the Persian empire. Kobâd showed spirit in the first encounter of Persia with an enemy destined in later ages to be more than once a scourge to her people. At the head of a hundred thousand men he attacked and utterly overthrew their army and captured immense spoils.

But Kobâd made a false step about the time that he appeared entering upon a prosperous reign. Mazdâk, a high priest of magianism, proclaimed himself to be a reformer of Zoroastrianism. The essential point of his doctrines was the equality of all men, including the king and the nobles. As a logical deduction from this principle, he asserted that none had a right to possess more than others, and hence a community of all property was essential. Women were to be, in his system, wives of all, and the social vices, which necessarily result from the existence of marriage laws, were abolished by the very fact of the abolition of marriage which he proposed. To these remarkable views Mazdâk added abstinence from animal food, with the exception of milk and eggs, and great simplicity of dress.

There is no reason to doubt the sincerity of this

founder of a creed intended, if successful, to abolish almost all the conditions which men in all ages have agreed to consider important for the well-being of man; for he had nothing to gain by changes which only tended to lower the exalted position he already occupied. And it was this very honesty of Mazdâk, his genuine enthusiasm, which gave him such success. All ages and ranks crowded to hear him, and multitudes accepted his doctrines. What is more strange and unaccountable, King Kobâd became a convert to the persuasive eloquence of Mazdâk, and by his influence did much to bring about a state of things that, if unchecked, would reduce Persia to a condition of anarchy and ruin.

The mobeds or magian clergy, together with the nobles, were overwhelmed with dread of the results of this tremendous revolution, unless decisive measures were speedily adopted to put an end to disorders which must prove fatal to the country if allowed to continue. The protection extended by the sovereign added enormously to the danger. The Armenians themselves were also incensed to such a degree by the attempts of the governor appointed by Kobâd to force the new religion into Armenia, that they summoned the emperor at Constantinople to invade Persia and rescue it from one of the most dangerous attacks yet made on social order and law.

This was no time for hesitation; the nobles of Persia assembled in council and solemnly agreed to depose King Kobâd, whose protection had encouraged the new movement to such dimensions. Kobâd was helpless when not a nobleman in the empire was on his side. He was thrown into the Castle of Oblivion, a fortress such as every Oriental capital possesses, and his brother, Zamasp, was chosen king in his stead. After this Mazdâk was seized, but when he was about to be executed, his followers arose and rescued him. Owing to their numbers, it was considered prudent to leave him unmolested, on condition that he remained in retirement.

Zamasp was urged to put his brother out of the way; but he was of a merciful disposition, and soon learned to his cost that mercy may sometimes be ill placed. Kobâd succeeded in effecting his escape from confinement, and fled to Kush-nevaz, king of the Ephthalites, who gave him his daughter in marriage, and thirty thousand stout warriors to restore him to his throne. Zamasp declined to contest a position he doubtless felt rightfully belonged to Kobâd, and peacefully resigned the sceptre. But, according to Procopius, a reliable historian, he was cruelly blinded by Kobâd.

The second reign of Kobâd continued thirty years. He was careful not to risk the rebellion of the nobles a second time, and announced that, while he continued theoretically to believe in the doctrines of Mazdâk, he could not as a sovereign allow them to be put in practice. This was a shrewd device to soothe his conscience without forfeiting his position; but it had the effect of checking the growth of the new sect, which had thriven on the royal favor.

Peace had now continued between the Persian and the Roman empires for nearly eighty years. The Roman empire had by this time been divided into the eastern and the western empires, Rome being the capital of the latter, and Constantinople of the former, although both for some ages yet were under the rule of the emperor who made Constantinople his capital. Anastasius was emperor when war at last broke out between Persia and Rome. Kobâd was a general of more than average ability, and whenever he conducted the campaign in person, victory attended his arms. The capture of the important city of Amida, after a siege of eighty days, was creditable to the skill of Kobâd. While he remained at the head of his armies in the west, the advantages of the war were with Persia. But the Ephthalites, in the northeast, demanded his attention, and for ten years he was engaged in hostilities with them. As that was the most dangerous enemy to overcome, Kobâd left the charge of the war with Rome to his generals, who, without suffering a decisive disaster, allowed the advantages he had gained to be frittered away. The "Great King," therefore, proposed terms of peace, which were accepted, agreeing for a large sum of gold to abandon Amida; the Roman emperor, Anastasius, gave solemn promises in return to leave matters as they were, a compact he entirely failed to keep, by strengthening the Roman frontier with a series of fortresses he caused to be built at points that in any future war made it easier for Rome to attack her rival or to repel invasions. Russia, in our day, pursues an insincere policy in peace similar to that of the Græco-Roman emperor. Treachery finds expression in all ages.

Hostilities were about to be resumed between the

two empires, Justin having succeeded Anastasius, when the attention of Kobâd was again called to a renewal of the disturbances created by the arch-heretic Mazdâk and his followers. For twenty years, under the tacit protection of Kobâd, they had prospered. But as that monarch was growing old, they perceived that with his successor might come persecution and extinction. Kobâd had four sons, of whom three were bitterly opposed to the communism of Mazdâk, the more especially as the prophet had actually demanded of Kobâd one of his wives, the mother of Chosroës, in pursuance of his peculiar doctrines. Phthasuarsas, the third son, was a convert to the teachings of Mazdâk, but had no prospect of succeeding his father.

These sectaries agreed to persuade Kobâd to appoint Phthasuarsas as his successor if he would agree to continue the protection they then enjoyed. Before the scheme was ripe Kobâd learned of it, but in such a manner as to lead him to conclude that a plot was on foot to drag him from the throne. This was a conspiracy of a sort peculiarly offensive to an Eastern king, and Kobâd took his part accordingly and at once.

COIN OF VARAHRAN V.

He invited all the Mazdâkites to assemble in order to witness the investment of Phthasuarsas with royal honors. Troops were secretly posted to surround the unarmed multitude, and at a given signal, the entire assembly was put to the sword. Having in this emphatic manner proclaimed his return to Zoroastrianism, Kobâd entered into a war with Gurgenes, the Prince of Iberia, on the shores of the Black Sea, with the avowed purpose of forcing the Iberians to abandon Christianity for Magianism. A point about which Kobâd was especially strenuous was in regard to the last rites to the dead. The Iberians, according to Christian custom, had cemeteries, and laid the dead in graves. This custom the king wished them to abandon for the Zoroastrian method of leaving corpses within circular enclosures, but exposed to the open air uncoffined, to be devoured by ravens and vultures. Gurgenes was defeated, taking refuge in Lazica, a mountainous region of Circassia, and Iberia became a Persian province.

One of the last events of the long reign of Kobâd was the re-opening of hostilities with Rome. The celebrated Justinian had recently become emperor; the Persian armies were conducted by the sons of Kobâd. This war was chiefly distinguished by a crushing defeat sustained by the great Belisarius at the hands of Xerxes, a son of Kobâd, whose army was inferior in numbers to that of the Romans. This memorable battle took place near Nisibis, in 529 A.D.; it probably presented the only instance during a long career of victory, that Belisarius was forced to seek flight from the field. Belisarius retrieved his honor in the following campaign, by defeating the Persian army at Daras, commanded by Perozes and Barsamenes. The battle was long and obstinate, but at last terminated in the death of

Barsamenes and the rout of his army. This was the first great battle won by the Romans over the Persians for nearly two centuries, and Belisarius was too conscious of the prowess of his enemy to risk the laurels already won, by a pursuit of the retreating host. The following year the Persians, in turn, retrieved their fortunes and closed the war by another hard-won victory over Belisarius at Callinicus. Kobâd showed of what stuff he was made by expressing serious dissatisfaction with his general because he had not made his victory complete by capturing Belisarius and his army.

COIN OF CHOSROËS I.

Soon after these events, glorious in the history of Persia, Kobâd was seized with paralysis, and died at the age of eighty-two. His long reign had been active, and had materially contributed to strengthen the Persian empire and the house of Sassân. But the records describe this hero and statesman as a man cruel and capricious, greater in his conflicts abroad than in his personal relations at home. It is given to few men to be consistent under all circumstances.

XVII.

CHOSROËS I., SURNAMED ANURSHIRWAN.

The final act of the reign of Kobâd was one of injustice, in which he allowed an excusable love for the son of his favorite wife to interfere with the natural succession, and thus left to his country a legacy of civil war and blood. Kaoses or Kaoos was the eldest son, and seems to have been worthy to wield the sceptre. But, doubtless through the influence of the mother of Chosroës, that prince was named by Kobâd as his successor, in a formal will. The terms of the will were ratified by the magians and a majority of the nobles, and Chosroës or Khosrû became king. The results of this injustice, it must be admitted, were ultimately such as to contribute to the splendor of the empire; but Chosroës was not permitted to occupy his position without a struggle that leaves a stain on his great renown.

Besides the natural claims of Kaoses, Zames, the second son of Kobâd, was put forward by a number of nobles who considered him best fitted to reign, perhaps because of the known severity of Chosroës. But before the conspiracy had ripened it came to the ears of Chosroës. There was no weakness in his method of crushing the opposition. All his brothers and his uncle, together with all their male children, were condemned to die without delay, to the number of forty. But one escaped, a youth named Kobâd, who fled to Constantinople, where he remained the rest of his days. The great general, Chanaranges, was also executed for assisting Kobâd to escape. The same fate befell Mebodes, the noble who, by producing the will of Kobâd, had secured the throne for Chosroës; he had shown hesitation in obeying an order of the "Great King," who was determined to show that once on the throne he was supreme.

Chosroës continued the tremendous measures for securing order in his empire, by causing Mazdâk, who had escaped the massacre ordered by Kobâd, to be executed, together with no less than one hundred thousand of his followers, who had multiplied in spite of the persecutions visited upon them. No one but a man of preëminent ability could have survived such terrible deeds. Assassination or revolt would have hurled their author from power if a weak man. But Chosroës was a character so strong and possessed of such intellectual force that the people submitted to his authority without further opposition, recognizing, perhaps, the stern necessity which had driven the young king to commence his reign with such fearful acts of retribution. That this must have been partially the case, seems evident from the fact that by universal acclaim Chosroës has received the title of Just.

While ruling with an iron hand, this great monarch, unlike many Eastern kings, administered justice with discrimination. Penalties were carefully proportioned to the crime, and rewards were granted when deserved. An anecdote has been handed down which illustrates the general opinion of the justice of Chosroës; while it may excite a smile that a king should be praised for a forbearance which is simply in accordance with equity and law, it should be remembered that in despotic countries the wish of a king is equivalent to a command, and that whenever he so chooses he can make might right. It is related that an old woman had a small property adjoining the park of one of this king's palaces. To carry out his plans for beautifying the park, it was necessary to gain possession of the woman's plot adjoining. But she refused to part with it, saying that she had always lived there, and desired to occupy it until her death. The courtiers were amazed at the courage of a feeble woman, who dared to resist the wish of such a monarch, and urged him to seize it without her permission. But Chosroës declined to persist in the attempt to secure the desired plot of ground, and the old woman lived in her little garden until she died. Perhaps the monarch was moved by a grim humor at the spectacle of a weak and feeble woman having the courage to resist his will.

Since the time of Darius I. no sovereign of Persia did so much to improve the administration of the laws and the condition of the people. It is the universal opinion of the historians of this reign that the administration of internal affairs was of a high order. One of the most important changes introduced by Chosroës was in regard to the satrapies, which were so numerous that it was difficult for the sovereign to give a personal attention to all the quarterly and annual reports submitted to him by the satraps. He therefore separated the satrapies into four divisions, to each of which he assigned a head or viceroy. The satraps reported to the viceroys, who in turn presented general reports to the great king. In order to assure himself of the substantial truth of the reports concerning the condition of his people, Chosroës made frequent journeys through his dominions, and

PALACE OF CHOSROËS I., AT CTESIPHON.

employed an army of detectives to inspect matters, and to report to him in secret. Cases of mal-administration were not decided hastily by the caprice of the king, as so often happens in Oriental governments, but they were carefully examined and judged by courts of inquiry. The same severity was shown in cases of proved guilt against those who plotted to injure the people, as of those who conspired against the person of the king. This fact gave great satisfaction to the public, who were unaccustomed to see their rulers considering the interests of the people as of equal value to their own. A case is mentioned in which eighty tax-collectors were executed for extortion.

The establishment of a fixed tax on land was also an improvement over the old system, which required a certain proportion of the crops to go to the crown, and the farmer could not reap his crops until the officers of the government came and gathered the tax off the field. Great hardship was often produced by this method of collecting the imposts. Stated taxes were also placed by Chosroës on the fruit-trees and personal property. He also interested himself greatly in improving the condition of agriculture. The army was likewise remodelled, and a paymaster-general was appointed to inspect the troops, and see that they received what they were entitled to—no more and no less. Frauds had often been perpetrated on the royal treasury through the looseness of the military organization, and the reforms of Chosroës were intended to prevent further robbery of the revenues, as well as to increase the discipline and efficiency of the army.

The roads over the empire were carefully repaired during this reign, and as the country was but thinly peopled in many parts, post-houses were erected and guards stationed at many points to afford comfort and security to travellers. Chosroës also, unlike most Orientals, encouraged the entrance and settlemen of foreigners in his dominions.

Indeed his appears to have been one of those rare

minds which seek all knowledge for their portion and find expansion in almost every form of experience and activity. What encouragement the arts found from his patronage we may learn from the remains of the great palace he erected at Ctesiphon, of which an illustration is given in this volume. The central arch of this wonderful structure is 85 feet high, 72 feet wide, and 115 feet deep. Although nothing now exists of this palace but the façade, we may judge from this what must have been the size and beauty of the structure before it had been destroyed by time and war.

Chosroës also found leisure to gratify his taste for literature and philosophy; and as a patron of all learning, founded a large university at Shapoor. He is said to have given considerable attention to a study of the Greek classics. It was doubtless the breadth of his mental vision that made him tolerant of all religions. The persecution of the Mazdâkites was in all probability because of their crimes against the state, rather than their beliefs. He early stated it as a maxim of his government, that it was with the deeds and not the thoughts of men that he concerned himself. This shows a very extraordinary character of mind, when we consider what crimes have in all ages been committed in every European country in the name of religion under forms of law. The king permitted one of his wives to practise the Christian religion in his own palace; and when her son professed the same faith, Chosroës only forbade him to go abroad, lest he should become a proselyter. The prince ill-requited his father for exhibiting a tolerance that was altogether unknown elsewhere in that age. Learning from a false rumor that the king had died on a distant campaign, the royal youth escaped from the palace and summoned all the Christians in Persia to arise and overthrow the Zoroastrians. The rebellion made considerable headway before it was defeated. According to some records the prince fell on the field, and according to others he was captured and taken before Chosroës, who allowed him to live but maimed in such manner that he could not, according to Persian law, inherit the succession.

The reign of Anurshirwan the Just was the Augustan period of Persian history previous to modern times. The greatness of this sovereign as an administrator would alone have made his fame secure. But his capacity was still further exhibited by the fact that he was, in addition to all his other talents, the greatest general of his time, and one of the greatest Persia has produced. His exertions for the improvement of his people and the cultivation of his own tastes were expended during brief intervals snatched from the long campaigns against Romans and barbarians. Wherever his stern eye surveyed the field of action, whether in the protracted march, the siege, or the battle, success perched on the leathern banner of Persia, and added to her renown.

Repeatedly Justinian, the Emperor of Constantinople, was forced to purchase a peace by agreeing to pay tribute annually to Chosroës. This was done on the plea that the great king agreed with the money to keep the Ephthalites, or White Huns, out of the

Roman dominions; but in reality it was a tribute paid to keep Chosroës himself out of the territories of Justinian. This was undoubtedly the case with the treaty concluded in the year 557 A.D.

It was after that treaty allowed him to turn his attention to other quarters that Chosroës undertook the expedition for the expulsion of the Abyssinians from Arabia. Newly converted to a sort of hybrid Christianity, and burning with zeal, the Abyssinians had crossed the Red Sea and established themselves in Arabia Felix, in the province of Yemen, whence they ruled most of the peninsula. If permitted to remain there they might soon become a formidable foe, who would, in alliance with Rome, attack the Persian armies on the flank when engaged with that power. Chosroës, therefore, listened cordially to the entreaties of the Arabians, and sent an army to their assistance by sea. The Abyssinians were totally defeated and expelled from Arabia, which, under a marzpân, or Persian viceroy, became a vassal of Persia.

In the wars with the Ephthalites, or White Huns, Chosroës was also completely successful; they were driven back with great losses, including the death of their king on the battle-field. In only one quarter was Chosroës unsuccessful; this was in Lazica, on the shores of the Black Sea. He desired to gain a foothold at that point, with the hope of annoying the Romans by the fleets he proposed to launch on the Euxine. The very great importance of preventing the " Great King " from gaining such a tremendous advantage, led the Romans, on the other hand, to make almost incredible exertions to prevent the success of his designs on Lazica. Notwithstanding this, Chosroës would have won his point but for the untimely death of the great general, Mermeroës, who died of old age at the moment when the final triumph was at hand. His successor, Nachorogan, wasted the advantages previously gained, and Chosroës, declining to throw away any more armies in so distant a quarter, resigned Lazica to Justinian for a payment of gold.

The Lazic war was signalized by many heroic incidents. The defence of the rock-fortress of Petra is one of the most remarkable in history. The Persians had captured it after great effort, and it was garrisoned with fifteen hundred men when the Romans appeared before it. The siege continued until only three hundred of the garrison survived the furious assaults of the enemy. The besieged were at the last gasp when Mermeroës came to its relief with thirty thousand men. The Romans hastily broke up the camp, and the place was garrisoned with three thousand fresh troops and victualled for five years.

In the following year a large Roman army under Bessas succeeded in outmanœuvring the Persians, and sat down before the walls of the redoubtable fortress. Every device then known in war was employed to capture or to defend the place. The garrison made large use of the naphtha and petroleum with which the Caucasus abounds.

The place finally fell by a combination of accidents. A point hitherto considered inaccessible was scaled by the assailants at the moment that the long-battered walls crumbled at two other points. When the Romans entered they found scarcely a man left able to offer resistance. The character of the defence is shown by the losses suffered by the garrison. Out of three thousand men only seven hundred and thirty were taken alive, and of these only eighteen were unwounded. Seven hundred fell during the siege; one thousand and seventy were slain in the final assault; the remaining five hundred threw themselves into the cita-

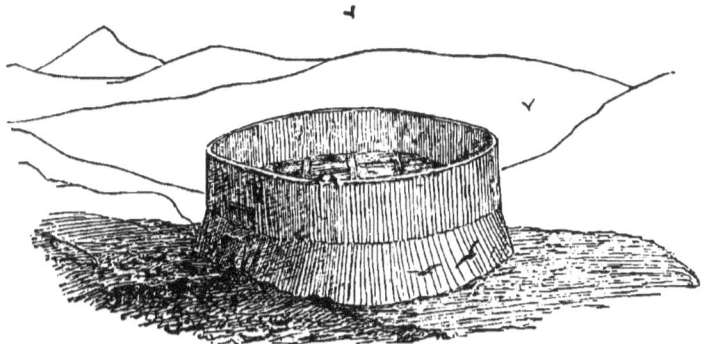

A CEMETERY OF THE ZOROASTRIANS.

del, and, rather than surrender, fought until by flame and sword they perished to the last man. The siege of Petra is alone a sufficient proof of the indomitable heroism of the Persian soldier when led by brave and competent generals.

Among the last military exploits of the aged Chosroës was the expulsion of the Turkish hordes, who were now beginning to make a figure in history and had ventured across the frontiers of Persia. Soon after this event he conducted in person the siege of Daras, the most important Roman fortress in the southeast, and captured it after a desperate resistance of five months. Alarmed by the success of the "Great King," whom the Romans supposed to be too old to exhibit his former prowess, their emperor, Justin, hastened to purchase a truce, of which one condition was the payment by Rome of an indemnity of forty thousand gold aurei.

Soon after these events the venerable Anurshirwan the Just died in his palace at Ctesiphon, after a reign of forty-eight years, during which he had carried the empire of Persia to the highest pinnacle of glory and power.

XVIII.

CHOSROËS PARVEEZ.

Chosroës I. was succeeded by his son Hormazd or Hormisdas, the son of the Turkish princess, Fakim. He ascended the throne without opposition and at the outset of his reign exhibited a most promising disposition, notwithstanding that, like too many Oriental sovereigns, he put his brothers to death, as a measure of precaution. But he is said to have shown impartiality in his treatment of the rights of the poor against the great; he also announced his purpose of tolerating all religions, and advised the magians, instead of persecuting the Christians, to pay more attention to practising the maxims of their own faith. It is difficult to decide what were the exact causes that led to the final unpopularity and downfall of Hormazd; possibly it was a want of knowledge of character in dealing with men, or his head may have been turned by too much power. But whatever the cause, he capped the climax by degrading the great General Bahram Shobeen for losing a battle. This captain was the head of the powerful house of Mihrân and could ill brook the insult offered him by the king, who sent to the victor in so many campaigns a distaff and cotton with a woman's dress, ordering him to give up war for spinning.

The grizzled veteran called on his troops to revenge the insult offered to them as well as to him. The army proclaimed him king of Persia, and he at once proceeded to march southward against the capital. An army which was sent against him mutinied against the king, but, true to instincts of law, refused to fight for a pretender not of blood-royal, and declared instead for Chosroës, the son of Hormazd. The greatest disorder now prevailed, and chaos seemed about to bring about the destruction of the empire. The people were infuriated against Hormazd for the conduct which had wrought such dire results. It was not a time for making nice distinctions, or considering too carefully what was legal or illegal. The crisis required quick and stern treatment. The maternal uncles of Chosroës, Bindoe, and Vistam, aided by other nobles, deposed Hormazd and threw him into prison, where he was blinded in order to incapacitate him for reigning, and soon after murdered. Chosroës was appointed king in the place of his father. He has been severely judged for the deplorable events which led to his elevation to the throne, and condemned by historians as a parricide. But we have no certain knowledge that he ordered the death of Hormazd, or even knew of it until after the deed was done by which he profited. The situation of the country was such as to demand severe measures, and it is quite likely that his uncles took on themselves the responsibility for a crime which seemed a state necessity, hoping that their nephew would grant his approval.

The fact that after becoming strong on the throne Chosroës ordered their execution, seems to indicate that he was not a participant in the crime, and considered that subjects who dared to slay a king, not only merited punishment, but could not be allowed to live with safety to the tranquillity of the state. Kings receive sufficient blame from the judgments of history, and Chosroës has perhaps justly come in for his share. It is therefore only fair to give him the benefit of the doubt in regard to the murder of Hormazd.

The prince who was thus elevated to the throne of the house of Sassân by a tragedy that, whether he was to blame or not, has left an indelible stain on his name, was destined to the most remarkable career in the history of his dynasty, and one of the most extraordinary in the annals of time. It reads like a romance; the vicissitudes of its hero are almost without parallel, and the inconsistencies which his character displayed, are such as to baffle analysis and make it impossible to make a just estimate of the man. From some historians he receives unstinted blame; by others he is lauded as a great administrator. He mounted to power on the dead body of his father; he did more than any prince of Persia, except, perhaps, Shah Abbass, to stimulate the progress of the arts; the generals he selected expelled the Romans from Asia and Africa, and extended the empire of Persia to limits only equalled by Darius the Great; and in his unswerving love for one woman during a long reign, he probably stands alone among the kings of Persia; law and order reigned throughout his empire; and yet he left the reputation of having the most extensive harem in Persian annals; he lived to see Persia stripped of half her possessions; and he was murdered in prison—execrated by his people. Such is a brief statement of the contradictions we are to meet in reading the narrative of this extraordinary career.

Chosroës II., called by Persians Parveez, or the Conqueror, was crowned in the summer of 590 A.D. But while the events which led to his elevation were occurring, Bahram Shobeen was approaching the capital by rapid marches. He was a rival with whom the young king could not afford to trifle; and Chosroës appears to have acted with moderation and wisdom at this crisis.

An embassy was sent to Bahram to convey to him a conciliatory letter from the king. It was not his fault, urged Chosroës, but his father's, that Bahram had been insulted. As, therefore, no cause of grievance existed between them, Chosroës invited Bahram to abandon his hostile attitude and to return peacefully to the capital, where he was promised the second place in the empire. Chosroës further offered to confirm his promise by a royal oath, which, in Persia, made it impossible for a king to recede from a compact.

In addressing this letter, Chosroës styled himself, according to the custom of Persian monarchs of that period: "King of kings, lord of lords, master of masters, prince of peace, savior of mankind, a virtuous and immortal man before the gods, a most real deity in the sight of men, glorious beyond compare, a conqueror, rising side by side with the sun and furnishing eyes to the night, of glorious ancestry, opposed to war, benevolent, served by the genii, and guardian of the kingdom of Persia." This curious series of grandiloquent titles is thoroughly Oriental,

RATSCH-RUSTAM.

and, with some variations, is still employed by the sovereigns of Persia.

But it does not seem to have made much impression on Bahram Shobeen, who, in his reply, merely addressed the king as "Chosroës, the son of Hormazd," while he added a long list of titles to his own name. He replied in an insulting tone, chiding him for the course he had taken, and summoning Chosroës to abdicate the throne. He concluded by saying: "When you have done as I bid, come hither, and I will give you the government of a province. Else you will perish like your father."

Once more Chosroës showed a singular moderation, and wrote another letter, advising Bahram to submit rather than force the king to crush the rebellion with arms. No reply came to the second letter, and Chosroës found that the question would have to be settled on the field. He was able to collect a small army, and the opposing forces met at Holwan. The king had reason to suspect the fidelity of his troops, and therefore sought a personal interview with Bahram, which, however, resulted in increasing the bitterness of the rivals. Chosroës manœuvred for six days to avoid a decisive engagement, in order to allow time to suggest some turn of fortune in his favor. But on the seventh night, Bahram surprised the royalist camp, and by inducing the troops to desert Chosroës, forced him to fly for his life.

The king retreated to Ctesiphon, but dreading resistance against the host of Bahram he decided to seek assistance from one of the powerful neighbors of his country. The choice lay between Turks, Khazars, Arabs, and Romans. Accompanied by his wives and uncles and a slim escort of thirty horsemen, the fugitive king fled from Ctesiphon at night. Once on the open plain he let the reins fall on his horse's neck, leaving it to destiny to decide in what quarter he should seek safety and assistance. The intelligent animal turned towards the Euphrates and Chosroës accordingly crossed the river, and, although sharply pursued by Bahram, succeeded in finding an asylum within the walls of the Roman fortress of Circesium.

The fugitive king was received with due honor, and at once despatched a letter to Maurice, the Emperor of Constantinople, asking aid to put down his enemies. After considerable discussion as to the course most likely to benefit Rome, Maurice and his counsellors decided in favor of Chosroës. An imperial letter was sent to him, promising him the assistance he implored, and inviting him in the meantime to accept hospitality as the guest and son of the emperor. Persians, at that time prisoners at Constantinople, were released as a token of good-will, and a powerful army of seventy thousand men was sent, under the command of Narses, together with a large supply of funds, to assist Chosroës to recover his empire. But the wily Greco-Romans were not granting all these favors for naught. Under the cover of generosity Maurice exacted from Chosroës the restoration of Persarmenia and part of Mesopotamia, together with the very important fortress of Daras, which had been one of the last trophies won by Anurshirwan the Just.

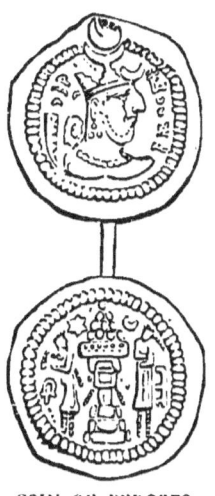

COIN OF PEROZES.

During the progress of these negotiations Bahram had occupied the capital and announced himself king of Persia, meeting with little opposition from the people, although there appears to have been but little interest taken by them in supporting a pretender whose aim was to supplant the great Sassanian dynasty. But when tidings came that Chosroës, the lawful sovereign, was returning home with a powerful army to claim his own, then conspiracies and rebellions broke out in many quarters against the usurper.

The first engagement between the two armies was the surprise of Bryzacius, who commanded the advance guard of Bahram near the Euphrates. He was defeated and captured, and barbarously tortured and slain in cruel sport to amuse the Persian and Roman generals at a banquet. Zoroastrians and Christians alike enjoyed the bloody entertainment.

Having only a force inferior to that of his antagonist, Bahram was outmanœuvred and obliged to leave the capital unprotected; Chosroës, by a flank movement, re-entered Ctesiphon, and was at once accepted by the people as the true sovereign. A usurper without the capital was rendered doubly weak, as Bahram now found to his cost. But he showed his able generalship by a masterly resistance, and was only overcome at last by the treachery and desertion of his best troops in a decisive battle in the north of Persia. At a critical moment six thousand of his army went over to the enemy. There was nothing left but to fly; his wives, his children, his treasures, and the crown were lost. He found a temporary refuge with the Turks, only to be followed hither by the emissaries of Chosroës, who caused him to be slain by a poisoned dagger. Bahram Shobeen was induced to rebel under very great provocation, after serving his country and king long and well; such was the condition of the government when he revolted that his ability and experience gave reasonable promise that his attempt to seize the crown would be attended with success. His failure furnishes another proof of the great difficulties that every one must encounter who undertakes a revolt against the established order of things. The instincts of order in every people sooner or later demand the vindication of law.

Chosroës Parveez commenced his second reign, 591 A.D., and he continued in possession of the crown for thirty-seven years. Success had thus far crowned the efforts of Parveez, but he had great difficulties to contend with still before he could feel himself secure. The method by which he had attained to power—the murder of his father, even if he were innocent of it, and the aid of the hereditary enemy, Rome—caused his subjects to exhibit apathy, or hate. The murmurs of the people, by which he was accused of parricide, reached his ear. He felt that it was necessary to vindicate his name and pacify the country by forgetting the debt of gratitude he owed to Bindoe and Vastam, the uncles who had murdered Hormasd, and shown such devotion towards Chosroës during his afflictions. He therefore decided to order the execution of the former and commanded the latter to leave his satrapy in the north and return to the court. But Vastam suspected the purpose of his nephew, and instead of obeying, revolted, and established a separate government in Media with Rheï for his capital. There Vastam succeeded in maintaining himself for several years, until Chosroës by promising to marry the wife of Vastam induced her to assassinate her husband. Such dark examples of domestic intrigue are unhappily not rare in history, especially of the East.

It is quite impossible, with the imperfect records we have concerning a large portion of Persian history, to form a conclusion as to the conduct of Chosroës in these transactions. But it certainly seems as if something must be allowed in his favor as after this he gained the esteem of his people and carried the empire to the highest point of splendor, prosperity, and power which it has reached during the twenty-six centuries that have elapsed since the birth of Cyrus. This, too, in spite of the fact that he was inclined to favor Christianity, if he did not actually profess that religion. He adopted Sergius, a Christian martyr, as his patron saint, and on one occasion at least gave the credit of the success of his arms to the influence of that saint.

The favorite wife of Chosroës, the celebrated Shireen, was a Christian. He was most tenderly attached to her, and it is the testimony of all the historians of the time that he continued true to her until his death. Indeed his untimely end was precipitated by his desire to name her son as his successor instead of the lawful heir. The love of Chosroës and Shireen is famous throughout the East; it has passed into legend and poetry, and the greatest poets of Persia have found it a congenial theme for their muse. Through her influence Chosroës was induced to allow her to build numerous churches and monasteries near the capital. When she died he immortalized her image in some of the noblest sculpture of the time, and sent her statue to the emperor of Rome and other sovereigns, both in her honor and to testify to his grief. Such conjugal affection reflects the highest credit on both, and shows, we think, beyond cavil, that this prince must have been possessed of some noble traits of character, that went far to redeem his fame from the attacks that have been made upon it.

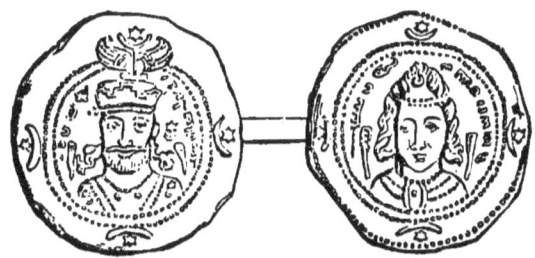

COIN OF CHOSROËS II.

Another fact shows the good that was in his nature. During the reign of the emperor Maurice, who had aided him to recover his kingdom, Chosroës Parveez refrained for twelve years from hostilities with Rome. On the contrary, the most friendly relations continued between the two sovereigns, until the deposition and assassination of Maurice by Phocas. But when Phocas sent an envoy to Chosroës to announce his coronation, the king threw the envoy, Lilius, into prison, and declaring his purpose to avenge the murder of one to whom he owed so much, commanded his armies to invade the territories of Rome.

Chosroës led the first campaign in person and defeated and slew the Roman general Germanus. He followed this victory by another at Arxamus, where a large part of the Roman army was forced to surrender. After these successes Chosroës opened the siege of the great fortress of Daras, and took it after nine months. Chosroës continued his triumphant progress by capturing stronghold after stronghold, and in 609 carried the war into Syria. These operations were conducted by Chosroës in person, and won for him the title of Parveez. We think they sufficiently disprove the charges of cowardice brought against him, and show that he had military ability of a high order.

If, after this, he preferred to leave the conduct of his campaigns to his generals, he only acted like many great monarchs who have shown that they knew how to select the men fit to fight the battles of the country, while the chief of the state remained at his capital to administer the internal affairs of the kingdom, which often require patience, skill, and wisdom. That Chosroës Parveez did so conduct the civil administration of his country while he was able to push his conquests over a vast extent of territory, is abundantly proved by the statements of historians who were not over friendly.

One of the greatest generals of Chosroës was Shahr Barz. He was a man of vast energy and great ambition, not easily discouraged by defeat. In 614 Shahr Barz captured Damascus, and invested

Jerusalem. The Holy City fell after a siege of eighteen days and was sacked. The churches were burned and the shrines stripped of their treasure. Over fifty thousand of the inhabitants were massacred, and thirty-five thousand carried into slavery, including the venerable patriarch, Zacharias. The True Cross, as it was reputed to be, was also carried to Ctesiphon and given to the charge of the fair Shireen, who preserved it with profound veneration.

In 616 Shahr Barz led the banners of Persia to Egypt, captured the great and wealthy city of Alexandria, and extended the authority of Chosroës Parveez as far as Æthiopia. The importance of this conquest may be realized if we consider the fact that over nine centuries had passed since the Egyptians had thrown off the yoke of Persia. During all that interval a Persian soldier had not been seen in Egypt.

While these operations were proceeding in the southwest, another Persian army was launched by Chosroës Parveez across Asia Minor. The victorious veterans of Persia, who in their chain armor and steel helmets had for so many ages marched from land to land upholding the glory of their race and religion, were now hurled over regions they had

DOMESTIC FIRE-ALTAR.

not trod since the time of Xerxes. The legions of Rome were driven back by the resistless advance of the Persian horse, led by the great general Shahên, until on the shores of the Bosphorus they looked down from the heights of Chalcedon on the glittering domes and spires of Constantinople, the very capital of the Roman empire. After a siege of several months Chalcedon fell, in the year 617.

It was a remarkable spectacle which now unfolded itself to the historian. After a war of fifteen years, of all the vast regions which the legions of Rome, led by Cæsar, Pompey, Lucullus, Antony, Aurelian, Trajan, Belisarius, and many other great captains, had conquered in Asia and Eastern Africa during successive ages, there now remained not a foot which Rome could claim as her own. It was the proudest hour in the history of Persia.

Chosroës Parveez, as he surveyed his empire from the towers of his sumptuous palace at Ctesiphon, could with justice assume that none before him on the Persian throne had held such vast power, and that for ages to come there would be hardly one to equal or surpass him for the splendor of his court, the vastness of his riches, the extent of his dominions, the influence of his great men in council, and the power of his armies in the field. At his audiences held in his magnificent pavilion at sunrise Chosroës Parveez, or the Conqueror, received dispatches from his governors in Egypt, Arabia, and Babylonia, in Syria, Asia Minor, and Mesopotamia, in Cordoyne, Armenia, and Media, in Parthia, Hyrcania, Bactria, Sogdiana, Arachosia, Gedrosia, Carmania, and Persis. About him were gathered in stately robes of office dark-bearded men, magians and nobles, wise men and generals of exalted rank, grave in deportment, of large experience, trembling at every utterance of him who sat on the throne, yet proud that one of such ability wielded the destiny of their country and reflected glory on them and their native land. Every moment, from the lofty gates of the palace swift horsemen dashed forth, carrying the decrees and the commands of the "Asylum of the Universe" to rulers, princes, and generals, in every corner of his vast dominions. Was it strange that he who had so many interests to consider, and whose decisions none dared dispute, should sometimes act unjustly and perhaps without intention show caprice or cruelty?

The spacious halls and saloons, the winter and summer apartments, the bowers and pavilions of his palace, were enriched with the spoils of empires; artists from all lands had wrought on the choice objects, the carvings, the embroideries, the mosaics, the paintings, which lent such voluptuous comfort and splendor to wall and ceiling and floor. The artisans of Greece had been invited to assist the Persian sculptor to decorate the marble pillars and emblazon the achievements of the "Great King" on the rocks of the everlasting hills. Carpets woven of soft woollen and silk and embroidered with pearls and gems covered the vast floors, sometimes over four hundred feet long in one piece, and the ceilings were supported on pillars of silver. What were the architectural and glyptic successes of the artists whose genius was encouraged by the patronage of Parveez, we may still judge in part by the sculptures of the triumphal arch at Tacht-i-Bostân, and the elaborate decorations of the palace of Machita, also constructed during this reign. These works and the description we have of others long since destroyed, serve to prove the breadth of mind possessed by Parveez. We have seen that he had military ability, and that in administration he showed not only energy but great executive genius. To this we now find that he added a refined love of the arts, and a mental expansion that enabled him to see the relations of things, and hence to desire to produce an equal development in the various powers and resources of his country.

It was probably only with a view to carry out the same purpose of symmetry in all the affairs of the empire that he gave to the domestic arrangements of the royal household a luxury that is unsurpassed in all the glowing records of Eastern courts. The account of the treasures found in his palace at Dastagerd baffles description, and would exceed belief did we not know from what sources and for how many ages Persia had been rifling the treasure-houses of the nations; and also consider as well that wealth in that period was far less distributed than at the present day.

The appointments of the court of Chosroës Parveez included 1,000 elephants, 12,000 white camels, and 50,000 horses, asses, and mules. These were rendered necessary for a royal escort when he rode forth, as well as to transport the tents and baggage when the "Great King" went to his hunting-grounds with wives and handmaidens,* of whom he had a more numerous supply than any sovereign of whom

---

* Even in our time the Shah of Persia maintains a large number of animals for his frequent excursions.

there is any record. In his harem were no less than three thousand concubines or inferior wives, who were attended by twelve thousand female servants. As the testimony of the historians of the time universally declares that Chosroës was true to his beloved Shireen until her death, there is every reason to believe that these concubines were kept by him for the purpose of adding to the ostentatious splendor of a great court. Although it is possible that after her death he may have abandoned himself to the seductive blandishments by which he was surrounded. If this were proved to be the case we should be the better able to explain the remarkable turn of fortune which in the end clouded the star of his destiny.

We have seen the power and magnificence of Chosroës Parveez, almost transcending the bounds of reality and bordering on the dazzling fancies of fiction. But we are now to see him under other circumstances so opposite, so dramatic, and so tragic that it is difficult to believe we are dealing with actual events. The action moves with the rapidity of a drama; scene after scene follows with unexpected force and cumulative power, until the final stroke of doom closes the tremendous tragedy.

In the year 617 we have seen the eager warriors of Persia within a mile of the capital of the Roman empire. Only a mile of water separated the victorious army from the trophy which, if captured, would have laid the world at the feet of Chosroës Parveez. The emperor, Heraclius, was in despair. He had actually placed his family and treasures on board ships to seek his fortune elsewhere. His galley had already sailed, and he himself was preparing to follow secretly, to join it at another port, probably with the intention of making Carthage his destination and there to make a final stand for the empire. But at the last moment his plans were suspected by the people he was about to forsake. A great tumult shook the imperial city, and the people, with the patriarch at their head, compelled the emperor to give a great oath in the Cathedral of Saint Sophia, that whatever might come he would not separate his fortunes from theirs, nor leave the capital of Rome except to return victorious.

Bound by this extraordinary predicament, Heraclius suddenly awoke to the consciousness of a genius which neither he nor his subjects had suspected. He resolved no longer to remain on the defensive, but to strike at once for the heart of the enemy's country. The plan was of so desperate a character that only a soldier of genius could have escaped speedy destruction in the attempt.

He embarked the few troops that remained to him on the fleet, and sailed southward leaving Constantinople to its fate, trusting to divert the enemy's attention before they could construct ships to transport their forces across the narrow strait. It was the Roman fleet which proved his salvation, and the lack of a fleet that prevented the Persians at this critical moment from intercepting the emperor and completing their magnificent career of conquest by the capture of Constantinople.

Heraclius sailed on Easter Monday, A.D. 622, on

the expedition that was to change the face of the world. The objective point of the fleet was the Gulf of Issus, in the northeast corner formed by Syria and Asia Minor, where Persia had already suffered a great defeat from Alexander the Great. The spot selected for landing was favorable for an army so reduced as that of the Romans; there they might hope to be able to meet the enemy on equal terms. The Persians did not hesitate to march to the encounter. Shahr Barz, the redoubtable hero of so many victories, hastened to crush Heraclius, and after some manœuvring the armies joined battle. The Romans were nerved by despair; to them it was life or death for Rome; and Heraclius himself displayed a skill that was equal to the emergency. After a long and desperate struggle the Persians were forced to retire, and the star of Persia began to wane from that hour. Although campaigns and battles followed after this before the triumph of Rome was assured, yet this was the decisive conflict of the war, because it encouraged the Romans and gave Heraclius opportunity to add to the resources needed for a continuation of the struggle.

COIN OF ISDIGERD III.

As winter was approaching Heraclius withdrew part of his army and returned to Constantinople. The following winter he devoted to active negotiations with his fierce Circassian allies, the Khazars, who agreed to aid him in the Persian war. In the spring he sailed with an army for Circassia, and, joined by the Khazars, invaded Persia with an army of one hundred and twenty thousand men. What he had expected now came to pass. Chosroës was forced to recall Shahen from Chalcedon and Shahr Barz from Syria, and ordered them to concentrate their armies to act in concert with the forty thousand men that he himself was leading against the great host of Heraclius.

Chosroës arrived at the strong city of Cauzaca, now called Tacht-i-Suleiman, where a decisive stand could probably have been made against the invaders if Shahr Barz and Shahen had coöperated in time. But this was exactly what Heraclius had foreseen and took measures to prevent by the extraordinary celerity of his movements. With a speed hitherto unknown in the military movements of that age, the Roman army poured like a torrent through the mountain passes of Northern Persia, sweeping all before it.

The pickets of the "Great King" were actually surprised and driven in by the speed of the Roman advance, when Chosroës gave the order to retreat, and moved southward to avoid the battle which Heraclius sought. The retreat turned into a flight; but Chosroës succeeded in eluding the pursuit of the enemy, while Heraclius dared not remain in the heart of a hostile country, and on the approach of winter returned to Constantinople. Chosroës has been severely blamed for his course in this campaign; but much may be said in his favor. His dispositions were properly made, and if supported as he had planned by his generals, he could reasonably ex-

TOMB OF AVICENNA.

pect a different issue. But with only forty thousand men against one hundred and twenty thousand led by a commander like Heraclius, and without a supporting army at hand to fall back on in the event of a reverse, it would have been exceedingly dangerous to the prestige of Persia to risk a battle, or a siege within the walls of Cauzaca. An overthrow there would be to risk the existence of the empire. It was the misfortune of Chosroës that circumstances suggested the expediency of retreating, while on the other hand, the farther the invaders were drawn away from their base, the greater the hazard of reverses to them in turn. That the retreat became a rout is due partly to the character of Oriental soldiers, to which we have already alluded, and partly perhaps to circumstances of which we have no certain knowledge.

This argument, however, does not alter the seriousness of the disasters which befell Persia during this campaign; and Chosroës was so well aware of this that he took the offensive early the following season, while Heraclius again invaded Persia on the line followed the previous campaign. This time the armies of Chosroës were manœuvred with such skill that Heraclius was hemmed in, and only escaped by a quickness and skill that remind one of the early campaigns of Napoleon. Feigning flight he turned on his course and in detail attacked and beat the Persian armies, and thus escaped. There was no lack of courage or generalship on their part; but their antagonist was probaby a man of greater genius, nerved by desperation.

The following year Heraclius changed the scene of

his operations to Asia Minor. The battles of this campaign were the fiercest in the long history of the wars between Persia and Rome; in several cases Heraclius only wrested victory from defeat by the most tremendous personal effort. At the end of the campaign the honors seemed to be equally divided. Chosroës Parveez still held all the territories he had captured, but to balance this he had to deal with a foe who had penetrated to the heart of his dominions, and whose armies were gaining in discipline and courage, which came from a hardy experience and frequent success.

The hour had come to act with unusual effort and decision. Undaunted by the unexpected spirit shown by Heraclius, the "Great King" resolved upon a final and gigantic effort to bring this protracted struggle to a close. That it did not succeed according to his plans can only be ascribed to an overruling Providence that willed it otherwise, for the plans of Chosroës were made with foresight and wisdom and conducted by the ablest generals in Persia commanding veterans inured to war for thirty years.

Negotiations were opened with the khan of the powerful Avars, who was to coöperate with a large army commanded by Shahr Barz. The allied force was to beleaguer Constantinople and capture it, while another army under Shahen was to engage the attention of Heraclius in Asia Minor. But the situation of the imperial city, as well as its fortifications, was such as to warrant Heraclius in feeling little fear for its safety. The Avars opened the siege with great energy, and assaulted its walls with fury, but without the aid of the Persian veterans they could accomplish nothing, and Shahr Barz was effectually prevented from crossing the Bosphorus by the enemy's fleet.

Theodore, the brother of Heraclius, was placed in command of the army of Asia Minor, and there again victory declared for the Romans, owing to an unforeseen incident. Similar accidents have more than once influenced great battles. The two armies engaged with great vigor, but a terrible hailstorm which arose at a critical moment drove full in the face of the Persian ranks, while the Romans, with it at their backs, were able to strike home unimpeded, and the Persians were defeated with great slaughter. Chosroës was so indignant at the ill-fortune of Shahen, that the victor of many a conflict died of a broken heart. Heraclius in the meantime repaired to Circassia to arouse the Khazars to a fresh invasion of Persia. He succeeded in gaining their assistance by promising his daughter in marriage to their chieftain, and the allied force laid siege to Tiflis. But the garrison made so gallant a defence that they were forced to retire.

While himself unsuccessful in this campaign, the operations of Heraclius' forces elsewhere had been of such a nature as to warrant him in undertaking a third and decisive campaign in the year 627. His aim was Dastagerd, north of Ctesiphon, where for many years Chosroës had held his court. To capture that city would be to strike such a blow at the prestige of Persia as to force her, in his opinion, to come to terms. But the movement to be successful must be rapid. Unlike Julian and other Roman invaders of Persia, Heraclius made this, as well as his previous attacks, from the north instead of from the west across Syria and Mesopotamia.

The measures taken by Chosroës to resist this invasion appear as usual to have been made on sound principles. He despatched a large army against Heraclius with orders to fight him at all hazards. By skilful manœuvring Rhazetes, the Persian general, got in the rear of the invading forces, and a great battle was the result near Nineveh. It lasted from dawn until noon without advantage to either side, until the death of Rhazetes and several of his leading officers obliged the Persians to retire. But they did so in good order, and remained all night on their arms, only two bow-shots from the ranks of the enemy, a fact which speaks well for the high state of discipline which they had reached. Reinforced soon after, the Persians advanced to give battle a second time; but with a boldness born either of great rashness or extreme confidence in his own powers, Heraclius had in the meantime marched southward with such despatch that they failed to reach him.

Chosroës, on learning of the approach of the Romans, despatched swift couriers to recall Shahr Barz and hasten the arrival of the army of Rhazetes. The latter was commanded to interpose itself between the enemy and the canal at Torua, and destroy the bridge across the canal, which seems to have been a point of the greatest importance in the dispositions made by Chosroës for the defence of his capital.

But for some reason his order for the destruction of the bridge was not executed, and Chosroës being outflanked by the Romans, fell back, and then fled in secret with his treasures of money and his best-beloved wives. We have no clear means of judging the course of Chosroës in not offering at least some resistance at this crisis, if for no other reason than to save his own reputation. But it is quite likely that he reasoned that, with the army he had with him demoralized, and no other reinforcements at hand but a rabble of household domestics, it was useless and worse than useless to resist the victorious legions. If he escaped, the task of the enemy would be incomplete; while if he were taken, such is the organization of an Oriental state, that the results to Persia might be the same as in the invasion of Alexander.

Heraclius sacked the magnificent palaces of Dastagerd, recapturing three hundred Roman standards, and then hastened forward towards Ctesiphon. But Shahr Barz was now approaching with a formidable army, and the approach of winter warned Heraclius to avoid the fate of Julian. He therefore hastened northwards and reached winter-quarters with little molestation.

In considering the latter campaigns of this terrible war, we are often confounded that it should have been attended with such results. Apparently there was no good reason for the defeat of the Persians. Their plans were excellent, and the courage displayed by them in the field was that of the best troops. But at certain critical moments we find that

SHAH ABBASS THE GREAT.

their movements were foiled by incidents beyond experience and calculation. The defeat of Shahên was owing to a hailstorm driving in the teeth of his army; the victory of Heraclius over the army of Rhazetes was owing to the death of that general in the moment of victory; the retreat of Chosroës from Cauzaca was due to the celerity of Heraclius, which was beyond precedent. Had the Romans failed in any one of these operations, the results of the war might and probably would have been entirely different.

The fate of Chosroës Parveez was now rapidly approaching. Both sides were weary of the war. Heraclius sought not conquest, but peace on condition of the restoration of the provinces which Chosroës had taken from Rome. The Persians also were disheartened; naturally, but unjustly, they threw the blame on their king, forgetting, in recent reverses, his long successes in administration and war. But Chosroës had not yet lost heart. As he did not live to retrieve his fortunes, historians have called his persistence in declining proposals of peace by the ugly name of obstinacy; but from what we know of his character and career, we are inclined to call his conduct at this crisis an heroic resolution, which might have led to a return of his good fortune but for the tragic events that now hastened his end.

It is hardly to be wondered at, however, that his soul should have been embittered by the astonishing reverses that had followed such an unexampled career of prosperity. It is not necessary to ascribe to the corruption of his character the harshness he showed towards Shahr Barz at this time. We have evidence that intriguers at court had poisoned the ear of the king against his general by statements which, whether true or false, were qualified to arouse suspicion. It is quite likely the blunt veteran had permitted himself to reflect the general discontent by using expressions derogatory to his master. At any rate Chosroës ordered his execution, which Shahr Barz evaded by the aid of secret information furnished him by the Romans. This circumstance suggests that there were Roman spies at the capital of Chosroës, and that perhaps the Romans were seeking to help their cause by fomenting rebellion against that sovereign.

But the measure which gave most displeasure to the Persian nobles, was the declared intention of Chosroës to designate Merdasas, the son of Shireen, for his successor in the place of Siroës, the legitimate heir. There was nothing unprecedented in such a measure. The kings of Persia had repeatedly done the same without arousing serious opposition; and it showed that even in the hour of trouble Chosroës still tenderly remembered his departed wife. But Shireen had been a Christian,—a fact the Persians had never forgiven,—and under the existing circumstances they were little disposed to humor the caprice of the king.

A conspiracy of twenty-two nobles was formed, headed by Guadanaspa, the commander of the garrison at Ctesiphon, and including two sons of Shahr Barz. The conspirators arose in favor of Siroës, who was not only knowing to the plot, but gave the order for seizing Chosroës and throwing him into a dungeon called the "House of Darkness." Here the "Great King" was closely confined, and fed on bread and water in meagre quantities. The officers of the guard even spat on him, to such depths had he fallen!

To complete the misery of this unfortunate prince, Merdasas, the son of his beloved Shireen, was brought into the dungeon, with several other children of Chosroës, and murdered before his eyes. On the fifth day, his tormentors, by order of Siroes, slew him with cruel tortures. He perished in 628 A.D., after a reign of thirty-seven years.

One of the greatest historians of Persia, Mirkhond, says: "Parveez holds a distinguished rank among the kings of Persia through the majesty and firmness of his government, the wisdom of his views, and his intrepidity in carrying them out, the size of his army, the amount of his treasure, the flourishing condition of the provinces during his reign, the security of the highways, the prompt and exact obedience which he enforced, and his unalterable adherence to the plans which he once formed."

Such an eulogy is in accordance with our own estimate of the character of Chosroës Parveez; and therefore it is that we are confounded by the events which immediately preceded the termination of his reign, and incline to consider his fate as an extraordinary example of the irony of destiny, for which no adequate explanation can be found, with our present knowledge of the powers which control the fortunes of man.

XIX.

THE MOHAMMEDAN CONQUEST OF PERSIA.

SIROES, or Kavadh, or Kobad the Second, as he was called after his coronation, succeeded Chosroës Parveez when the latter was thrown into prison. Four days later he ordered his father's execution. Persian historians affirm that he did this only at the urgent advice of the nobles, in order to ensure peace. The fact remains, however, that he yielded to this advice. Immediately after the consummation of this horrible tragedy, Kobad entered into negotiations with Heraclius, and a peace was soon concluded, by which each State returned to the limits it occupied before the conquests of Chosroës Parveez. It is worthy of note that notwithstanding the victories of Heraclius, Persia, at the death of Parveez, still retained her grasp on the provinces he had wrested from Rome. These were now resigned, to the contentment of the Persian people, who were weary of the war. Shahr Barz alone objected, perhaps with the intention of making this a pretext for the rebellion he instigated not long after these events. It appears to us that the fact that two of the sons of this great general were prominent in the conspiracy against Siroës, together with the early attempt made by their father to seize the crown, without an apparent cause except ambition, seems strong proof that Chosroës had good reason for suspecting the loyalty of Shahr Barz and ordering his execution.

Kobad was at first esteemed by his subjects, and seemed inclined to reign with moderation and justice. But he soon extinguished all the hopes of the people by one of the most wanton and atrocious deeds in the history of the house of Sassân. He caused all his brothers to be murdered; the number is variously stated, but does not seem to have been less than thirty. There was no known reason for this deed of horror, beyond the jealous fear of one who was intellectually their inferior. But instead of preserving order and peace in Persia, the assassination of so many princes, while Kobad himself had but one child, resulted, as we shall see, in disorders and wars for the succession that precipitated the ruin of the dynasty and the fall of Persia.

Kobad had allowed his sisters to survive the dreadful massacre of their male relatives, and two were at that time dwelling unmarried at the royal palace, Pirandocht and Azermidocht. Frantic with grief and horror, they rushed into the presence of the king, their brother, and, regardless of their own lives, reproached him in language that made him tremble. "Thou hast killed thy father and brothers to gratify thy ambition; thou hast thought thus to perpetuate thy power. But, even if thy life be long, die thou must at last. May God deprive thee of all the enjoyment of the power thou hast gotten in this wise!"

MOSQUE AT KOOM.

These bitter reproaches struck to the heart of this monster like a knife. Remorse made him her victim. He hung his head and dared not reply. A profound melancholy preyed on his soul, and in a few days he was buried by the side of the victims of his wickedness.

About this time a great pestilence added to the afflictions of Persia, sweeping away myriads—some historians say from one third to one half of the population. Kobad died in the year 629, and the troubles of Persia were continued by the accession of his son, a mere infant, one year old, named Artaxerxes III. The nobles elected Mihr Haziz as regent, and he held the reins of government with moderation and wisdom. Shahr Barz had in the interval been delaying the evacuation of Asia Minor and Syria by the Persian armies, and employed the opportunity of cultivating a personal friendship with Heraclius. He artfully managed these negotiations to arrange a separate secret treaty with that emperor, in which it was agreed that Heraclius should lend his aid to place Shahr Barz on the throne of Persia, in consideration of large sums to be paid by the Persian general in the event of his success, in order to indemnify the Romans for the great losses they had suffered from the Persian invasions. As an earnest of his sincerity, Heraclius agreed to the marriage of Niké, the daughter of Shahr Barz, and his son Theodosius, and of Gregoria, the daughter of Niketas, son of Shahr Barz, with Constantine, the heir to the throne of Rome. The names of the children of Shahr Barz are Greek, as given by the historians, and hence imply that he had become considerably Christianized, or at least influenced, by his long campaigns and viceroyalty in the Asiatic territories of the Greco-Roman empire.

Having completed the plans he had evidently been maturing for some time, Shahr Barz marched on Ctesiphon at the head of sixty thousand veterans. The capital fell into his hands; the infant king and the regent were slain, and every thing seemed to point to the permanent reign of the usurper and the foundation of a new dynasty on the ruins of the house of Sassân. But one of the strongest traits of Oriental character is respect for constituted authority. Were it not for this, so many Asiatic dynasties would not have continued to exist for ages, as they have done, long after they had become weak and degenerate.

We are not surprised, therefore, that after a reign of two months Shahr Barz found his position insecure. He had restored the last Roman province to Heraclius and sent an army to expel the Khazars from Armenia. To strengthen his hold on the sceptre he had also married Pirandocht, one of the daughters of Chosroës Parveez, when his ambitious career was brought to a close by a revolt of the garrison at the capital. He was in the open court of the palace when the guards pierced him with their swords, and dragged his corpse through the streets, crying out: "He who usurps the throne of Irân, not being of blood royal, shall share the doom of Shahr Barz!" Pirandocht was proclaimed the sovereign, the first woman who had ever occupied the throne of Cyrus and Ardeshir. She did not long enjoy her remarkable elevation to power, and on her death was succeeded by her sister Azermidocht, who was assassinated by one of the numerous pretenders to the throne.

Unmindful of the fate of Bahram and Shahr Barz, aspirants to the crown rapidly followed each other during the next four years. Anarchy was fast bringing this magnificent empire to perdition ; everywhere discord and blood distracted the unhappy country, when relief came from an unexpected quarter. It was discovered that a grandson of Chosroës Parveez was living obscurely and tranquilly near Istakr, most likely concealing his royal birth in order to escape the murderous attacks of usurpers. He was fifteen years old at this time, and the only living descendant of the house of Sassân. The nobles urged him forth from his retirement, and crowned him king with the name of Isdigerd III. Perhaps it would have been well for him if he had never left his obscure position, because, although he proved to be a worthy, patriotic, and heroic prince, it was his misfortune to be the last of his dynasty. During his reign Persia ceased for nine hundred years to be an independent power, and he himself was driven from province to province and fell by the hand of an assassin. "The stars in their courses fought against him," and resistance was vain.

Some years before this a new power had been looming up in the southwest, little regarded at first but destined to reverse the beliefs of half the known world, and shake the strongholds of Pagan and Christian alike to their very foundations. It was the power of Mohammed. During the wars between Chosroës and Heraclius the camel-driver of the desert had proclaimed a new religion whose arms were enthusiasm and war. His troops were the fiery tribes of Arabia, and the dreams of voluptuous bliss for those who fell in the cause of the new faith, inspired them with a contempt for death which made them irresistible, until they too, like other Oriental nations succumbed in turn to luxury and prosperity.

During the internal dissensions which followed the murder of Chosroës Parveez, the Arabs had expelled the Persian satraps from Arabia and had repeatedly overcome the veteran armies of Heraclius.

Burning with zeal, the Arabs or Saracens now turned their arms towards Persia. Isdigerd III. prepared to meet this new foe with spirit; he seems from the outset to have divined the character of the peril which now menaced his country and taken his measures to resist it with prudence and vigor. Nor were the Persians at all lacking in energy necessary to second the efforts of their sovereign. But the greatest difficulty Isdigerd had to encounter from the outset was the absence of generals fitted to cope with the skilful leaders and furious onset of the enemy. The long wars with Rome had for the time exhausted the military talent of Persia; while, on the other hand, the Saracens showed another example of the law that when a great revolution or change is about to occur in the history of the nations, men of unusual ability are provided to carry it to a successful issue.

The early operations of the campaign of the Arabs

against Persia were successful, chiefly for the reasons before mentioned; and a large and victorious army of the invaders at last encamped on the western Euphrates. The Persian army in that quarter was commanded by Bahman. The jewel-studded leathern apron of Kaweh, the standard of Persia for so many centuries, was there. Flushed by their victories the Mohammedans rashly ventured to cross the river and engage the Persians on their chosen field. But they met with a crushing defeat, and Abu Obeïdah, their commander, was trampled under foot by the elephants. This was the last victory won by an army bearing the standard of Kaweh. In another battle, which soon followed, the Persians were repulsed, and fell back in good order on Ctesiphon.

Isdigerd III., equal to the great emergency, made abundant preparations during the succeeding winter to bring about a decisive victory against the enemy in the attack which it was certain they would renew in the next campaign. Rustem, a man of experience, and the best Persian general of the time, was placed at the head of an army of one hundred and twenty thousand men. Rustem appears to have been a man of energy and courage, but deficient in devising plans best suited to meet the impending danger.

Instead of awaiting the attack of the enemy, whose inferior forces must eventually have been shattered against the Persian host,—and defeat for them meant utter ruin in that early stage of Islamism,—Rustem crossed the Euphrates, and assaulted the Saracens who were encamped at Kadesiyêh, under the command of Saad ibn Vakass. The dispositions for the battle made by Rustem were judicious, and the conflict was desperate, and inclined in favor of the Persians, until the Arabs succeeded in cutting the girths of the elephants and precipitating their riders to the ground. The Arabs thus relieved from the terrible onset of the elephants repulsed the Persian attack, and Rustem ordered a retreat to the camp. This day's battle is called by the Arab historians, the " Day of Concussion."

During the night and the following day, reinforcements frequently reached the Arabs, and it is therefore called the " Day of Succors." The battle was renewed at first with single combats, which generally resulted disadvantageously to the Persians, who lost in this way two of their best generals. Under the circumstances it was poor generalship for Rustem to allow his best material to be thrown away in this unscientific mode of carrying on war. The result of this day's fight was a drawn battle, with the advantage inclining towards the Arabs.

The third day of this great battle began at first by a successful charge of the Arabs, who had become accustomed to fighting elephants, and had been informed by a deserter that the quickest way to disable these huge monsters was to strike their spears at the eye or the proboscis. Although disconcerted by the fury of the elephants, which turned against their own ranks, the Persians rallied with great valor and repulsed the tremendous onset of the Arabs. But at night Rustem withdrew his army across the canal El Atik, placing that barrier between the two armies.

As the Persian army was still not defeated, it is conjectured that this movement was taken in order to obtain much-needed rest, after three successive days of severe fighting. The Persians were mostly raw recruits, and in any case were less hardy than the wiry and nervous Arabs. But the latter seemed to have suspected the motive of Rustem, and therefore prevented the Persians from resting by making loud noises and constantly renewing their attacks in small bodies, which gradually brought on a general battle at dawn of the fourth day. The Persians were at first successful, recrossing the canal and driving back the enemy. But at noon a wild wind arose from the desert, bringing with it clouds of sand which smote the Persians full in the eyes, while the Arabs felt it but little. Here, again, in a critical period of Persia's history, we find the elements conspiring to aid her overthrow. Hormuzen, who commanded one wing, fell back, which gave the Arabs an opportunity to drive their van like a wedge between the hitherto unbroken lines of the Persians, and enabled them to dash on the tent whence Rustem was directing the movements of his valiant troops. Before he could escape, he was injured by the falling of the tent-pole, and was immediately despatched by the sword of Hillal, the son of Alkama. Hillal shouted with stentorian tones, "By the lord of the Kaaba, I have slain Rustem!" As these fateful words rang over the battle-field, they struck terror to the exhausted ranks of Irân; a panic seized the Persian troops; they turned and fled. The four-days' battle was over. A few regiments stood their ground to

NADIR SHAH.

the last, and were cut down to a man. The leathern standard of Kaweh fell into the hands of the enemy for the first time,* and the destiny of Persia was decided.

In the desperate and protracted conflict of Kadesiyêh, we see a battle worthy of a great empire; if she was destined to fall, she fell covered with glory; as a later general has said, "All was lost but honor." † The tide of the battle was turned by the sandstorm, and not for lack of generalship or heroism.

Although the battle of Kadesiyêh was of such importance, it appears that the exhaustion of the Arabs after the battle was such that for a year and a half they abstained from active hostilities. But in 637 they resumed the offensive under the same general, Saad, with an army of sixty thousand men. The decisive character of the battle of Kadesiyêh was now apparent. The Persian generals advised Isdigerd to abandon his capital and make a stand in the mountain regions. The Arabs entered the great capital of the Sassanidæ and found there treasures so vast that the description of them bewilders the fancy. A fifth part of the booty was set aside and sent to the Caliph Omar, at Medina. What remained allowed each soldier twelve thousand dirhems, or nearly two thousand dollars.

Isdigerd concentrated over one hundred thousand men at Holwan. Haschem was sent against him,

---

* The soldier who took the standard sold it for thirty thousand dirhems, or five thousand, four hundred dollars. Its real value was upwards of one hundred and fifty thousand dollars, as they discovered when it was cut to pieces and its gems were appraised.

† Francis I. to his mother after the battle of Pavia.

as the Arabian historians assert, with only twelve thousand men. This statement of the relative force of the two armies we cannot fully accept, for the Arabs had already had sufficient proof of the courage of the Persians. But it may be assumed as true that the Arabs were inferior in number, for they consumed eight months in manœuvring before they could by stratagem get the Persian army into a position where they could be defeated and annihilated.

Isdigerd retired after the battle of Jolula to Rheï,[*] in the north of Persia, and made that ancient city his capital. He ordered his captains to remain on the defensive and hold Holwan at all hazards. But the commands of the king were rashly disobeyed, and the result was another crushing defeat and the loss of that important fortress. But soon after Saad ibn Vakass, the Arab general who had thus far conducted the campaigns against Persia, was removed on account of rumors that he was too rapidly learning to imitate the luxury of the Persians. Isdigerd took fresh heart on hearing of this event, hoping that with a change of commanders the enemy might be more easy to encounter, a hope in which he was strengthened by the magnificent resistance offered by Hormuz in the south. No less than eighty battles or skirmishes occurred in that quarter before that city yielded to the final assault.

Isdigerd collected an army, stated as high as one hundred and fifty thousand men, from all the north-

[*] Rheï, formerly Rhages, was near the present city of Teheran. Its ruins are still quite numerous; the tomb of a daughter of Isdigerd III. overlooks the ruins, near the cemetery of the fire-worshippers.

ern and eastern provinces of Persia, and in 641 concentrated his forces at Nehavend in Media. It must be admitted that this unfortunate monarch showed himself a worthy descendant of the house of Sassân. The command of this host was entrusted to Firoozân, who had been in the battle of Kadesiyêh. The enemy, to the number of thirty thousand, were led by Noman, who immediately sought to bring on a battle, aware how much depended on availing himself of the impetuosity of the Arabs. But Firoozân adopted a masterly policy of remaining on the defensive and thus exhausting the patience and provisions of the enemy. He entrenched himself at Nehavend, where the two armies faced each other for two months. During this period it is probable that Noman received reinforcements, which only tended to exhaust his provisions, and the position of the Arabs became critical.

In this emergency Noman resorted to a stratagem which completed the ruin of Persia. He spread a report that Omar the caliph was dead, and broke up his camp as if for a hasty retreat. Firoozân fell into the trap, for which he could hardly be blamed, and set out in pursuit, which probably was disorderly. On the third day he overtook the enemy, whom he found on the plain, not flying, as he expected, but drawn up in battle array, and a tremendous conflict ensued. The Arabs charged with their fierce cry, "Allah Acbâr!" and forced the lines of the Persians with the furious onset of the cavalry of the desert. Firoozân was killed, and, it is said, that one hundred thousand of the routed army fell in the disorderly flight. The fury of the Arabs was increased by the death of their own general. They halted not until they reached Hamadan, which surrendered without a blow, and Persia lay bleeding at the feet of Islam.

Isdigerd III. fled eastwards, and for ten years maintained a desultory warfare in the mountains. He was at last assassinated by a servant for his clothes and jewels, and the house of Sassân came to an end 415 years after it was founded by Ardeshir Babegân.

The coins bearing the face of Isdigerd III. indicate a prince of handsome features and mild disposition. The long resistance he made against the invaders shows that he also had firmness and courage. We do not agree with the historians who assume that he was necessarily weak or pusillanimous because he did not personally lead his armies to battle. It was becoming the custom for kings to delegate the military command to their generals, and if he were conscious that his ability was rather that of the administrator than the soldier, it would have only made matters worse for him to take the field. His education when he took the throne, at the early age of fifteen, certainly had not been such as to train him for war. It must also be considered that in no country attacked by the Mohammedans, in the early period of their conquests, did they meet a resistance as obstinate and heroic as in Persia. It should be remembered that in many instances chieftains and kings elsewhere submitted to the Arabs, and gained security and honor by embracing Mohammedanism. But Isdigerd disdained such a course and struggled with spirit, against his destiny to the end. It is also in his favor that historians have charged him with none of the terrible crimes which stained the record of his line. The disasters which overwhelmed him and his country were rather the result of a combination of circumstances. The storm had been long gathering; wherever it struck it carried all before it. Persia presented no exception to the uniformity of the success of the Arabs; but although weakened by foreign wars and internal strife, none exceeded her in the heroism she exhibited in this great crisis of her history.

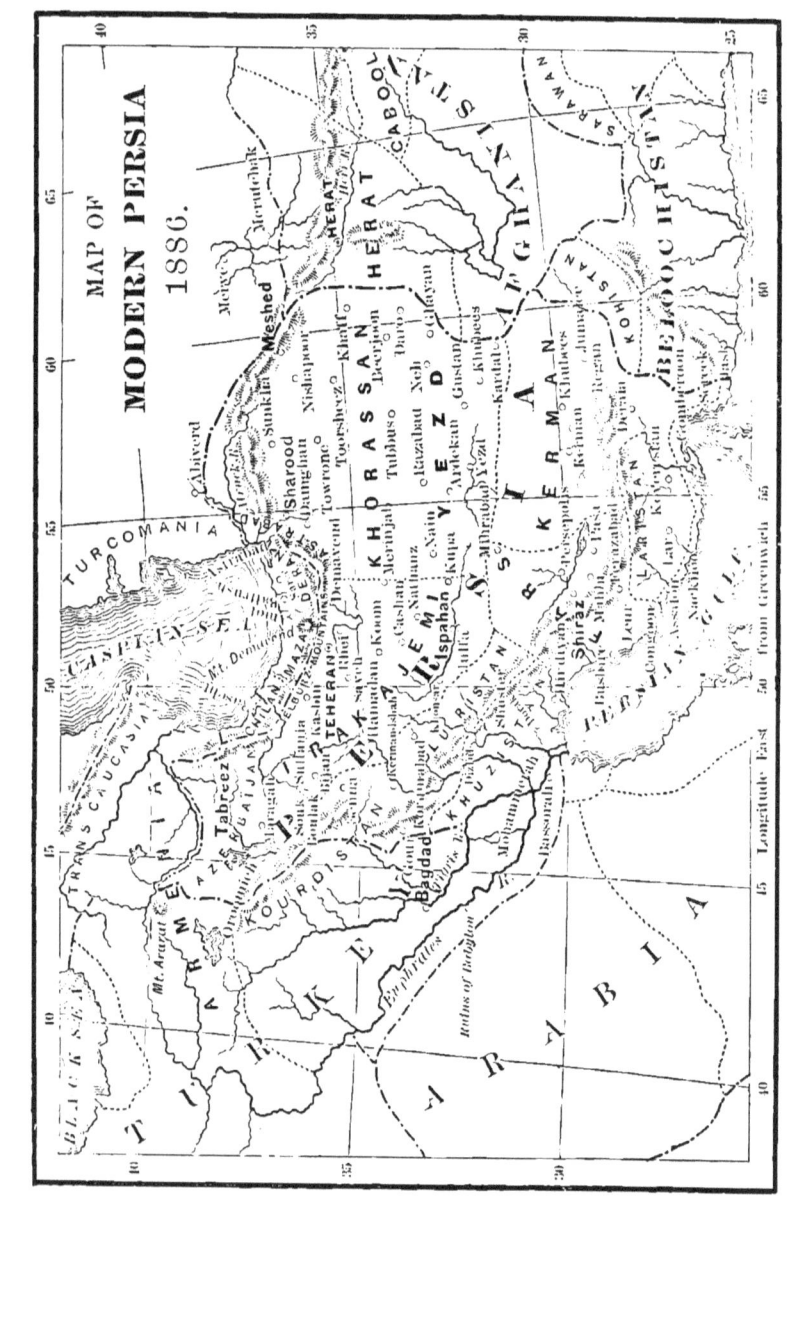

CHAPTER XX.

PERSIA UNDER THE MOHAMMEDANS.

THE Arabs carried their religion wherever they carried their victorious arms; and thus after frequent outbreaks in various parts of Persia, and violent persecutions, they succeeded in crushing Zoroastrianism as a national faith. A number of the fire-worshippers fled to India, where their descendants now live under the name of Parsees or Persians. A few contrived to survive the general proscription of their sect and continue in their native land, where they received from their conquerors the opprobrious name of Kaffeer or Guebre, which means infidel. Their descendants in Persia number perhaps thirty thousand at the present day, and are allowed to live unmolested.

With the national religion also went the national independence of Persia for over eight centuries. The history of that long interval is one of wars and invasions; of dynasty rapidly following dynasty; of vast calamities like the overwhelming hordes of Zenghis Khan, and Timoor Lane,* sweeping like a hurricane over the country. In one or two cases there are instances of Persian dynasties like the Deïlamee,

* This name is more properly spelled Timoor Lenk, or Timoor the Lame.

which ruled for three quarters of a century over the northern part of Persia, in Parthia. But, as a rule, the period to which we allude presents a dreary monotony of Saracen, and Tartar, and Turkish tyrants, none of whom attained to any permanence, but who vied in crushing the independence of the great Aryan race of Irân.

But during these ages of obscurity and dependence it is interesting to note how the Persian mind continued to find expression, how it insisted in preserving its vitality, and looked forward to the time when a deliverer of their own race should once more give freedom to the Persians. It was during that period that the great poet, Firdoüsee, composed, in the pure language of Persia, the noble historical epic, or poetical chronicle, of the legends of Persia, prepared at the court of Mahmood of Ghiznéh. Soon after flourished Nizamee, the poet of the heart and the passions, and the lyric poet Hafiz. Then too Omar Khayâm, composed his celebrated philosophic verses, and arranged the calendar for Shah Rokh, and Djamee, sang of the loves of Yusûf and Zuleika. The celebrated physician and philosopher Avicenna, likewise belongs to that brilliant epoch. The architectural and keramic arts also flourished in the hands of the brilliant artisans of Persia, and the Saracens borrowed from her the ideas which in Egypt and Spain served them as the foundation of the so-called Saracenic school of art.

To narrate the history of Persia during this period of subjection, while in parts romantic and brilliant with stirring events, would be in general tedious,

AGA MOHAMMED KHAN.

complicated, and frequently to repeat only episodes in the career of conquerors who found elsewhere the principal theatre of their deeds of splendor and blood.

But at last the independence of Persia came in a manner that would have been least predicted when she was subjugated by the Mohammedans. It was by that very religion which overthrew the Sassanid dynasty that Persia once more arose from her ashes.

At an early period in the rise of Islamism, the followers of Mohammed became divided on the question of the succession to the caliphate, or leadership, vacated by the death of Mohammed. Some, who were in majority, believed that it lay with the descendants of the caliph, Moawiyêh, while others as firmly clung to the opinion that the succession lay with the sons of Alee and Fatimeh, the daughter of the prophet, Hassân and Housseïn, and their descendants. In a desperate conflict on the banks of the Euphrates, nearly all the male descendants of the prophet were slain, and almost the entire Mohammedan peoples, from India to Spain, thenceforward became Sunnees—that is, they embraced belief in the succession of the line of the house of Moawiyêh, called the Ommiades. But there was an exception to this uniformity of belief. The Persians, as has been seen, were a people deeply given to religious beliefs and mystical speculations to the point of fanaticism. Without any apparent reason many of them became Sheähs, or believers in the claims of the house of Alee and Fatimeh, and considered pilgrimages to the tomb of Alee at Kerbelah as little less meritorious than the pilgrimage all true believers endeavor to make to the tomb of Mohammed at Mecca. Koom and Mesched, where many Sheäh saints are buried, are also considered extremely holy, and are the resort of many Pilgrims.

The Persian Sheähs also held in great veneration the twelve Holy Imâms, who were direct descendants of the Prophet, and famed for their wisdom and sanctity. The twelfth Holy Imâm mysteriously disappeared under persecution, but is expected to reappear and once more lead the Islamites to victory against the cross. Naturally for centuries the Sheähs suffered much persecution from the Sunnees, as the rulers of Persia, until the fifteenth century, were generally Sunnees. But this only stimulated the burning zeal of the Sheähs, and in the end resulted in bringing about the independence of Persia under a dynasty of her own race.

In the fourteenth century there resided at Ardebil a priest named the Sheïkh Saifus, who was held in the highest repute for his holy life. He was a lineal descendant of Musa, the seventh Holy Imâm. His son, Sadr-ud-Deen, not only enjoyed a similar fame for piety, but used it to such good account as to become chieftain of the province where he lived. Junaïd, the grandson of Sadr-ud-Deen, had three sons, of whom the youngest, named Ismaïl, was born about the year 1480.

When only eighteen years of age, the young Ismaïl entered the province of Ghilân, on the shores of the Caspian, and by the sheer force of genius raised a small army, with which he captured Baku. His success brought recruits to his standard, and at the head of 16,000 men he defeated the chieftain of Alamut, the general sent against him, and, marching on Tabreez, seized it without a blow. In 1499 Ismaïl, the founder of the Sefavean dynasty was proclaimed Shah of Persia. Since that period, with the exception of the brief invasion of Mahmood the Afghan, Persia has been an independent and at times a very powerful nation. The establishment of the Sefavean dynasty, also brought about the existence of a Sheäh government, and gave great strength to that sect of the Mohammedans, between whom and other Islamites there was always great bitterness and much bloodshed. Ismaïl speedily carried his sway as far as the Tigris in the southwest and to Kharism and Candahar in the north and east. He lost one great battle with the Turks under Selim II. at Tabreez, but with honor, as the Persians were outnumbered; but it is said he was so cast down by that event he never was seen to smile again. He died in 1524, leaving the record of a glorious reign. His three immediate successors, Tahmasp, Ismaïl II., and Mohammed Khudabenda, did little to sustain the fame and power of their country, and the new empire must soon have yielded to the attacks of its enemies at home and abroad, if a prince of extraordinary ability had not succeeded to the throne when the new dynasty seemed on the verge of ruin.

Shah Abbass, called the Great, was crowned in the year 1586, and died in 1628, at the age of seventy, after a reign of forty-two years. This monarch was one of the greatest sovereigns who ever sat on the

FETH ALEE SHAH.

throne of Persia. He was great in war, as shown by his conquests in every direction, conquests which carried Persia to the highest pinnacle of renown. He was an able administrator—improving the revenues, regulating his armies, beautifying Ispahan, his capital, to a degree that has carried its fame to all lands; and constructing good roads, bridges, and inns all over his dominions. He was a patron of letters, and by establishing schools of art he did more to cultivate the progress of the arts in Persia than any sovereign of whom we have any record. To crown all these qualifications that entitled him to the respect and love of his people to all time, Shah Abbass the Great was a prince of wide and generous views, anxious to promote friendly and commercial relations with all nations; and unlike every other sovereign of his time, he was tolerant of all religions and beliefs. It is probably to the times and circumstances in which he lived that we must chiefly attribute the acts of cruelty which stained his name in the later years of his reign.

It was the misfortune of Persia that the Sefavean line rapidly degenerated after the death of Shah Abbass, and it only adds to his glory that the empire held together for so many years after his death, a result due at least in part to the admirable improvements he originated in the system of administering the internal affairs of the empire. Taking advantage of the low state of the Sefavean dynasty, Mahmood, an Afghan chieftain, invaded Persia in 1722 with an army of fifty thousand men. Such was the condition of the empire that he had little difficulty in capturing Ispahan, although it had a population of six hundred thousand. He slaughtered every male member of the royal family except Houssein the weak sovereign, his son Tahmasp, and two grandchildren; all the artists of Ispahan and scores of thousands besides were slain. That magnificent capital has never recovered from the blow.

Mahmood died in 1725, and was succeeded by his cousin Ashraf. But the brief rule of the Afghans terminated in 1727. Nadir Kuli, a Persian soldier of fortune, or in other words a brigand of extraordinary ability, joined Tahmasp II., who had escaped and collected a small force in the north of Persia. Nadir marched on Ispahan and defeated the Afghans in several battles; Ashraf was slain and Tahmasp II. was crowned. But Nadir dethroned Tahmasp II. in 1732, being a man of vast ambition as well as desire to increase the renown of Persia; and he caused that unfortunate sovereign to be made away with some years later. Soon after Nadir Kuli proclaimed himself king of Persia with the title of Nadir Kuli Khan.

Nadir was a man of ability equal to his ambition. He not only beat the Turks with comparative ease, but he organized an expedition that conquered Afghanistan and proceeded eastward until Delhi fell into his hands, with immense slaughter. It is said one hundred thousand people were massacred in one day in the streets of Delhi. After the marriage of his son to the daughter of the Mogul emperor, Nadir returned to Persia with vast spoils, including the famous peacock throne now in the royal treasury at Teheran, and valued at not less than thirteen millions of dollars. He was assassinated in 1747. Nadir Kuli Khan was a man of great genius, but he died too soon to establish an enduring dynasty, and after his death civil wars rapidly succeeded each other until the rise of the present or Khajâr dynasty, which succeeded the reign of the good Kerim Khan the Zend, who reigned twenty years at Shiraz.

Aga Mohammed Khan, the founder of the Khajâr dynasty, succeeded in 1794 in crushing the last pretender to the throne, after a terrible civil war, and once more reunited the provinces of Persia under one sceptre. He was a man of great energy and decided genius for government and war. But he was also one of the most terrible monsters who ever held power in the East.

Aga Mohammed Khan was succeeded, after his assassination, by his nephew Feth Alee Shah, a monarch of good disposition and some ability. It was his misfortune to be drawn into two wars with Russia, who stripped Persia of her Circassian provinces, notwithstanding the stout resistance made by the Persian armies.

Feth Alee Shah was succeeded by his grandson Mohammed Shah, a sovereign of moderate talents. No events of unusual interest mark his reign, excepting the siege of Herât which was captured in the present reign from the Afghans. He died in 1848, and was succeeded by his son Nasr-ed-Deen Shah, the present sovereign of Persia, who is a man of excellent motives and decided intelligence. He has sincerely desired to improve the administration of his empire and has generally exhibited a clemency

A YOUNG PERSIAN GOVERNOR (MODERN).

hitherto rare with Oriental sovereigns. But he occupies a peculiar position owing to the situation of Persia, which is the seat of the intrigues of Russia and England, the former power undoubtedly intending sooner or later to extend her sway over Persia. We hardly think this will be soon accomplished, but whatever be the result of the ambition of Russia, enough has been recorded in this volume to indicate the great vitality of the Persian race, and to show that even when for a time Persia falls under foreign influence and rule she has in the character of her people elements that promise again to lead her to assert her supremacy under more favorable circumstances.

Although her present area is far less than in the time of Darius I. or the House of Sassân, yet Persia is still a large country, being more than twice the extent of Germany. The climate although warm is generally healthy; the soil is fertile wherever it is irrigated; and the progressive tendencies of the present dynasty, combined with these advantages, indicate conditions that promise a renewal of the greatness of Persia when she has emerged from the transitionary period through which she is now passing. The long-continued existence of the Persians as an active and intellectual race offers a strong ground for belief that she has yet before her a prosperous future.

INDEX.

A

Abbass, Shah, the Great, crowned, 288; character and beneficence of, 290
Abtin, executed by Zohâk, 6
Achemenes, *see* Achemenian dynasty.
Achemenian dynasty, origin of, 88; termination of, 146
Æschylus, opinion of concerning Darius, 110; apostrophe of, on the defeat of Xerxes, 124
Afrasiab, slays Newder, 36; invades Persia, 37; invades Persia during captivity of Keï Kaoos, and defeated, 42; treachery of, toward Sohrab, 45; invades Persia a third time, 89; receives Siawusch, 71; deals treacherously with Siawusch, 75; spares Keï Khosroo, 77; defeated by Rustem, 80; slain by Keï Khosroo, 81
Aga Mohammed Khan, reduces Persia to one government, 292; character of, 292
Alamut defeated by Ismaïl, 288
Alee, son-in-law of the Prophet, 286
Alexander the Great, invades Persia, 143; destroys Persepolis, 145; measures to secure his empire, 147; fate foretold by a plane-tree, 148; death, 149; composition of his army, 150

Amida captured by Kobâd, 222
Amyrtæus expels the Persians from Egypt, 129
Anastasius infringes treaty with Persia, 222
Antigonus usurps the throne, 151
Arabs, *see* Saracens.
Arbela, battle of, 143
Arda Virâf reduces Zoroastrian beliefs to writing, 175
Ardeshir, *see* Artaxerxes.
Ariobarzanes crushes a rebellion, 136
Armenia, incorporated into the Persian empire, 211; destroys altars of fire-worshippers, 218
Arsaces I. founds a dynasty and the kingdom of Parthia, 156
Arsacidæ, *see* Arsaces I.
Artabanus, slays Xerxes, 125; executed, 126
Artabanus, king of Parthia, overthrows armies of Rome, 170; defeated and slain by Artaxerxes, son of Sassân, 174
Artaphernes defeated at Marathon, 108
Artaxerxes Longimanus, ascends the throne, 126; subdues rebellion in Egypt, 126; clemency towards Megabyzus, 127; character and death, 127
Artaxerxes II., crowned, 130; defeats his brother Cyrus at Cunaxa, 133, death, 136

295

Artaxerxes Memnon, *see* Artaxerxes II.
Artaxerxes III., accession to power, 136; reduces Egypt and Cyprus, 138; destroys Sidon, 138; designs on Greece, 139; assassinated, 139
Artaxerxes or Ardeshir, son of Sassân, revolts and founds Sassanian dynasty, 173; defeats Artabanus, 173; reforms Zoroastrianism, 174; persecutes heretics, 177; maxims, character, and death, 178
Artemisium, battle of, 117
Arts, fine, in Persia, under Sapor, 183; borrow ideas from China, 188; from Byzantium, 189; in time of Shah Abbass, 291
Ashraf succeeds Mahmood the Afghan, 291
Astyages, overthrown by Cyrus, 88
Atossa, slain by Cambyses, 100
Avars besiege Constantinople, 259
Avicenna, physician and philosopher, 284
Azermidocht reproaches Siroës for his cruelty, 268; ascends the throne, 272; assassinated, 272

B

Babylon, description of, 91; besieged and taken by Cyrus, 92
Bactria, Greek colonists of, revolt and found independent kingdom, 154; character of, 154; facts relating to its history, 155; revolts from Persia, 181
Bagoas, assassinates Artaxerxes III., 139; crowns and murders Arses, 139; elevates Darius III., 140; executed, 140
Bahman defeats the Saracens, 274

Bahram, *see* Varahran.
Bahram Shobeen, affronted by Hormazd, 237; revolts and seizes the throne, 240; defeats Chosroës Parveez, 242; defeated, 244; assassinated, 245
Balas, or Valasgash, reign of, 218; pacifies the Ephthalites, 218
Barman delegated by Afrasiab to accompany Sohrab, 46
Behistoon, rock of, 103
Belshazzar, gives a festival in his palace by night, 94; sees a strange portent, 94; slain by the Persians, 95
Bessas captures Petra, 234
Bessus, murders Darius III., 146; sets up an independent government, 148
Bindoe murdered by Chosroës Parveez, 245

C

Cambyses, ascends the throne, 98; invades Egypt, 99; conduct towards the Egyptians, 99; murders Smerdis, 100; slays Atossa, 100; death by fall from his horse, 101
Cassius invades Parthia, 169
Chalcedon captured by Shahên, 250
Chosroës or Khosru, surnamed Anurshirwan, awarded the sceptre, 226; crushes revolt of his brothers, 227; anecdote of, concerning garden of an old woman, 228; character of his administration, 228; qualities of his mind, 231; military genius, 232; forces Justinian to pay tribute, 232; expels Abyssinians from Arabia, 233; defeats the Ephthalites,233; loses Lazica, 234; expels Turkish hordes, 235; captures Daras, 236; death, 236
Chosroës II., or Parveez,

crowned, 238, 240 ; character, 239 ; negotiations with Bahram Shobeen, 240 ; forced to fly, 242 ; seeks assistance from Emperor Maurice, 243; defeats Bahram Shobeen, 244 ; commences second reign, 245 ; executes his uncles for murder of Hormazd, 245 ; character and religion of, 246 ; love for his wife Shireen, 246 ; opens hostilities with Phocas, 247 ; defeats Romans and takes Daras, 248 ; successes of his generals, 248–50 ; invades Egypt, 249 ; dominions of, 250 ; splendor of his court, 251, *et seq.*; defeated at Cauzaca, 256 ; retreats from his capital, 262 ; deposed from his throne, 265 ; murdered, 266 ; eulogy of, 266
Christians, persecuted by Isdigerd I., 208
Clearchus, bad generalship of at Cunaxa, 153 ; assassinated, 154
Constantinople, threatened by Shahên, and besieged by Avars, 259
Crassus, invades Parthia, 162 ; overthrown by Surenas, 163
Crœsus, character of, 90 ; defeated by Cyrus, 90 ; fate of, 91
Ctesiphon, or Taisefoon, made capital of Parthia, 164 ; besieged by Julian, 199 ; captured by the Saracens, 278
Cunaxa, battle of, 133
Cyaxares, conquests of, 86 ; invents military organizations, 86 ; expels Touranians from Media by stratagem, 87
Cyrus, or Kei Khosroo, or Kur, proper spelling of name of, 82 ; childhood of, 84 ; overthrows Astyages, 88 ; character of, 89 ; invades Asia Minor, 89 ; conquers Crœsus, 91 ; besieges and captures Babylon, 91 ; military genius of, 96 ; death of, 96 ; tomb of, 96–7 ; epitaph of, 97
Cyrus, surnamed the Younger, plots against his brother, 130 ; pardoned, 130 ; plots a second time against Artaxerxes II., 131 ; defeated and slain at Cunaxa, 133

D

Damascus, captured by Shahr Barz, 248
Daniel, interprets the mysterious writing for Belshazzar, 95
Daras, captured by Chosroës I., 236 ; captured by Chosroës Parveez, 248
Darayavalm, *see* Darius.
Darius, or Darayavalm, elected to the throne, 102 ; age of, when crowned, 103 ; executes Intaphernes, 103 ; invader Scythia, 105 ; territories under his dominion, 106 ; wins battle of Ladé, 106 ; invades Greece, 107 ; defeated at Marathon, 108 ; character of, 110 ; death, 111
Darius II., called Ochus and Nothus, usurps the throne, 128 ; loses Egypt, 128
Darius III., called Codomanus, crowned, 140 ; attacked by Alexander of Macedon, 141 ; defeated, 142, *et seq.*; seeks refuge in Bactria, 146 ; murdered by Bessus, 146
Darius, son of Xerxes, murder of, 126
Datis defeated at Marathon, 108
Deeve Sefeed overthrown by Rustem, 38
Deeves, war with Kaiomurs, 2 ; make bricks, 2
Deïlamee dynasty, 283
Demavend, Mount, Zohâk chained there, 10

Demetrius III., surrenders to Mithridates, 161
Deodatus founds Greek kingdom of Bactria, 154
Djamee, the poet, 284
Djemsheed, Shah, account of what he accomplished for Persia, 2 ; character of, 3 ; slain by Zohâk, 5 ; daughters of, rescued by Feridoon, 9
Djendil, searches for wives for sons of Feridoon, 12 ; proceeds to Yemen, 12

E

Ecbatana or Hamadan, 83
Egypt, invaded by Cambyses, 99 ; revolts from Persia, 127 ; subdued by Megabyzus, 127 ; throws off Persian yoke, 128 ; reduced by Artaxerxes II., 138 ; invaded by Chosroës Parveez, 249
Elborz, region of, 84
Ephthalites or White Huns, invade Persia, 211 ; defeated by Varahran V., 213 ; defeat Perozes, 217 ; pacified by Balas, 218 ; defeated by Chosroës, 233
Eumenes elected to throne of Alexander, 151

F

Fars, definition of, 83
Fatimeh, daughter of the Prophet, 286
Ferenguiz, marries Siawusch, 73 ; a son born to her, named Keï Khosroo, 76 ; intercedes for Piran Wisa, 81
Feridoon, birth of, 6 ; drives Zohâk from the throne of Persia, 8 ; mace of, 9 ; rescues daughters of Djemsheed, 9 ; asks blessing of his mother, 10 ; finds wives for his three sons, 12 ; advice to his sons when going to Yemen, 13 ; goes forth to meet his sons and their brides, 17 ; divides his empire among his sons, 17 ; laments the death of Iredj, 22 ; eulogy of by Firdoûsee, 23
Feth Alee Shah, reign and character of, 292
Firanêk gives birth to Feridoon, 6 ; flies with her child to Elborz mountains, 6 ; honored by Feridoon, 10
Firdoûsee, the poet, saying of, concerning husbandry, 2 ; allusion to, 284
Fire-worshippers or Parsees, the Persians first became, 2 ; fate of, after the Mohammedan conquest, 283 ; present number of, 283
Firoozân, commands third army of Isdigerd against the Saracens, 280 ; slain at Nehavend, 280

G

Gang, capital of Afrasiab, 72
Gang-i-Siawusch, founding of, 73
Gordian defeats Sapor, 181
Gouderz pacifies wrath of Rustem, 50
Granicus, battle of, 142
Greek mercenaries, 129
Guebre, definition of the term, 283
Guerschap, repels Turkish invasion, 36 ; death of, 37
Guersiwez, betrays Siawusch, 74 ; slain in battle, 81
Guiv bears royal message to Rustem, 50 ; incurs wrath of Keï Kaoos, 51 ; goes a-hunting with Thous, 66
Gurdaferid, daughter of Guzdehem, challenges Sohrab to combat, 46 ; ruse to escape capture, 48
Guzdehem, chieftain of the White Castle, 46

INDEX.

H

Hafiz, the poet, 284
Hamadan, see Ecbatana; also description, 86
Hamaverâm, king of, revolts, 39; treachery of, towards Keï Kaoos, 39; defies Rustem, 41; defeated, 42
Harpagus, treachery of, towards Astyages, 88
Hassân and Houssein, fate of, 286
Hatra, under the Parthians, 164; betrayed by daughter of Manizen, 180
Hedjir, captured by Sohrab, 47; felled by Sohrab, 56
Heraclius, emperor, resolves to fly his capital, 254; changes his purpose, 254; invades Persia, 255; defeats Shahr Barz at Issus, 255; invades Persia a second time, from the north, 256; defeats Chosroës Parveez at Cauzaca, 256; third campaign against Persia, 258; captures Dastagerd, 262; concludes peace with Persia, 267; aids Shahr Barz, 270
Hit captured by Julian, 197
Hormazd or Hormisdas, injudicious conduct of, precipitates his downfall, 237; affronts Bahram Shobeen, 237; deposed and slain, 238
Hormisdas II., 191
Hormuz, battle of, 173
Houman delegated by Afrasiab to lead auxiliaries to Sohrab, 46
Houscheng, reign of, 2
Hyrcania, defined, 84

I

Imâms, the twelve Holy, 287
Intaphernes executed by Darius, 103
Irâk, see Irân.

Irân, limits and location of, 83
Iredj assigned kingdom of Irân, 18; slain by his brothers, 21
Isdigerd I. takes charge of Theodosius, 208; persecutes the Christians, 208
Isdigerd III., advanced to the throne, 272; prepares to resist the Saracens, 273-4; makes Rhages his capital, 279; flies eastward after battle of Nehavend, 281; assassinated, 281; character of, 281
Ismaïl, Shah, commencement of his career, 287; founds Sefavean dynasty, 288; conquests of, 288; loses battle of Tabreez, 288; death of, 288
Ismaïl II., Shah, 288
Ispahan, made the capital of Persia, 290; beautified by Shah Abbass, 290; sacked by Mahmood the Afghan, 291
Issus, second battle of, 255

J

Jerusalem taken and sacked by Shahr Barz, 249
Jolula, battle of, 279
Jovian, elected emperor, 202; ratifies peace with Sapor, 203
Julian, character of, 194; invades Persia, 194; retreats, 199; defeated and slain, 202
Junaid, father of Shah Ismaïl I., 287
Justin purchases peace with Chosroës, 236
Justinian pays tribute to Chosroës. 232

K

Kabool, capital of Mihrab, 26
Kadesiyêh, battle of. 274, et seq.
Kaiomurs, founder of Persia, 1; wars with the Deeves, 2; death of, 2
Kaweh, demands justice of Zo-

hák, 7; raises a revolt, 8; apron of, made the national standard, 8
Kaweianee, or apron of Kaweh, 8; used in campaign against the Saracens, 274; captured and destroyed, 278
Keï Kaoos ascends the throne, 37; attacks Mazanderan, 37; rescued by Rustem, 38; goes against king of Hamaveram, 39; marries Soudabêh, 39; cast in a dungeon, 40; returns to his capital, 43; learns of the invasion of Sohrab, 49; proceeds against Sohrab, 51; marries the mother of Siawusch, 67; confounded by conduct of Siawusch, 72; sends an army to avenge Siawusch, 78; death of, 80
Keï Khosroo, birth of, 76; left in charge of a shepherd, 76–7; slays Afrasiab, 81. *See also* Cyrus, 77
Kei Kobad, reign of, 37
Kerim Khan the Zend, reign of, 292
Khazars, defeated by Kobad, 219; assist Heraclius against Persia, 255
Khshathrapavan, *see* Satraps.
Kobad, defeats the Khazars, 219; accepts doctrines of Mazdâk, 219; deposed, 221; marries daughter of Kush-newaz, and resumes the sceptre, 221; captures Amida, 224; defeats Belisarius, 225; death of, 225
Kobad the Second, *see* Siroës.
Kush-newaz, king of the Ephthalites, 218

L

Ladé, battle of, 106
Lazica lost by Nachoragan, 234
Leonidas fights and is slain at Thermopylæ, 116

M

Macrinus defeated by the Parthians, 170
Madjin, isles of, 6
Mahaferid, mother of Minoutchehr, 22
Mahmood the Afghan, invades Persia, 290; atrocities of, 291; death of, 291
Manee, career of, 185; brings art ideas from China, 188; fate of, 190
Manizen, daughter of, betrays Hatra, 180
Marathon, battle of, 108
Mardas, father of Zohâk, 3; killed by Zohâk, 4
Mardonius incites Darius to invade Greece, 107; defeated at Platæa, 122
Mark Antony, defeated by Phraates, 166
Massagetæ, described, 84
Maurice assists Chosroës Parveez, 243
Mazdâk, doctrines of, 219; seized by orders of Zamasp, 221; followers of, massacred, 223; executed by Chosroës, 226
Mebodes executed by Chosroës, 227
Media, 83, 86
Megabyzus, subdues Egypt, 127; revolts and is pardoned, 127
Mercenaries, Greek, 129
Merdasas murdered, 266
Mermeroës dies in Lazic war, 234
Mihrab, king of Kabool, opposes marriage of Roodabeh, 27
Miltiades wins battle of Marathon, 108–9
Minoutchehr avenges the murder of his father, 23; ascends the throne, 24; wars against the rebels in the north, 26; puts the powers of Zal to the test, 32; death of, 36

Mithridates the Great of Parthia, conquest and coins of, 161
Mohammed Khudabenda, Shah, 288
Mohammed Shah, reign of, 292
Mohammedanism, sects of, 886
Musa, seventh Holy Imâm, 287

N

Nachoragan defeated in Lazica, 234
Nadir Kuli Khan, usurps the throne, 291 ; captures Delhi, 291 ; assassinated, 292
Nasr-ed-Deen Shah, succeeds to the throne, 292 ; character of, 292
Nehavend, battle of, 280
Newder, ascends the throne, 36 ; tyrannizes his subjects, 36 ; slain by Afrasiab, 36
Nisibis captured by Sapor, 181
Nizamee, the poet, 284
Noman wins battle of Nehavend, 280

O

Ochus, *see* Darius II.
Odenathus, king of Palmyra, harasses Sapor, 182
Omar Khayâm, 284
Ormuzd, 175
Orodes, becomes king of Parthia, 162 ; wars with Rome, 162 ; assassinated, 164 ; title of, 164

P

Parni, *see* Parthians.
Pars, *see* Fars.
Parsees, *see* Fire-worshippers.
Parthia, founding of, 156 ; invaded by Mark Antony, 166 ; invaded by Trajan, 168 ; invaded by Cassius, 169
Parthians, origin of, 155, 156 ; character, religion, customs, coins, and military organization, 159, 160
Parysatis, wife of Darius II., character of, 128 ; intercedes for Cyrus the Younger, 130
Passargad, capital of Persia, 97
Passargadæ, *see* Passargad.
Pehlevee language defined, 176
Perdiccas, regent of Alexandrian empire, 150
Peri Sabor, or Firooz Shapoor, besieged by Julian, 198
Perozes defeated and slain by the Ephthalites, 217
Persarmenia, *see* Armenia.
Persepolis, destruction of, 145
Persia, limits of, at birth of Cyrus, 83 ; when founded, 86 ; influenced by Median civilization, 88 ; present limits and condition of, 294
Persian names, origin of mode of spelling, 102
Persian soldiers, quality of, 204
Pestilence sweeps over Persia, 270
Petra, sieges of, 234 ; heroic conduct of Persian garrison of, 235
Phædyma detects the false Smerdis, 101
Phericles, Satrap of Parthia, overthrown, 156
Phocas, emperor, attacked by Chosroës Parveez, 247
Phraates, murders his father and usurps the throne, 164 ; removes his capital, 164 ; wars with Rome, 165 ; defeats Mark Antony, 166
Phraortes ascends the throne, 161 ; murder of, 162
Phthasuarsas invested with royal honors, 223
Pirandocht, reproaches Siroës for cruelty, 268 ; married to Shahr Barz, 271 ; proclaimed sovereign of Persia, 271
Piran Wisa welcomes Siawusch, 72 ; gives Ferenguiz to Sia-

wusch, 73 ; befriends Kei
  Khosroo, 76 ; slain, 81
Pitho, claimant to regency, 150
Platæa, battle of, 122
Poets of Persia, 284
Prexaspis murders Smerdis, 100
Purmajeh, the cow, nurses Feridoon, 6 ; head of, used as a talisman in Persia, 9

R

Rhages, or Rheï, capital of the Arsacidæ, 157 ; made the capital of Isdigerd III., 279
Rhazetes slain in battle, 261
Resaina, battle of, 181
Rheï, *see* Rhages.
Roodabeh, falls in love with Zal, 27 ; marriage of, 33 ; gives birth to Rustem, 33 ; welcomes Rustem from victory, 35
Rustem, birth of, 33 ; captures Sipend, 35 ; finds his charger Raksch, 37 ; goes in search of Keikobad, 37 ; rescues Kei Kaoos in Mazanderan, 38 ; overthrows Deeve Sefeed, 38 ; adventures in war with king of Hamaveram, 41 ; drives Afrasiab from Persia, 42 ; visits Semenjan, 43 ; marries Tehmimêh, 44 ; token left by him with Tehmimêh, 44 ; summoned to resist the invasion of Sohrab, 49 ; altercation with Keï Kaoos, 50 ; slays Zendeh Rezm, 52 ; single combat of, with Sohrab, 57 ; slays Sohrab, 62 ; returns to Seistan, 64 ; storms Balkh, 70 ; slays Soudabeh, 78 ; marches to avenge Siawusch, 78
Rustem, general of Isdigerd III., encounters the Saracens at Kadesiyêh, 274 ; slain, 276

S

Saad ibn Vakass defeats the Persians at Kadesiyêh, 275

Saccæ described, 84
Sadr-ud-Deen Sheikh, 287
Sahm, gives his adhesion to Minoutchehr, 24 ; house of, 24 ; a son born to him, 24 ; indignation of, on learning of his son's white hair, 25 ; exposes his son, 25 ; rescues him, 26 ; attacks the northern rebels, 26; arranges for the marriage of Zal, 30 ; receives a royal missive, 33 ; bestows robe of honor on herald of good news, 35 ; refuses the crown, 36
Salamis, battle of, 118
Samarah, battle of, 201
Sapor or Shapooree, succeeds to the throne, 179 ; renews hostilities with Rome, 181 ; captures Nisibis, 181 ; defeated by Temistheus, 181 ; forces Valerian to surrender, 182 ; promotes the fine arts, 183 ; character, 189 ; death, 189
Sapor II., crowned, 191 ; character of, 191 ; attacks Constantine, 192 ; wars with Rome, 193 ; prepares to meet Julian, 196 ; defeats Julian, 202 ; makes advantageous peace, 203 ; military character of, 203 ; death, 209
Saracens, invade Persia, 273 ; defeated by Bahman, 274 ; encounter the Persians at Kadesiyêh, 274 ; at Nehavend, 280 ;
Satraps or Khshathrapavan, character of their office, 104
Scythians described, 84
Sefavean dynasty, founded, 288; degenerates, 290
Seleucia, founding of, 151 ; destruction of, 169
Seleucidæ, dynasty of, 151
Seleucus surnamed Nicator, founds a dynasty, 151
Selm, assigned part of Persian empire, 18 ; slays Iredj, 21 ; killed by Minoutchehr, 23
Serv, king of Yemen, course fol-

lowed by, when his daughters were asked in marriage, 12; receives the three princes, 14; enchantments of, 15; grief at parting with his daughters, 16
Shahen, captures Chalcedon, 250; threatens Constantinople, 259; defeated in Asia Minor, 264; death from mortification at reproaches of his king, 265
Shahr Barz, takes Damascus and Jerusalem, 248; invades Egypt, 249; defeated at Issus by Heraclius, 255; usurps the throne, 271; marries Pirandocht, 271; slain by the guards, 271
Shahr-i-Veramin, 157; *see also* Rhages Shapooree; *see* Sapor
Sheähs, or Persian Mohammedans, 286; veneration of the Holy Imâms, 287
Sheikh Saifus, 287
Shireen, love of Chosroës Parveez for her, 246
Shushan, *see* Susa.
Siamek, slain in war with the Deeves, 2
Siawusch, birth of, 67; subjected to temptation, 68; put to the ordeal of fire, 69; leads an army against Afrasiab, 69; storms Balkh, 70; resists the commands of Keï Kaoos, 70; goes to the court of Afrasiab, 71; marries Ferenguiz, 73; founds cities, 73; betrayed by Guersiwez, 74; murdered by Afrasiab, 75
Siawuschgird, founding of, 73
Sidon destroyed by Artaxerxes III., 138
Simurgh, the bird of the Elborz, protects Zal, 25; assists at the birth of Rustem, 33
Sindocht, opposes marriage of Roodabeh, 27; waits on Sahm with gifts, 31
Siroës, or Kavadh, or Kobad the Second, advanced to the throne and concludes peace with Heraclius, 267; massacres his brothers, 268; death of, 270
Smerdis, murder of, 100
Smerdis, the Magian, or the False, usurps the throne, 101; slain, 101
Sohrab, birth of, 44; character of, 45; finds a worthy warhorse, 45; organizes an invasion of Persia in search of his father, 46; attacks the White Castle, 46; combat with Gurdaferid, 47; surveys the Persian host, 54; fells Hedjir to the earth, 56; assaults the Persian camp, 56; encounters Rustem in single combat, 57; slain by Rustem, 62; funeral of, 64
Soudabêh, given in marriage to Keï Kaoos, 39; prefers captivity with Keï Kaoos, 40; attempts to seduce Siawusch from virtue, 69; slain by Rustem, 78
Sunnee sect of Mohammedans, 286
Surenas, character of, 162; defeats Crassus, 163; fate of, 164
Susa, or Shushan, capital of Cyrus, 97

T

Tabreez, battle of, 288
Tahmasp, Shah, 288
Tahmasp II.; dethroned, 291
Taisefoon, *see* Ctesiphon.
Tehmimêh, falls in love with Rustem, 43; marries Rustem, 44; a son, Sohrab, born to her, 44; reveals to Sohrab the name of his father, 45; laments the death of Sohrab, 65; death of, 65
Ten Thousand, retreat of the, 135
Thaïs incites the burning of Persepolis, 145

Thamauras, succeeds Houscheng, 2
Themistocles, stratagem of, at Salamis, 118
Thermopylæ, battle of, 117
Thous, goes a-hunting and finds a maiden in the woods, 66; struck dead by Rustem, 51
Tigranes, defeated by the Parthians, 161
Timasitheus wins the battle of Resaina, 181
Tissaphernes, intrigues with the Greeks, 129; betrays Cyrus the Younger, 130; treachery towards the Greek generals, 134
Tour, assigned part of the Persian empire, which takes its name from him, 18; murders Iredj, 21; slain by Minoutchehr, 23
Tourân, limits of, 34, 83
Touranians, 84; how named by the Greeks, 84; expelled from Media by Cyaxares, 87
Trajan invades Parthia, 168

V

Valerian, captured by Sapor, 182; fate, 183
Varahran I. or Bahrâm, executes Manee, 190; ascends the throne, 190
Varahran V. or Bahram Goor, crowned, 210; makes Armenia a Persian province, 211; organizes secret expedition against the Ephthalites, 212; defeats the Ephthalites, 213; anecdote of, concerning the lady and the cow, 214; lost in a quicksand, 216; character of, 217
Vastam, revolts, 246; assassinated by his wife, 246
Volosges I., character of, 168

Volosges III., defeated by Cassius, 169

W

White Huns, see Ephthalites

X

Xerxes, character of, 112; crushes revolt of Egypt, 114; invades Greece, 114; number of his host, 114; at Thermopylæ, 116; defeated at Salamis, 118; returns to Persia, 121; assassinated, 125
Xerxes II., assassination of, 128
Xenophon, accompanies expedition of Cyrus the Younger, 134; assumes command of Greek army, 135; masterly generalship of, 135

Z

Zal, birth of, 24; visits king of Kabool, 25; marries Roodabeh, 33; places Zeff on the throne, 36
Zeff, reign of, 36
Zendavesta, or holy book of Persia, 176
Zendeh Rezm, slain by Rustem, 52
Zenobia, 182
Zerduscht, see Zoroaster.
Zohâk, tempted by the Evil One to slay his father, 4; deceived by the Evil One, 4; invades Persia, 5; horrible cruelties of, 5; dreams an evil dream, 6; driven out of Persia, 7; chained on Mount Demavend, 10
Zoroaster, or Zerduscht, founds his religion, 87; doctrines of, 88
Zoroastrianism, doctrines of, 88; reformed and systematized by Artaxerxes, the Sassanid, 174

The Story of the Nations.

MESSRS. G. P. PUTNAM'S SONS take pleasure in announcing that they have in course of publication a series of historical studies, intended to present in a graphic manner the stories of the different nations that have attained prominence in history.

In the story form the current of each national life will be distinctly indicated, and its picturesque and noteworthy periods and episodes will be presented for the reader in their philosophical relation to each other as well as to universal history.

It is the plan of the writers of the different volumes to enter into the real life of the peoples, and to bring them before the reader as they actually lived, labored, and struggled—as they studied and wrote, and as they amused themselves. In carrying out this plan, the myths, with which the history of all lands begins, will not be overlooked, though these will be carefully distinguished from the actual history, so far as the labors of the accepted historical authorities have resulted in definite conclusions.

The subjects of the different volumes will be planned to cover connecting and, as far as possible, consecutive epochs or periods, so that the set when completed will present in a comprehensive narrative the chief events in the great STORY OF THE NATIONS; but it will, of course, not always prove practicable to issue the several volumes in their chronological order.

The "Stories" are printed in good readable type, and in handsome 12mo form. They are adequately illustrated and furnished with maps and indexes. They are sold separately at a price of $1.50 each.

not always prove practicable to issue the several volumes in their chronological order.

The "Stories" are printed in good readable type, and in handsome 12mo form. They are adequately illustrated and furnished with maps and indexes. They are sold separately at a price of $1.50 each.

The following is a partial list of the subjects thus far determined upon:

THE STORY OF *ANCIENT EGYPT. Prof. GEORGE RAWLINSON.
" " " *CHALDEA. Z. A. RAGOZIN.
" " " *GREECE. Prof. JAMES A. HARRISON,
                            Washington and Lee University.
" " " *ROME. ARTHUR GILMAN.
" " " *THE JEWS. Prof. JAMES K. HOSMER,
                            Washington University of St. Louis.
" " " *CARTHAGE. Prof. ALFRED J. CHURCH,
                            University College, London.
" " " BYZANTIUM.
" " " *THE GOTHS. HENRY BRADLEY.
" " " *THE NORMANS. SARAH O. JEWETT.
" " " *PERSIA. S. G. W. BENJAMIN.
" " " *SPAIN. Rev. E. E. and SUSAN HALE.
" " " *GERMANY. S. BARING-GOULD.
" " " THE ITALIAN REPUBLICS.
" " " HOLLAND. Prof. C. E. THOROLD ROGERS.
" " " *NORWAY. HJALMAR H. BOYESEN.
" " " *THE MOORS IN SPAIN. STANLEY LANE-POOLE.
" " " *HUNGARY. Prof. A. VÁMBÉRY.
" " " THE ITALIAN KINGDOM. W. L. ALDEN.
" " " *MEDIÆVAL FRANCE. Prof. GUSTAVE MASSON.
" " " *ALEXANDER'S EMPIRE. Prof. J. P. MAHAFFY.
" " " *THE HANSE TOWNS. HELEN ZIMMERN.
" " " *ASSYRIA. Z. A. RAGOZIN.
" " " *THE SARACENS. ARTHUR GILMAN.
" " " *TURKEY. STANLEY LANE-POOLE.
" " " PORTUGAL. H. MORSE STEPHENS.
" " " MEXICO. SUSAN HALE.
" " " *IRELAND. HON. EMILY LAWLESS.
" " " PHŒNICIA.
" " " SWITZERLAND.
" " " RUSSIA.
" " " WALES.
" " " SCOTLAND.
" " " *MEDIA, BABYLON, AND PERSIA.
                                            Z. A. RAGOZIN.

* (The volumes starred are now ready, September, 1888.)

G. P. PUTNAM'S SONS
NEW YORK   LONDON
27 AND 29 WEST TWENTY-THIRD STREET   27 KING WILLIAM STREET, STRAND

www.ingramcontent.com/pod-product-compliance
Lightning Source LLC
Chambersburg PA
CBHW022018240426
43667CB00042B/935